AN H. G. WELLS COMPANION

Frontispiece H. G. Wells, *circa* 1900, a photograph taken by his wife Jane

AN H. G. WELLS COMPANION

A guide to the novels, romances and
short stories

J. R. HAMMOND

First published 1979 by
THE MACMILLAN PRESS LTD
London and Basingstoke
Associated companies in Delhi
Dublin Hong Kong Johannesburg Lagos
Melbourne New York Singapore Tokyo

Typeset in Great Britain by
VANTAGE PHOTOSETTING LTD, SOUTHAMPTON
and printed by
REDWOOD BURN LTD, TROWBRIDGE AND ESHER

British Library Cataloguing in Publication Data

Hammond, J. R.
    An H. G. Wells companion
    1. Wells, Herbert George – Criticism and
    interpretation
    I. Title
    823'.9'12   PR5777

    ISBN 0–333–24698–5

His generous unwisdom in the cause of human progress was Wells's artistic undoing. But when all his plans and pamphlets have blown away, the best of the novels, the scientific romances and the short stories are still there—wonderful and indestructible. They are alive and kicking.

JOHN RAYMOND

Wells will not be remembered for his teachings. He will be remembered for his novels, some of which are the only ones in English that come near to rivalling those of Dickens. This would have annoyed him very much. But there is no escaping one's destiny, despite Wells's many attempts to do so.

A. J. P. TAYLOR

Contents

Contents

List of Plates and Map

For the provision of illustrations, and permission to reproduce them, grateful acknowledgements are made to: Mr. Frank Wells (Frontispiece); Mrs. Gwen Tilly (1a, 8); Bromley Central Library (2a, 2b, 3); Mr. Rodney Hampson (4a, 4b); the National Trust (6). Nos. 7a, 7b, 9a, 9b are the author's and the copyright in them is his.

Preface

H. G. Wells was one of the most prolific writers of modern times, producing over a span of fifty years some thirty novels, an equal number of scientific romances, and seventy short stories, in addition to a considerable output of non-fiction writings and copious journalism. He was the author of a number of outstanding novels in the English radical tradition of Dickens and Thackeray, of which the most well-known are *Love and Mr. Lewisham, Kipps, Tono-Bungay.*and *The History of Mr. Polly.* He was a short-story writer of genius, creating tales of humour, pathos, horror and mystery. He was a pioneer of science fiction, writing stories of interplanetary travel and aerial warfare even before the turn of the century. He wrote children's books, essays, satires and romances. Faced with the sheer volume of Wells's literary range, it is hardly surprising that many readers find difficulty in assimilating it, or that critics find him such an extraordinarily difficult writer to assess dispassionately.

The purpose of the present guide is to provide a key to the vast corpus of his fictional writing. I have deliberately excluded any discussion of the non-fiction works, although I am aware that by doing so I may offend some Wells devotees; my reasons for this exclusion are three-fold. First, the bulk of the sociological and political works have been out of print for many years and are now virtually unobtainable; second, to have embraced the whole range of his work would have meant enlarging the scope of this *Companion* to an unmanageable length; and thirdly, since much of the fiction has endured and seems destined to continue in popularity it is these works—the novels, romances and short stories—which will be familiar to most readers.

I am conscious that Wells is not the most fashionable of writers at the present time, and that since the height of his fame in the early decades of the twentieth century other literary idols—Hardy, Conrad, Lawrence and Joyce—have ousted him from the commanding position he once shared with Bennett and Galsworthy. It is my hope that the present *Companion* will assist in the process of re-evaluating Wells and demonstrate that, despite the unevenness of his work, he remains a major novelist and a writer of unusual imaginative power.

I am indebted in particular to the following critical works: Geoffrey West's admirable *H. G. Wells: A Sketch for a Portrait* and *H. G. Wells: A Bibliography, Dictionary and Subject Index*; Lovat Dickson's illuminating study, *H. G. Wells: His Turbulent Life and Times*; and *The Time Traveller: The Life of H. G. Wells*, that most readable and fascinating biography by Norman and Jeanne Mackenzie. These four works have been constantly at my elbow throughout my researches, and whilst the conclusions I have formed are entirely my own, it would be ungracious not to acknowledge my indebtedness to them. Their stimulus in suggesting fruitful lines of enquiry, identifying elusive quotations and illuminating the background of his life and times has been invaluable.

I am grateful to Professor G. P. Wells and to the Executors of the Estate of H. G. Wells for permission to quote from Wells's works, which are all still in copyright. My debt to Wells's writings and in particular to his *Experiment in Autobiography* will be immediately apparent. It would not be too much to say that my respect and admiration for them has deepened as work on the *Companion* has proceeded.

I also wish to acknowledge my thanks to the following: A. J. P. Taylor and the Estate of the late John Raymond for permission to quote from their work; the Bromley Central Library for their assistance with illustrations; Rodney Hampson for placing at my disposal his unrivalled knowledge of the topography of the Potteries; Patrick Parrinder for his encouragement and advice; T. M. Farmiloe for his courtesy and help on behalf of the publishers; and my wife and sons for their constant encouragement and interest.

I trust that this *H. G. Wells Companion* will be found helpful and stimulating, and that the reader will find as much pleasure and interest in browsing through it as I did in its preparation. Above all I hope that its use will enable the reader to study and enjoy Wells's writings with a keener appreciation. He is surely one of the most underestimated novelists of this century.

J. R. HAMMOND

Part I

Background

To the popular mind the name H. G. Wells signifies a famous writer of science-fiction, and his fame and reputation rest primarily on a handful of stirring scientific romances. These books—*The Time Machine*, *The War of the Worlds*, *The First Men in the Moon* and others—have carried his name literally throughout the world. Even those who have read none of his works have heard something of his reputation as a prophet and as a writer of strange fantasies of the future. They may have seen his epic film *Things to Come*. They will have heard of the adjective 'Wellsian'—a term almost of abuse, indicating pseudo-scientific planning, soulless uniformity and plastic utopias.

Yet few writers have been so misunderstood or have been judged so widely on the basis of hearsay. He was, of course, very much more than a writer of scientific romances and humorous novels. He himself regarded his early literary efforts as 'droppings by the way'. In fact, he wrote 120 books—more than Dickens and Shakespeare added together—on a vast range of subjects including education, sociology, history, science and political thought. It is rather ironic that Wells's fame rests on a mere handful of his immense output and that the works he particularly wished to be remembered by —*A Modern Utopia*, *Joan and Peter*, *The Undying Fire*, *Mr. Blettsworthy on Rampole Island*, *The Science of Life* and many others—have been out of print for many years and to the reading public are largely unknown.

For two generations of readers, in the English-speaking world and beyond, he became one of the great prognosticators of the future, one of the foremost opponents of the morality of his day and a renowned iconoclast and leader of thought. His influence on the social and intellectual climate of the twentieth century has probably been more extensive than that of any other single writer, with the possible exception of Bernard Shaw.[1] He was the last of the great Utopists.

What were the forces which helped to mould him as a man and as a writer? In order to answer this question it is necessary to consider briefly his life and background, and the influence of his environment on the formulation of his ideas.

*   *   *   *   *

Herbert George Wells was born at Bromley, Kent, on 21 September 1866. Bromley was at that time a separate community, but has since become virtually a suburb of London. A vivid description of the process of suburbanisation and its impact on a sensitive mind can be found in the 'Bromstead' chapter in *The New Machiavelli*.

His father, Joseph Wells, kept a small, struggling hardware shop and was also a professional cricketer. His mother, a conventional, devoted woman of rather limited imagination, had been in domestic service before her marriage. A lively description of his parents and their profound influence on his life and ideas is given in his *Experiment in Autobiography*. Thinly veiled portraits of them both can be found in *The New Machiavelli* and *The Dream*, of his mother in *In the Days of the Comet*, and his father in *The History of Mr. Polly*. He had a deep affection for them both, and each in their different ways affected his outlook on life and basic attitude of mind.

His mother was deeply religious and orthodox. From his earliest years she attempted to impart to him a theology of the most limited, conventional sort. But Wells was born 'blasphemous and protesting'. He was 'exceptionally deficient in the religious sense',[2] he rebelled, secretly at first, at last openly. Her religion became for him the embodiment of orthodox Christianity, with its belief in original sin, the Doctrine of the Fall, and the Doctrine of the Trinity. It was a pious, submissive code which was anathema to his questioning, sceptical mind. Yet he loved his mother deeply and his debt to her was immense. He records in his autobiography that 'she loved and slaved for us intensely, beyond reason': 'nothing could exceed the grit and devotion of her mothering'. Some inkling of his feelings for her can be gauged from the moving account of her death in *Tono-Bungay*.

Her life was one long drudgery: an endless struggle against disappointments and disillusionments, hardships and vexations. The crockery shop was semi-bankrupt. The house in Bromley High Street was dirty, ugly and infested with bugs. She could not understand how 'vast unsuspected forces beyond her ken were steadily destroying the social order ... to which all her beliefs were attuned and on which all her confidence was based'.[3] The fixed, stable social order of her youth was visibly crumbling to pieces throughout her adult life. And as the crowning blow her beloved daughter Fanny died in 1864 at the age of nine.

Joseph Wells was mentally more akin to Herbert George ('Bertie' as he was called) than his wife. He had a sceptical, agile, enterprising mind. He read freely and discursively, and from him H.G. inherited a taste for reading which opened up new worlds to his imagination.

It is noteworthy, too, that the physical resemblance between father and son was striking. There was the same jutting lower lip, the same broad forehead, the same visionary quality of the eyes. Joseph Wells brought books home from the Literary Institute and from sales, so that there was always some miscellaneous reading matter around the house. At the age of seven H. G. Wells broke his leg—a cardinal event in his life—and for some weeks was confined indoors with a continually replenished supply of books, pictures, paper and pencils. When presently his leg healed the reading habit had got him securely. Among the books he devoured was Wood's *Natural History*, the life of the Duke of Wellington, a geographical work in two volumes, and bound volumes of *Punch* and *Fun*. All these played their part in stimulating and developing his imaginative framework. Perhaps the most important as a formative influence was Wood's *Natural History*. After studying the woodcuts of animals and birds 'curious premonitions of evolution crept into my thoughts'. In later years he wrote 'I did come upon something then that made a distinctive, new and fruitful beginning in my thoughts. I was in bed with a broken leg. But the book made me forget my splints. I was absorbed by it. My mind was born anew.'[4] His mind was awakened to the fact that nature had 'rules'; that there were classes and orders, and that the animal kingdom followed a definite pattern. This was his first crude intimation of evolution, in the days when 'it would have been considered improper to mention the word Evolution in a book intended for family reading'.

His father was in many ways a remarkable man. He was a gardener of some determination, and had succeeded in growing a thriving grape vine against the back of the house. He was a cricketer of no mean skill, being employed intermittently as a professional bowler and cricket instructor. He was clever with his hands and brain, and keenly observant of his natural surroundings. Wells records that 'his was a mind of inappeasable freshness, in the strangest contrast to my mother's'.[5] There can be little doubt that, given a more promising start in life and greater opportunities to use his latent talents, Joseph Wells would have achieved distinction.

H.G. was sent to school locally, first to a dame school at 8 South Street, Bromley (the cottage is still in existence) and later to an establishment called Morley's Commercial Academy for Young Gentlemen, where he remained until the age of thirteen. Here he received an education which by modern standards would be considered woefully deficient, but which in later years he thought reasonable considering the eighteenth-century traditions from which Mr. Morley derived. A satirical account of Morley's Academy is sketched in the description of Mr. Polly's schooling in *The History of Mr. Polly*, and in 'On Schooling and the Phases of Mr. Sandsome', an essay reprinted in *Certain Personal Matters*. Corporal punishment was liberally administered, and little or no effective tuition took place. He acquired a hatred of arithmetic because an undetected astigmatism made addition a nightmare, but he was a precocious child and made the most of what little teaching there was. This 'Academy for Young Gentlemen' was a private school catering for the sons of middle-class parents, and Mrs. Wells, as the wife of a small tradesman, felt it proper that her sons should attend this school rather than the National School for working-class children.

The inevitable rivalry between the two schools occasionally expressed itself in pitched battles fought with sticks and staves. Wells's distrust and fear of the working class can be traced directly to these schoolboy days in Bromley. His antipathy towards manual workers and lack of understanding of their ways was an important part of his basic mental attitude.

As a boy he had a facility for drawing and caricature, and amused his friends by writing epic serials, copiously illustrated by himself. These juvenilia derived partly from his private imaginings and partly from his reading, including old copies of *Punch* and his only children's book, *Struwwelpeter*. One of these productions, *The Desert Daisy*— a quite remarkable *tour de force* written at the age of twelve—was published in facsimile by the University of Illinois in 1957. It reveals many significant anticipations of the mature Wells, including indications of his irreverent habit of mind and a distinct relish for poking fun at the government, the army and authority generally.

In 1880 the Wells family found itself in acute financial difficulties, and the dissolution of the home became inevitable. His mother was offered and accepted a post as housekeeper to her former employers at Up Park, near Petersfield, where she remained until 1893. His father remained alone in the hardware shop on Bromley High Street. His elder brothers Frank (born 1857) and Fred (1862) were already working away from home, as draper's assistants. Herbert George was apprenticed to a draper in Windsor, but left after two months. For a very short time he acted as pupil teacher at a school at Wookey (Somerset), and was then a chemist's assistant at Midhurst for one month. The chemist's speciality was a 'universal cure', which may have been the germ of the idea of his novel *Tono-Bungay.* Certainly he drew very largely on this experience for his description of Edward Ponderevo's shop in 'Wimblehurst', and in the account of the chemist's in *The Dream.*

In April 1881 he was again apprenticed to a firm of draper's, this time at Southsea. He was bitterly unhappy and after two years of monotonous toil insisted on cancelling his indentures and left. His impressions of life as a draper are vividly recounted in *The Wheels of Chance*, *Kipps*, and *The History of Mr. Polly.*

It is worth digressing here to describe Up Park, since this house and its 'atmosphere of unhurried liberal enquiry'[6] was destined to have a profound influence on his outlook and ideas. Wells gives a faithful impression of Up Park in the 'Bladesover House' chapter in *Tono-Bungay*, and in the description of Burnmore Park in *The Passionate Friends*. It is one of the most famous and beautiful English country houses built in the late seventeenth century, and a symbol *par excellence* of the squirearchy of the Age of Reason. He stayed at Up Park frequently whilst his mother was housekeeper there, and the house played a very important part in stimulating his youthful imagination.

The house had been in the hands of the Featherstonhaugh family for many years, and Sir Harry Featherstonhaugh, who died in 1846 at the age of 92, was a free-thinker. As a boy Wells spent many happy hours looking through the library of Up Park, and there he discovered many of Sir Harry's books—books which had an inspiring effect on his enquiring mind. Here, for example, he read Tom Paine, an unexpurgated edition of *Gulliver's Travels*, and Plato's *Republic*. The latter work, in particular, was to have a deep influence on the development of his imagination—an influence which bore fruit in his own description of an ideal community, *A Modern Utopia*. Here, also, in the attic, he discovered an old Gregorian telescope, which revealed to him something of the wonder and fascination of the starry sky—a theme he was to return to frequently in his novels. His mother found him in the small hours of the morning studying the craters of the moon.

There are some large gratings let into the ground in front of the entrance to the house, and if one stares down these gratings it is apparent they are not part of the drains or dungeons, but serve as

ventilators and skylights for underground passages. These connect
the big house with the kitchen building and the stable block. These
gratings bear an extraordinary resemblance to the circular wells he
described so vividly in *The Time Machine*, and it is quite feasible
that Wells may have derived the germ of the idea for those ventilating shafts from the gratings he must have seen as a boy at Up Park.
Indeed, at a time when so many people of Wells's class spent so
much of their working lives 'below stairs', it is hardly surprising
that he conceived the idea of a division of the human race into two
distinct species: the Eloi, living above the ground, and a labouring
class, the Morlocks, living underground. Almost all the large
houses of this kind had underground kitchens, into which the light
of day very rarely filtered. The shop at Bromley also had an
underground kitchen.

He remembered a great deal about Up Park and thought of it, in
later years, with affection. He regarded it as one of the great houses
where people in the past had been able to read, talk, think and write
in an atmosphere of dignity, leisure and independent thought, and
that England had gained much because of them. He thought also
that the estate and the sharply defined farms and villages of the
countryside below caught him at just the right stage of mental
development to awaken a sense of history and social relationships
that might never have been roused if he had remained surrounded
by suburbs.

'For me at any rate the house at Up Park was alive and potent.'[7]
To Wells, it was 'the clue to all England', and the key to almost all
that is distinctively British and puzzling to the foreign inquirer.
'There have been no revolutions, no deliberate restatements or
abandonments of opinion in England since the days of the fine
gentry, since 1688 or thereabouts, the days when Bladesover was
built; there have been changes, dissolving forces, replacing forces,
if you will; but then it was that the broad lines of the English system
set firmly.'[8]

George Ponderevo, the narrator in *Tono-Bungay*, develops this
idea until Bladesover House becomes a symbol of 'the Bladesover
system': the system of great country houses and landed gentlefolk,
depending for its existence on a subordinate toiling class. 'Grasp
firmly that England was all Bladesover two hundred years ago. . . .
Everybody who is not actually in the shadow of a Bladesover is as it
were perpetually seeking after lost orientations.'[9]

There had arisen in these country houses a spirit of scepticism,
curiosity and free deliberate thought. Many of these prosperous,
independent people had made important contributions in the

fields of education, science, literature, research and art. The country house was 'the experimental cellule of the coming Modern State'.[10]

One day in August 1883, Wells, then a boy of nearly seventeen, walked the seventeen miles from Southsea to Up Park to present an ultimatum to his mother. He told her that he hated the Southsea Drapery Emporium, and begged her to let him go to Midhurst Grammar School as a student-assistant. His mother was dismayed beyond measure, but he was firm, threatening that suicide would be the answer if not Midhurst Grammar School. This walk to Up Park and the parley with Mrs. Wells was undoubtedly one of the turning points in his life, and he wrote afterwards that 'I felt then most desperately wicked, and now I know that it was nearly the best thing I ever did'.[11]

Mrs. Wells relented and he was allowed to go to the Grammar School as an assistant master, a post which enabled him to pursue a considerable amount of private reading and study in his free time. Here he remained for one year (1883–4): a year of hard work but great happiness and mental growth. He had succeeded in escaping at last from the world of drapery, in which he might otherwise have been imprisoned for the rest of his days. He was very much attracted to Midhurst and the town subsequently figured in many of his novels. It is portrayed as Whortley in *Love and Mr. Lewisham* and Wimblehurst in *Tono-Bungay*. There is also a careful description of Midhurst in *The Wheels of Chance*, in which his landlady, Mrs. Walton, appears as 'Mrs. Wardor'.

It was about this time that he first read Plato's *Republic* and Henry George's *Progress and Poverty*—two very different books which had a fermenting influence upon his mind. Strands of Shelley intermingled with his perfervid reading, and ideas gleaned from copies of the *Freethinker* and the *Malthusian*. Under the stimulus of Plato's Utopianism he came to a vision of a world rebuilt: a world of free-living, free-loving rational beings, united in their knowledge that progress was inevitable and that the millennium was plainly ahead. He was, in fact, passing through that phase of intense idealism which many sensitive adolescents embrace on the way to maturity. He saw the world with 'divine simplicity';[12] he had not reckoned as yet with the power of inertia in human life, or the immense obstacles to progress engendered by irrationality and prejudice.

He records that 'before I was eighteen, the broad lines of my adult ideas about human life had appeared—however crudely'. He was moving towards 'religious scepticism, socialism and sexual rationalism'.[13] He realised in later life that multitudes of English minds were moving in exactly the same direction, but at the time he was quite unaware of the general drift about him. He thought he was thinking independently.

It is interesting to note one or two dates in relation to Wells's life. Darwin's *Origin of Species* was published in 1859, and *The Descent of Man* in 1871, when Wells was five. Huxley's thought-provoking book *Man's Place in Nature* had appeared in 1863. Ruskin's *Unto this Last* was published in 1861, and William Morris's *News from Nowhere* in 1890. The Fabian Society was founded in 1884, the same year in which Wells left Midhurst for London. In the summer of that year he was awarded a scholarship of one guinea a week at the Normal School of Science, South Kensington, now the Imperial College of Science and Technology. For three years he studied physics, chemistry, geology, astronomy and biology—the latter under the inspiring tuition of Professor T. H. Huxley. These were years of fundamental importance in his mental development. To him, the year he spent in Huxley's course in comparative anatomy was 'beyond all question, the most educational year' of his life.[14] About that course as a nucleus he 'arranged a spacious digest of facts. At the end of that time I had acquired what I still think to be a fairly clear and complete and ordered view of the ostensibly real universe.'[15] He had come to a vision of life as a complex biological and ecological process. 'I had man definitely placed in the great scheme of space and time. I knew him incurably for what he was, finite and not final, a being of compromise and adaptions.' He had traced the whole process of man's evolution, and had measured man's place in the universe by the scale of the stars. The course left him with a hatred of slovenly thought and arbitrary statements, and a desire for coherence and logic which he upheld as the distinctive feature of the educated mind. Some indication of his physical and intellectual atmosphere at this time can be derived from 'A Slip Under the Microscope' (1896), a very carefully written short story, and his novel *Love and Mr. Lewisham* (1900). Whilst at South Kensington, he helped to found the *Science Schools Journal* and became its first editor. Throughout his student years he was a frequent contributor of humorous and satirical essays to the *Journal*, and it was in this magazine that 'The Chronic Argonauts', the original draft of *The Time Machine*, appeared in the year 1888. The idea had come to him in the students' Debating Society—in which he was a regular participant—while listening to a paper on the fourth dimension.

During these years in London he attended a number of socialist gatherings, some at William Morris's home at Hammersmith and others under Fabian Society auspices. It was at these meetings that he first encountered Bernard Shaw and Graham Wallas. During his last year at Kensington, distracted from his studies by his lack of interest in geology, he discovered such works as Carlyle's *French Revolution*, the prophetic works of William Blake, and the writings of Tennyson, Goethe, Shakespeare and other philosophers and poets. He read 'not only a voluminous literature of propaganda but discursively in history, sociology and economics'.[16] He was reading widely in English prose and sharpening his mind against anyone's with whom he could start a discussion. Although he failed his final examination, he continued with his studies and in the following year was awarded the diploma of licentiate of the College of Preceptors. In October 1890 he took a B.Sc. degree with first class honours in zoology at the University of London.

On leaving the Normal School of Science, he became assistant master in a school at Holt, near Wrexham, North Wales. There he had a severe football accident which resulted in a crushed kidney, from the effects of which he suffered for many years. He returned to Up Park to convalesce, and remained there for nearly four months. 'It was an interlude not only of physical recovery but mental opportunity. I read, wrote and thought abundantly.'[17]

By skilful treatment a young doctor who was staying in the house at the time, Dr. William Collins, succeeded in arresting the haemorrhage, although he warned Wells that his damaged kidney was of doubtful stability and that there was a possibility of diabetes in later life—both diagnoses which proved accurate. He continued his convalescence in the Five Towns. A fellow student, William Burton, was now working as a chemist with Wedgwoods the potters, and invited him to stay at his new home at Etruria. Wells accepted this invitation very eagerly. He had already determined that he must find temporary employment 'while learning to write',[18] but welcomed the opportunity of a rest while thinking out his next move. The complete change of environment, coupled with the books and conversation of the Burtons, proved a stimulating experience. During his three months' stay at Etruria he explored much of the topography of the Potteries, and his writing began in earnest. He planned an ambitious melodrama in the setting of the Five Towns, of which a fragment survives as 'The Cone'. He retained in his memory an acutely vivid impression of the Potteries, which later bore fruit in *In the Days of the Comet* and the Staffordshire section of *The New Machiavelli*. The description of Remington's uncle in the latter novel is a brilliant sketch of a Potteries 'self-made man': a description which Arnold Bennett himself could hardly have bettered.

His spirits were now greatly improved. 'I am now a broken-down invalid,' he wrote to a friend. 'I have merely had a revolution in my constitution—on the principle that a man who would revolutionize the world must first revolutionize himself.'[19]

He returned to London in the summer of 1888 in a mood of some determination. For six months he eked out a precarious living, coaching in biology and preparing wall diagrams for lecturing purposes. During this period he came near to complete bankruptcy, and frequently had to skimp his meals. This phase in his life was perhaps the nearest he ever came to Grub Street.

Early in 1889 he joined the staff of Henley House School at Kilburn. Alfred Harmsworth, later Lord Northcliffe, was an 'old boy' of this school, and A. A. Milne and Batsford the publisher were pupils at that time. In the summer of 1890 he left Henley House and—armed with a degree with first class honours in zoology and second class honours in geology—joined the University Correspondence College as a biology tutor. He conducted classes in Red Lion Square and was also responsible for correspondence tuition.

In October 1891, he married his cousin Isabel Mary Wells. This first, unsuccessful, marriage affected profoundly his views on sexual morality and his whole personal credo and attitude of mind. The importance he attached to it may be judged from the long account of his estrangement in *Experiment in Autobiography* and *Tono-Bungay*.

In July of that year he had published a serious philosophical essay, written during a month's holiday at Up Park following a breakdown. This was 'The Rediscovery of the Unique', his 'first quarrel with the accepted logic'.[20] At the end of 1891 he became a Fellow of the College of Preceptors.

During the years 1892–3 he worked on a series of textbooks, which were his first full-length works: *Textbook of Biology, Honours Physiography* (written in collaboration with R. A. Gregory), and *Textbook of Geography*. The latter was never completed, but it is possible that the manuscript still survives.

Even in these early textbooks there were hints of the 'Wellsian' style of the novels and scientific romances. Consider, for example, this passage from *Textbook of Biology*: 'The great things of the science of Darwin, Huxley, Wallace, and Balfour remain mainly untold. In the book of nature there are written, for instance, the triumphs of survival, the tragedy of death and extinction, the tragi-comedy of degradation and inheritance, the gruesome lesson of parasitism, and the political satire of colonial organisms. Zoology is, indeed, a philosophy and a literature to those who can read its symbols. . . . And at last, in the place of the manifoldness of a fair or a marine store, the student of science perceives the infinite variety of one consistent and comprehensive Being—a realisation to which no other study leads him at present so surely.'[21]

In the summer of 1893 a serious haemorrhage of the lungs ended his career as a biology coach and forced him to take a long rest. While recuperating from this illness at Eastbourne he wrote a humorous article, 'On the Art of Staying at the Seaside', which was accepted by the *Pall Mall Gazette*. This was the first of a long series of facetious and satirical essays, most of which were subsequently reprinted in two books, *Select Conversations with an Uncle* (1895) and *Certain Personal Matters* (1897). He also wrote numerous short stories and commenced work on a novel. Within two months he was earning more money than he had ever done as a teacher. Success came swiftly and reassuringly. After all the false starts, setbacks and disasters his 'idler flounderings with material fortune were over'.[23]

During January, 1894, he left his cousin and went to live in lodgings with a former student of his, Amy Catherine Robbins. She became his wife in the following year following his divorce, and until her death in 1927 was the most important single influence in his life. His debt to her was incalculable. For many years she was his secretary, business manager and steadfast helpmate. She typed his novels, administered his financial affairs, supervised his household and shielded him from many of the petty irritations which afflict the life of a successful novelist. He wrote of her 'She stuck to me so sturdily that in the end I stuck to myself. I do not know what I should have been without her. She stabilised my life.'[23] In his introduction to *The Book of Catherine Wells*, he paid a moving tribute to her and all that she meant to him. It is clear that, but for her, he might have been a very different person indeed. She was a steadying influence on his inherently anarchic and rebellious temperament. She schooled his indiscipline and gave his life a stability and dignity it would have otherwise lacked. She organised his affairs with competence and understanding, and it is doubtful whether he would have written so consistently or at such a standard without her resolute support. Without her as his wife during the most creative years of his life he would probably have run amok and dissipated his literary genius in less enduring forms. He would certainly have never produced a work of the stature of *Tono-Bungay*.

Wells was by nature impatient, untidy, sceptical and unruly. He would not conform. 'Jane' Wells with her quiet dignity, graciousness, methodical temperament and intolerance of disorder was just the balancing influence he most needed. She was shy and preferred to remain in the background, yet no account of his life and ideas is complete without an acknowledgement of her unique contribution to his success.

With the publication of his first novel, *The Time Machine* (1895), his literary career had begun in earnest. This was the prelude to a brilliant series of romances which established his reputation as a writer of extraordinary imagination and vision. The same year saw the publication of a volume of essays, *Select Conversations with an Uncle*, a collection of short stories, *The Stolen Bacillus and Other Incidents*, and a second novel, *The Wonderful Visit*.

Wells did not hesitate to introduce unconventional themes into his stories: *The War of the Worlds* describes an invasion of the earth by creatures from the planet Mars; *The Wonderful Visit* describes a visit of an angel to the earth; *The Sea Lady* tells of the discovery of a mermaid. But in each case it is not with the idea itself that the author is primarily concerned. It is with the impact of the idea upon established society and traditions. The device of the critical visitant from another world was Wells's vehicle for satirising Victorian England. In common with his novels, each of these romances had a definite didactic intent—they were not simply *stories*—yet each can be read straightforwardly as a story and nothing more. Some of them—such as *The Island of Doctor Moreau* and *The Food of the Gods*—are really fables: satires written in the form of an allegory. Orwell's *Animal Farm* is a modern instance of the same technique. To Wells the novel was a vehicle for the discussion of ideas, and although this became much more evident in his later works the serious intent was there from the very beginning.

It should also be noted that the strain of pessimism which runs through so much of his later work was already apparent in his earlier writings, from the 1890s onwards. In 'The Extinction of Man', published in 1894, he questioned man's complacency and optimism and pointed out that 'in the case of every other predominant animal the world has ever seen, the hour of its complete ascendency has been the eve of its entire overthrow'.[24] This was a theme he was to return to again and again in his immense output of novels, tracts, outlines and blueprints for world revolution written over a period of fifty years.

The Island of Doctor Moreau (1896) was one of his most pessimistic works. It is a grisly parable of the beast in man, and a grim reminder of the animal nature which lurks beneath the thin veneer of civilisation. *The Croquet Player* (1936) is a later parable on the same theme.

When the Sleeper Wakes (1899) is a nightmare description of a soulless despotism, which anticipates much of the drab uniformity and regimentation of Aldous Huxley's *Brave New World* and Orwell's *Nineteen Eighty Four*. The belief that Wells preached the inevitability of progress conveniently overlooks all these pessimistic writings.

At the same time as he was writing these tales of fantastic drugs, space travel and the coming of the aeroplane, he was writing romantic novels in the Dickensian tradition. Each was coloured with his rich and essentially English sense of humour; each contained a simple yet profound message for mankind. As Shaw was to the play and Chaplin to the film, so was Wells to the novel. At once his versatility became apparent: one has only to compare *The Wheels of Chance* with *The Island of Doctor Moreau* to appreciate the extraordinary range of style at his command. One finds it almost unbelievable that these are the work of one and the same author. In fact they were both published in the same year.

There is, too, a deeply human touch pervading all his early fiction. The description of the Philosophical Tramp in *The Wonderful Visit*, the Smallways family in *The War in the Air*, the wedding and funeral feasts and the Larkins sisters in *The History of Mr. Polly*, the garden party in *Tono-Bungay*, Remington's childhood in *The New Machiavelli*—all these are drawn with a Dickensian eye for detail and an infectious delight in the sheer wonder and joy of life. Wells's characters are not mere ciphers, as is sometimes alleged, but are drawn with a complex pen. Such figures as Cavor in *The First Men in the Moon* are no more ciphers than Arthur Kipps or George Ponderevo. Cavor is a vivid portrait of a deeply individual personality. Human touches abound in these early romances. After the Martian cylinder had landed on Horsell Common, 'an enterprising sweet-stuff dealer in the Chobham Road had sent up his son with a barrow-load of green apples and ginger-beer'.[25] And on the following morning the author's neighbour 'came up to the fence and extended a handful of strawberries, for his gardening was as generous as it was enthusiastic'.[26]

As Cavor and Bedford sit in the sphere on their journey to the moon, Bedford reads a newspaper advertisement stating that 'a lady in distress wished to dispose of some fish knives and forks, a wedding present, at a great sacrifice'.[27] And the first making of Cavorite happens quite unexpectedly because of a dispute between the joiner and the gardener as to whether coal is wood or soil.

This is the genius of the scientific romances: that they present a skilful word picture of the world we know—a tangible, familiar world—as the frame and starting point of the extra-terrestrial and the unknown. The Martians do not invade a world of depersonalised human beings. *The War of the Worlds* is peopled with characters like the 'shrivelled old fellow' pathetically trying to rescue his beloved orchids from the coming holocaust, and obstinately refusing to believe that destruction is imminent.

For Wells the years 1894–1900 were years of intensive literary activity. During this period he published eight novels and six volumes of short stories and essays. In 1900 he bought a house at Sandgate (Spade House), near Folkestone, which remained his home for nearly a decade. His health had now greatly improved, he was a successful writer, and by all his previous standards an extremely wealthy man. His name was becoming world famous. With the publication of *Anticipations* in 1901, his first serious sociological work, he was fairly launched upon his career as novelist, iconoclast and man of ideas.

* * * * *

During the years prior to 1914 Wells made some of his most enduring contributions to English literature including *Kipps* (1905), *Tono-Bungay* (1909), *Ann Veronica* (1909), and *The History of Mr. Polly* (1910). In 1908 he confided to Frederick Macmillan: 'As I told you long ago I want to specialise as a novelist. I think now my opportunity is ripe, and that if new novel follows novel without anything to distract people's attention—any other sort of work by me, I mean—it will be possible to consolidate the large confused reputation I have at the present time.' There is no doubt that Wells at this time regarded himself as primarily a novelist and only secondarily a writer on sociological problems. In the preface to *A Modern Utopia* he had gone so far as to state that he had intended *Anticipations* 'to be my sole digression from my art or trade (or what you will) of an imaginative writer' and that he regarded *A Modern Utopia* as in all probability the last of his sociological writings. Yet again and again he was distracted from his literary objectives by his intense curiosity about human affairs and his interest in social and political matters. He became a member of the Fabian Society in 1903 and for some years was an active speaker and writer on aspects of socialism.

In 1909 Wells sold Spade House and moved to London (17 Church Row, Hampstead) and in 1912 bought Little Easton Rectory, near Dunmow, Essex. This house, which he renamed Easton Glebe, remained his home until his wife's death in 1927. It is the 'Dower House' of *Mr. Britling Sees it Through.*

The outbreak of the First World War in 1914 proved to be a crucial turning point in Wells's affairs, and from this point onwards he was increasingly preoccupied with the need for world unification. The thesis which he expounded with mounting emphasis during the last thirty years of his life was that man must adapt his political and educational institutions to the sweeping changes in material conditions brought about by his expanding knowledge, or perish. This, in Wells's view, involved the creation of federal world institutions to enforce disarmament and ensure peace, and the setting up of planetary bodies for the conservation of natural resources, the co-ordination of transport, and so on. He devoted a considerable proportion of his energies to advocating the teaching of history on a world rather than a national basis and wrote *The Outline of History* (1920) and *A Short History of the World* (1922) to demonstrate that it was possible to relate 'the human adventure' as a single continuous narrative. *The Science of Life* (1929) and *The Work, Wealth and Happiness of Mankind* (1932) were conceived as companion volumes: these encyclopaedic compilations were intended to provide an outline of history, biology and economics for the common man.

During the inter-war years Wells travelled much and for some years spent his winters in the south of France. From 1923 to 1933 his winter home was near Grasse in Provence—first in a rented villa called Lou Bastidon and then in a more permanent home, Lou Pidou. Here he planned and wrote *The World of William Clissold*, a long and ambitious novel which gives a fascinating picture of his mental world at this time. In 1934 he published his two volume autobiography *Experiment in Autobiography*, a work which contains some of his freshest and most engaging writing.

Despite his preoccupation with his non-fiction writings Wells remained a novelist throughout his life and after 1926, when he was sixty, produced no fewer than six major novels. These are *Mr. Blettsworthy on Rampole Island* (1928), *The Bulpington of Blup* (1932), *Brynhild* (1937), *Apropos of Dolores* (1938), *Babes in the Darkling Wood* (1940) and *You Can't be too Careful* (1941). Opinion is sharply divided on the merits of these novels. Some critics regard them as being devoid of any literary merit; others see in them abundant evidence of his extraordinary abilities as a creative writer.[28] My own reading, as I hope to show, supports the latter view.

At the same time he was writing imaginative romances in the vein of his earlier work. These included *The Shape of Things to Come* (1933), *Star Begotten* (1937), and two film scenarios which were subsequently adapted for the screen, *Things to Come* and *Man who Could Work Miracles*. During these years Wells also produced a considerable quantity of journalism and lectured in the United States, Australia and elsewhere. From 1933 to 1937 he lived at various addresses in London, finally settling in an elegant Nash house at 13 Hanover Terrace, Regents Park. Here he remained throughout the war years, refusing to move in spite of air raids. He wrote numerous articles and pamphlets on the issues of war and peace, and in *The Fate of Homo Sapiens* (1939) and *The Common-sense of War and Peace* (1940), reiterated his advocacy of world order and the ending of national sovereignty. In 1943 he was awarded the degree of D.Sc. by the University of London, submitting in its support a 'Thesis on the Quality of Illusion in the Continuity of the Individual Life'.

His health deteriorated with increasing seriousness from 1944 onwards and for some time he lived the restricted life of a semi-invalid. Something of the quality of his life and surroundings during this period may be gleaned from *The Happy Turning*, a serene collection of essays written simultaneously with *Mind at the End of its Tether*. The latter work, frequently cited as evidence of his culminating pessimism, was not in fact his last word. In 1944–5 he was at work on a collection of articles, *Exasperations: The Last Testament of H. G. Wells* (now preserved at the Wells Archive at the University of Illinois) and in July 1945 appeared 'The Betterave Papers',[29] a delightful essay in which he looked back, with frankness and charm, on the whole of his literary career. 'Reviewers might praise him [Wells],' he wrote, 'and a dwindling band of dupes might get his books. They vanished from the shop windows and from the tables of cultured people. . . . People whom once he had duped would perhaps mention him as a figure of some significance in English literature, but the established reply of the people who no longer read him and had nothing to say about him, was simply the grimace of those who scent decay. "Oh, *Wells!*" they would say, and leave it at that. So that Wells decays alive and will be buried a man already forgotten. . . .'

On the afternoon of Thursday, 13 August 1946 he died, quite alone, at 13 Hanover Terrace. He was cremated at Golders Green three days later.

*   *   *   *   *

Wells was an uneven writer, capable at his worst of writing in a repetitive manner. But at his best he could write novels of the stature of *Tono-Bungay*, *The History of Mr. Polly* and *The Dream*; he could write brilliant fantasies such as *The Time Machine*, *The War of the Worlds* and *The First Men in the Moon*; inspiring visions of the future such as *A Modern Utopia* and *Men Like Gods*; blueprints for a new world order such as *The Open Conspiracy* and *Phoenix*; he could write summaries of the human adventure such as *The Outline of History*; above all, he could inspire and stimulate his readers, create a sense of wonder and an awareness of the limitless possibilities of the universe.

We ought not to be ungrateful. In the best of the novels, romances and short stories he made a permanent contribution to English letters and opened up new horizons of life and behaviour which will be appreciated by generations yet to come. He inspired countless thousands of readers with his fresh, invigorating, humanitarian vision. He brought new insights to the English novel in a way which had not been attempted before. It is indeed through the novels and romances rather than the vast corpus of his non-fiction writing that his name and ideas will be kept alive. These will live through the sheer vitality of their imagination, the force of their writing and their incomparable breadth of vision. These are his literary inheritance.

Wells's Literary Reputation

H. G. Wells was the *enfant terrible* of English letters. He refused to conform to any of the established canons of literature, preferring to call himself a journalist and insisting that his work was only of transitory value.

'This world, says Sir James Jeans, is going on for a million million years. I wave the striving immortals onward, and step aside. Sir J. C. Squire doubts if I shall "live", and I cannot say how cordially and unreservedly I agree.'[1]

The chief flaw in his make-up was a tearing impatience: a combination of restlessness with a furious energy which led him to produce book after book at prodigious speed. His three encyclopaedias alone—*The Outline of History, The Science of Life* and *The Work, Wealth and Happiness of Mankind*—would be considered the life's work of any normal man. Yet he wrote more than a hundred books in addition to these. The immensity of his output meant inevitably that his work suffered in lack of finish and in repetitiveness. Some of the later novels, such as *The Secret Places of the Heart* and *The Autocracy of Mr. Parham*, are marred by pages of dull writing, and even the early novels are not altogether free of untidiness and occasional clumsiness of structure. With one or two notable exceptions—*Love and Mr. Lewisham* and *Tono-Bungay*, for example—he did not take great pains over his writing. Much of the laborious work of proof-reading and searching for grammatical errors was executed by his faithful wife, Jane.

What, in fact, was his attitude to the novel? In a revealing passage from *Tono-Bungay* he set out his approach with transparent clarity:

> My ideas of a novel all through are comprehensive rather than austere. . . . I've found the restraints and rules of the art (as I made them out) impossible for me. I like to write, I am keenly in-

terested in writing, but it is not my technique . . . do what I will I fail to see how I can be other than a lax, undisciplined story-teller. I must sprawl and flounder, comment and theorise, if I am to get the thing out I have in mind.[2]

One may argue that in this statement he was doing less than justice to himself, for if the expression 'a born novelist' has any meaning then he was certainly that. And yet how true this confession is. Even in *Tono-Bungay*, which represents Wells the novelist at the height of his creative powers, the reader is almost overwhelmed by the sheer force of the IDEAS the author is continually advancing. The novel, for him, was a vehicle for the discussion of ideas. It had value so long as these ideas had relevance to society, and after that its living interest ceased. His output was littered with novels of the calibre of *Joan and Peter* (1918) and *Babes in the Darkling Wood* (1940), relevant and topical in their day but less readable to the world of the 1970s. They were not written with an eye on posterity at all: they were designed to meet the immediate needs of the moment, to portray the mood of the times and to capture the social and intellectual climate of a passing phase. *Mr. Britling*, whilst appearing extremely 'dated' today, proved to be an extremely popular book and earned for its author a considerable sum of money. It met a popular demand and interpreted the First World War as no other novel of that period did.

There are, of course, exceptions. *Tono-Bungay*, *The New Machiavelli* and *The Dream* are still readable and fascinating today because of their vitality and power as authentic social documents. In them the climate of an age is portrayed with a brilliant and searching pen. But these are untypical of his work as a whole. Save for a few rare exceptions he did not consciously aim at survival into futurity. One wonders what his reaction would have been had he known that *The Time Machine* would still be in print eighty years after its original publication. The hastily written hybrid fiction of his later years—such works as *The Autocracy of Mr. Parham* and *The Holy Terror*—is nowadays completely forgotten. It was written to serve a purely transitory end and Wells was quite indifferent to its fate once that limited end had been served.

His lack of patience with men and institutions was certainly a grave weakness, both in his temperament and his thought. He himself had no illusions about his shortcomings.

I am a far less stable creature than she [Jane Wells] was, with a driving quality that holds my instabilities together. I have more drive than strength, and little patience; I am hasty and incompetent about much of the detailed business of life because I put too large a proportion of my available will and energy into issues that dominate me. Only in that way do I seem able to get on with these issues that dominate me. I have to overwork, with all the penalties of overworking in loss of grace and finish, to get my work done.[3]

Here we touch the core of Wells's attitude of mind. At the root of his temperament he was an unstable creature, driven by storms of restlessness and claustrophobia, which at times almost overwhelmed his life.[4] Lurking in the deep recesses of his nature was a tendency to run amok: a driving impatience with the world of reality and a desire to escape from it into an ideal world of his dreams.

His friends nicknamed him 'the fiery particle'. He was consumed by a dynamo of hectic nervous energy, and his temperament compelled him to pour his energies into whatever project was on hand with fanatical zeal. He frequently commenced work on a new book before completing its predecessor and on many occasions was writing two entirely dissimilar books simultaneously. This instability in his make-up proved to be a serious flaw. In *The New Machiavelli*, Remington's close friend Willersley (Graham Wallas) observed: 'You're a strange man, Remington, with a kind of kink in you. You've a sort of force. You might happen to do immense things. . . . Only—.'[5]

Wells simply had not the patience for any sustained academic discipline, or to work closely with others over a period of time. *The Outline of History*, with its glaring defects but thrilling sweep and power, was the utmost he could go towards sustained intellectual effort. He had no staying power, no ability for consistent unrewarding labour. He was in too much of a rush to abandon what was on hand and begin work on the next thing.

His conception of all creative work was essentially anarchic. 'Organisation and genius are antipathetic. The vivid and creative mind, by virtue of its qualities, is a spasmodic and adventurous mind; it resents blinkers, and the mere implication that it can be driven in harness to the unexpected. It demands freedom.'[6] For this reason he refused to be bound by canons and formulas, declaring that there was no such thing as THE novel and that each writer must be absolutely free to interpret his work in his own way. There is more than an element of Cockney cheek in his unruliness. There is a deliberate defiance of authority, an impish rebelliousness, an irreverent cocking the snook at established conventions and accepted morality. Any suggestion that there could be uniform standards in literature or that the novel had certain definable limits was completely rejected. An invitation from Henry James to join the Academy of the Royal Society of Literature was politely but firmly refused.

His conception of the novel was, in essence, that it had a vital role to play in society: a role which no other medium of discussion could adequately fulfil. He had no respect for what he called the 'Weary Giant' theory: the idea that a novel should be light and should avoid serious issues since the reader would be too tired for anything else. The novel was a vehicle for the criticism of life as it is—not simply for *describing* life as it is, *à la* Arnold Bennett.[7] In his essay 'The Contemporary Novel' (1911)[8] he argued that 'Before we have done, we will have all life within the scope of the novel.' He withdrew this statement in his autobiography, but there could be no doubt of the wide claims he was making. Politics, religion, philosophy, sexual morality—all these were legitimate fields for comment and discussion by novelists, and in his own work he did not hesitate to defy the social code and outrage the conventions of his day.

Ann Veronica (1909) was his first serious breach of the established order. His heroine, who was in many respects drawn from actual life, had the effrontery to elope with a married man and live with him in a state of defiant happiness. This was contrary to all the prevailing ideas of the time and the furore aroused by this book led to attempts to ostracise Wells from public life. Many libraries banned it and angry sermons were preached against it. But *Ann Veronica* was a lusty infant and it has survived, alive and kicking, into the present day. It is still in print at the time of writing. To this day, babies are still named after Ann Veronica in honour of her cheerful rebellion against narrow-mindedness.

Hardly had the dust settled after this controversy than he published *The New Machiavelli* (1911), which hammered home the same points from a slightly different angle. In the closing sections of this novel he elaborated his attack on the accepted sexual morality into a vigorous criticism of the entire code. This was followed by *The Passionate Friends* (1913) which continued the attack in even more unmistakable terms. After 1914 Wells claimed to have cut himself adrift from literature altogether—if, indeed, he had ever wholly belonged to the mainstream of English letters. After this date he became, by his own choice, a 'journalist'. He had burned his literary boats in the cause of the salvaging of civilisation.[9]

His quarrel with Henry James has been fully documented

elsewhere[10] and there is no need to repeat it here. It was basically a dispute between men of profoundly divergent temperaments whose attitude of mind and outlook upon life differed beyond any prospect of reconciliation. The gulf which separated them mentally and emotionally was as wide and unbridgeable as that between himself and the Webbs. Henry James was a perfectionist, an artist in the classical sense. He was meticulous, methodical, painstaking and deeply interested in literary style; Wells was none of these things. Their close friendship, begun in 1898, became increasingly strained as their differences grew more apparent. It was finally severed by the publication of *Boon* (1915) in which Wells ridiculed James and all he stood for in a biting parody which James never forgave. Wells apologised profusely for his tactlessness and lack of manners but by then the friendship was definitely at an end.

It may be questioned whether they had ever really understood one another. For some years they had maintained a frequent correspondence and never lost an opportunity of meeting, but their thought processes were so dissimilar and their basic outlook so foreign that it is doubtful if any real intellectual intimacy ever existed. As with the Webbs, the substance of their thoughts was wholly different.

Many years later Wells observed that throughout their quarrel he had had the peculiar feeling that they were both right,[11] and indeed there can be no final judgement on their dialogue. The debate between the scientist and the artist, the empiricist and the perfectionist, will continue so long as man endures. But how far is this a false division? Are the two attitudes completely incompatible? Wells's own personality was far more complex than this simple division into mutually negatory terms would suggest. There was a fundamental contradiction in his mind between the attitudes of the scientist and the artist: an inner conflict between classical and romantic elements. Neither was uppermost throughout his life. Rather was his work and thought a continual interplay of the two attitudes. In his franker moments he was aware of this contradiction. He rarely confessed as much in his own person, but preferred to express it from the viewpoint of his fictional heroes. William Clissold, for example, admitted that his disposition was diametrically opposed to his philosophy,[12] and the conflict is evident at many points in *Tono-Bungay*, particularly when George confesses he is 'a hard and morally limited cad with a mind beyond my merits'—'a spiritual guttersnipe in love with unimaginable goddesses'.[13]

*   *   *   *   *

It is significant that as a scientific romancer Wells's reputation is still high, as a novelist his fame (in common with that of Galsworthy and Bennett) has declined very considerably, and as a thinker and social theorist his standing has fallen to almost zero. Yet these assessments are in inverse ratio to his own scale of values.

He wrote nearly fifty novels, from *The Time Machine* in 1895 to *You Can't Be Too Careful* in 1941, but scholarly discussion has centred almost entirely on a mere handful of these: *Love and Mr. Lewisham*, *Kipps*, *Tono-Bungay* and *The History of Mr. Polly*. These four have been frequently dissected and analysed, whilst the remainder of his output has been permitted to fall into almost total neglect. Admittedly, Wells wrote hastily and often ill. He acknowledged that 'certain streaks of slovenliness' were inseparable from his temperament and that he rarely took pains over his writing,[14] and it is undeniable that much of his later work is uneven and poorly constructed. But this is by no means true of all his fiction, and at least five of the later novels deserve serious reassessment: these are *The Passionate Friends* (1913), *The Dream* (1924), *Mr. Blettsworthy on Rampole Island* (1928), *The Croquet Player* (1936), and *You Can't be too Careful* (1941).

The Passionate Friends is memorable for its profound insight into the author's hidden personality. The chapter entitled 'Boyhood', describing Stephen Stratton's childhood at Burnmore Park and his secret thoughts and speculations, is one of the most intimate and authentic self-portraits in any of the novels. It contains the clue to the wayward, sceptical, rebellious nature of Wells's innermost temperament, and the entire work is permeated with a mood of philosophical detachment rare in such an ebullient writer. *Tono-Bungay* and *The New Machiavelli* belong to the same phase of self-criticism and burning social purpose.

The Dream is an intense criticism of life as it is and, in common with *In the Days of the Comet* (which it resembles in many respects), contrasts the freedom and happiness of an ideal world with the confusion and disorder of the present. The book is saturated with the idealism which was so characteristic of his work and, as with all his finest writing, has the capacity to stimulate thought, to suggest ideas, and to inspire by its visionary quality. On its publication it was hailed by the *Daily News* as 'the richest, most generous and absorbing thing that Mr. Wells has given us for years and years', and it certainly contains some of the most living characters among the later novels.

In a totally different category is *Mr. Blettsworthy on Rampole Island*, one of the most remarkable works ever to fall from his pen. This marks a return to the style of *Doctor Moreau*, satirising with biting wit such venerable institutions as the monarchy, the church, the army and the law. The opening, non-allegorical chapters contain some of his most vivid impressions—the description of Blettsworthy's childhood at Harrow Hoeward, of his uncle the Rev. Rupert Blettsworthy, of his love for Olive Slaughter and of Oxford in those remote, placid days before 1914. Then the long account of the sea voyage, strangely reminiscent of Edward Prendick's sojourn in *Doctor Moreau*, culminating in the strange adventure of Rampole Island. It is at this point that the allegory begins, from the moment of his arrival and the first sight of 'the Great Goddess welcoming her slaves' (the Statue of Liberty) to his final return to the ostensible world. The satire is wickedly barbed from beginning to end. One sees life in terms of a squalid, narrow gorge, the monarchy as a cage of tree sloths, ancient organisations and institutions as the dreary Megatheria, and politicians as 'loud-croaking bull-frogs'. Wells recorded in his autobiography that he laughed aloud when writing it. The note of sarcasm remains long after the narrator has returned to civilisation. On the outbreak of war Blettsworthy enlists in the army and shortly afterwards embarks for France. Then follows a bitter and moving description of the battlefields of death, written with all the anger of a deeply sensitive man outraged by military stupidity and shortsightedness. For all these reasons *Mr. Blettsworthy* merits far more serious consideration than it has yet received. The quality of writing in both this and in *The Croquet Player* lifts them well above the mainstream of his later work and demand a permanent niche among his masterpieces.

You Can't be too Careful, his last novel, is an amalgam of all his many-sided talents in a single work. Much of it is reminiscent of *The History of Mr. Polly*, and the first half at least is told with Dickensian humour and imagination. At the same time the book is pervaded by an austerity and dispassionate realism unusual in his fiction. Mankind, he urges, is not yet *Homo sapiens* but only *Homo Tewler*—a feeble, blundering misfit struggling against an environment which has changed beyond all recognition, and 'a ruthless urgency calls upon him to adapt his mind and his way of living to these vast demands and become *Homo sapiens* indeed, before utter disaster overwhelms him'.[15] As a novel in the conventional manner *You Can't be too Careful* is perhaps a failure; as a salutary warning of impending disaster it is unforgettable.

These, at least, must be added to the canon, and alongside them should be placed the opening chapters of *In the Days of the Comet* and *The New Machiavelli*—both fascinating glimpses into his boyhood. But in the last analysis any attempt to confine him to a selection of titles fails because of his extraordinary vitality. He was the faithful observer of a particular period in time, recording with unforgettable clarity the social, political and intellectual forces of his day and portraying with warm compassion the lives and loves of inconspicuous folk.

A fact which has escaped the attention of literary critics almost completely is that Wells was in reality a regional novelist. He was the delineator of a particular region of England—London and the Home Counties—and he rarely strayed far in his novels from the Weald and South Downs which he loved. Even of the scientific romances this is true. *The Time Machine* is set entirely in the valley of the Thames; *The Invisible Man* is set in Iping (Sussex) and London; *The War of the Worlds*, for all its cosmic implications, is fought out on the familiar terrain of Surrey, and the opening and closing chapters of *The First Men in the Moon* are set firmly on the Kentish coast. In all his enormous output of fiction the only major exceptions to this rule are *The Island of Doctor Moreau*, *In the Days of the Comet*, *The World of William Clissold* and *Meanwhile*. Though in his ideas and breadth of vision he ranged far and wide, as a novelist he remained almost exclusively provincial.

There is also a rather curious limitation to the 'types' portrayed in his fiction. He re-created extremely well the kind of people he KNEW—Kipps, Polly, Uncle Ponderevo, Harry Mortimer Smith—but nearly all his heroines (with the exception of Ann Veronica and Dolores, both of whom were drawn from life)[16] are unconvincing. He could describe with conviction clerks, tramps, draper's apprentices, scamps and frauds; all these he knew from bitter and intimate experience. But he was less skilful at IMAGINING character or presenting realistic sketches of types outside his immediate range of knowledge.

Nowhere, in any of his novels, is there a convincing picture of a manual worker: even in *In the Days of the Comet*, which is an acutely perceptive description of life in the Potteries, the hero, Willie Leadford, works in a pot-bank office, and the reader is given no details of his daily routine. In *A Modern Utopia* we are given a brief description of work in a wood-carving factory, but this account bears little relevance to earthly experience. Most of his heroes are drapers, shop assistants, school teachers—even tramps—but very rarely is there any reference to the 'other side' of life: miners, factory workers, agricultural workers, and so on. This lack of contact with manual workers and ignorance of their mode of living was one of his most important blind spots. He had an intimate knowledge of the life of a draper and could also write convincingly of shop assistants, clerks and research workers: all aspects of life which he knew closely from his own personal experience. But his knowledge of industrial organisation and trade unionism was slight. By his own definition he was an aristocrat, not a democrat, and he had no hope of any constructive initiatives from the common man. Consistently throughout his writings recurs his dream of mankind being salvaged by a creative minority of leading men and women—'the vast complex of powerful people, clever people, enterprising people, influential people, amidst whom power is diffused today'.[17] It has been said of him that he wanted to see the whole world become one gigantic middle class, and it is certainly true that there was little room in his planetary Utopias for the purely manual worker.

In fairness it should be said that he made strenuous efforts to understand the character and psychology of the English working man, and certainly had the gift of mingling with all social classes on terms of complete equality. During his visit to Nottingham in 1937 he went out of his way to meet miners and labourers in the public houses of Radford, an area Alan Sillitoe was to make famous in *Saturday Night and Sunday Morning*. He confided to a friend that it was the first time in his life he had met 'real people'. He was also familiar with such works as Bart Kennedy's *A Man Adrift* and *A Sailor Tramp*, and was fully aware of the need for a sympathetic understanding of the navvy and the labourer. Yet the fact remains that he failed to communicate this concern through the medium of his novels and, either deliberately or unconsciously, created the impression of indifference to their fate. This gap in his vision, together with its corollary, an intrinsic distaste for social democracy, was probably his gravest limitation as a thinker.

He was also a curiously egoistic writer. All his leading characters—Hoopdriver, Kipps, Polly, George Ponderevo, Remington, Trafford, Stratton, Mr. Britling, Clissold—all these and many others were reincarnations of Wells himself, projections of his own personality in one guise or another.

He was a vivid writer with extraordinary gifts of evocation and inspiration, whose books had a highly stimulating effect on millions of his readers. One of his publishers said of him: 'His influence upon his generation, and especially upon youth, was profound.' And yet his standing as a literary figure remains ambiguous. New idols have ousted him from the literary scene. In the West his reputation slumped disastrously during the years following his death and, in his own words, only 'a dwindling band of dupes' still read his books.[18]

An additional factor must surely be that he tended to over-simplify issues which are in reality complicated and difficult. He was not a practical man. Like Robert Owen before him he was a visionary, a man of ideas. He had little sympathy with democratic techniques. He could not work as a member of a committee. He resigned in a huff from almost every organisation he joined. As Margaret Cole remarks, 'the rage may always have been well-founded, since organisations are apt to be exasperating, but the result was a trifle anarchical'.[19] He lacked the patience or temperament to engage in slow, dogged spade work in bodies such as the Labour Party or the Fabian Society; he had a restless nature, alternately bored and furiously active, and was constitutionally incapable of succumbing to a sustained academic discipline. If illness had not obliged him to abandon teaching and research work for journalism it is fairly certain that his own temperament would have forced him out of it sooner or later.

He was also inconsistent as a prophet and as an educator. This was partly because his books were written over a long period of time and his views naturally changed over the years, but the confusion in the mind of the reader was no less real. His views on religion fluctuated very widely, alternately giving alarm to the Rationalist Press Association and the Roman Catholic Church. His forecasts of the future were often woefully wrong—witness his comments on the submarine in *Anticipations*, and his remarks on broadcasting in *The Way the World is Going*. And it must be said frankly that some of his romances and speculations were incredibly naïve: *The World Set Free* contains a glib description of the establishment of a world government by a council of wise politicians. In *In the Days of the Comet* mankind is converted to sanity by breathing a gas from outer space. There is a tendency in much of his writing to skate round difficult problems and to take short cuts to his desired end. His books are deeply inspiring, but they lack practical guidance on how to bring about the better world of his dreams. There is no satisfactory answer to the question: 'What can *I* do to help bring about a world state?' This was, of course, partly deliberate. Wells's novels, like Shaw's plays, did not set out to offer a detailed blueprint for practical action, but rather to suggest ideas, to stimulate thought, to set in motion thinking and discussion on the problems facing humanity and the ways in which they can be overcome. He wished to be regarded not as an inspired prophet, but rather as a writer who supplied a point of departure.

At his worst, his writings were verbose and repetitive. *The Autocracy of Mr. Parham* and *The Soul of a Bishop* are examples of his style when it touches bottom. *Crux Ansata* falls into the same unhappy category. A few more novels of the calibre of *Tono-Bungay* or *The Time Machine*, and a few more non-fiction works of the standard of *First and Last Things* or *The Open Conspiracy*, would have done more to establish a lasting reputation for him than a dozen books like *The Research Magnificent*. Only a small proportion of his enormous output will survive to carry his name forward into posterity. The bulk of his non-fiction writings will fade into oblivion.

*   *   *   *   *

Yet it remains true that to discuss the novels without discussing the ideas which animate them is to misunderstand the whole approach of the writer to his art. It is frequently assumed that there were two distinct Wellses: the literary craftsman of 1895–1914, and the propagandist of 1914 onwards. This is not so. Wells was very definitely a preacher from the time of his earliest novels, and *The Island of Doctor Moreau* is just as didactic in intent as *The Croquet Player*. All the scientific romances were conceived as allegorical media for the presentation of his ideas—*The Time Machine* and *The War of The Worlds* as a counter to the prevalent spirit of optimism and a grim reminder of human solidarity; *The Island of Doctor Moreau* as a fable on the evil within man: *The Invisible Man* and *The War in the Air* as a warning of the tragic consequences following upon the misuse of science for selfish or warlike ends; *The First Men in the Moon* as a satire on over-specialisation; and *The Food of the Gods* as a plea for the sweeping enlargement of local and national boundaries.

The early novels, too, each had their message. *The Wonderful Visit* is a satire on human cruelty and mismanagement; *The Wheels of Chance*, in spite of its whimsical gaiety, contains many passages of dialogue which anticipate the rebellious note of *Ann Veronica*; *Love and Mr. Lewisham* is a perceptive study of the problems of courtship and marriage in the lower middle-class.

Any attempt to dichotomise Wells is therefore quite false. From his earliest literary efforts to his unpublished *Exasperations: The Last Testament of H. G. Wells*, from the facetious irreverence of *The Desert Daisy* to the angry, doom-laden utterances of his last days, he sought to convey, illustrate, expand and disseminate his ideas through the medium of his books.

His influence on the modern novel has been profound, and though he has been eclipsed by a new generation of later writers—novelists of character rather than ideas—his place among the giants of English literature is secure. For the scientific romances, the short stories and the best of the novels posterity has reason to be grateful, and for these alone he merits a permanent place in our affections. The indications are, indeed, that his fall from favour is merely temporary. Literary fashions change rapidly and, as with any major writer, there was an inevitable decline in fame in the years immediately following his death. One may confidently predict therefore that before this century has run its course scholarly and popular interest in him will have revived and he will be once again one of the most widely read authors in our literature. The first signs of that revival are already discernible.

The process of assessment was bound to be a slow one. He was such a prolific writer and lived so abundantly that it is only now, thirty years after his death, that we are in a position to digest his achievement and attempt a dispassionate appraisal of it. We can now see that he was the Rousseau of our age, embracing in a single mighty span the scientific austerity and sense of world crisis of the twentieth century and the intellectual curiosity of the enlightenment. Perhaps the most fascinating question for the historian of ideas is to ask which of his books, if any, will carry his name beyond the year 2000. One would hope that future generations will remember him at least for the short stories, *The Time Machine*, *The History of Mr. Polly* and *Tono-Bungay*, that they will think of him as one of the most original and prosilient writers of his day and as the apostle of a new pattern of living for mankind.

As a novelist in the accepted sense his supreme achievement remains *Tono-Bungay*. This is a sweeping panorama of the social life of England in the years before 1914, and in its pages he came near to bringing all life within the scope of a single epic. Here is Wells both in his strength and in his weakness, and this fascinating novel, containing as it does the essence of his personality and the light of his vision, will carry his name beyond the confines of our own century into that unknown futurity he yearned to explore.

Part II

AN H. G. WELLS DICTIONARY

An H. G. Wells Dictionary

This dictionary is an alphabetically arranged guide to the titles of all the novels, romances, short stories and fictional essays by Wells published in book form. It does not include references to the unreprinted journalism—of which there is a very considerable quantity—with the exception of those short stories not included in any published collection.

The following abbreviations are used throughout the dictionary:

CB: *The Country of the Blind and Other Stories.*
CSS: *The Complete Short Stories of H. G. Wells.*
CPM: *Certain Personal Matters.*
DW: *The Door in the Wall and Other Stories.*
PS: *The Plattner Story and Others.*
SB: *The Stolen Bacillus And Other Incidents.*
SCU: *Select Conversations with an Uncle.*
TD: *Twelve Stories And A Dream.*
TST: *Tales of Space and Time.*

ADVENTURES OF TOMMY, THE. An illustrated short story written in 1898 whilst Wells was convalescing at New Romney following an illness. It was written to amuse Marjorie Hick, the daughter of Wells's doctor. The story was published in book form in 1929.

AEPYORNIS ISLAND. Short story, first published in the *Pall Mall Budget*, Christmas 1894. Included in SB and CB. The narrator, Butcher, hatches out the egg of the aepyornis, an extinct bird, on an atoll in the Indian Ocean.

AESOP'S QUININE FOR DELPHI. An unpublished appendix to *Mind at the End of its Tether* (1945), consisting of additional fables supposedly written by Aesop. The following extracts are included in *H. G. Wells: Journalism and Prophecy*, edited by W. Warren Wagar (Houghton Mifflin, 1964):

'Old Aesop Resuscitated'; 'The World in slippers'; 'The Everlasting Nay'; 'The Culminating Man'; 'The Insignificant Man Ends History'.

ALL ABOARD FOR ARARAT. A parable based on the story of Noah's Ark, first published in 1940. The central character, Noah Lummock, sets sail in the ark, bound for the new world of post-war reconstruction.

AMATEUR NATURE LOVER, THE. First published under the title 'Out Banstead Way' (*Pall Mall Gazette*, 25 November 1893) and reprinted in CPM. The essay describes an autumn walk over Epsom Downs from Banstead to Sutton, interspersed with reflections on life and nature.

ANN VERONICA. Novel, published in 1909. Based in part upon Wells's friendship with Amber Pember Reeves, the book caused a furore on publication because of its frankness on sexual matters and the uninhibited behaviour of the heroine, who professes her love for a married man. (See *The Time Traveller* by Norman and Jeanne Mackenzie, ch. 16.)

ANSWER TO PRAYER. Short story, first published in the *New Statesman*, 1937, and reprinted in *Turnstile One*, edited by V. S. Pritchett (Turnstile Press, 1948). Not included in CSS. A bishop, in the act of prayer, receives an answer from God.

APPLE, THE. Short story, first published in *The Idler*, October 1896. Included in PS. A schoolmaster is given an apple from the Tree of Knowledge.

APROPOS OF DOLORES. Novel, published in 1938. Based in part upon Wells's friendship with Odette Keun, *Apropos of Dolores* is one of the finest and wittiest of the later novels. The story is analysed in detail in *Anatomies of Egotism: A Reading of the Last Novels of H. G. Wells* by Robert Bloom (University of Nebraska Press, 1977).

ARGONAUTS OF THE AIR, THE. Short story, first published in *Phil May's Annual*, 1895. Included in PS. An early forecast of flight, which anticipates the experiments with flying machines described in *Tono-Bungay* (1909).

ART OF BEING PHOTOGRAPHED, THE. First published in the *Pall Mall Gazette*, 1893, and reprinted in SCU. The uncle advises George that 'a man should go very softly to a photographer's, and he should sit before the camera with reverence in his heart and in his attitude, as if he were in the presence of the woman he loved'.

AT A WINDOW. *See* THROUGH A WINDOW.

ATLANTIC EDITION. A uniform edition of Wells's works in 28 volumes, issued simultaneously in 1924 by Fisher Unwin Ltd., London, and Charles Scribners and Sons, New York. The edition was limited to 1670 sets, the first volume in each set being autographed by Wells. Wells wrote a special introduction to each volume and a general preface to the collection as a whole.

AUTOCRACY OF MR. PARHAM, THE. Novel, published in 1930. The story contains caricatures of a number of politicians and public figures of the time, including Winston Churchill and Mussolini.

BABES IN THE DARKLING WOOD. Novel, published in 1940. Wells's introduction, 'The Novel of Ideas', needs to be read in conjunction with Chapter 7, Part 5 of *Experiment in Autobiography* ('Digression about Novels'), and also his essay 'The Contemporary Novel' (Chapter 9 of *An Englishman Looks at the World*). Both are reprinted in *Henry James and H. G. Wells*, edited by Leon Edel and Gordon N. Ray (London, Rupert Hart-Davis, 1958). See also Wells's preface to *Stories of Men and Women in Love*.

BAGARROW. Essay, first published in the *Pall Mall Gazette*, 1894, and reprinted in CPM: a light-hearted sketch of a well-meaning but priggish idealist.

BAGSHOT'S MURAL DECORATIONS. First published in the *Pall Mall Gazette*, 2 May 1894, and reprinted in SCU. The uncle criticises Bagshot's taste for decorating his walls with reproductions of the old masters.

BARDLET'S ROMANCE, A. *See* IN THE MODERN VEIN.

BEALBY. Novel, published in 1915. Describes the picaresque adventures of Arthur Bealby, a servant boy who flees from a life of domestic servitude and becomes involved in a series of escapades.

BEAUTIFUL SUIT, THE. Short story, originally published in *Collier's Weekly*, April 1909 (under the title 'A Moonlight Fable') and reprinted in DW and CB. A man has a beautiful suit made for him by his mother; on wearing it one moonlit night he falls accidentally and is killed.

BETTERAVE PAPERS, THE. Three satirical essays (ostensibly written by Wilfred B. Betterave 'at the uncalled for insistence of H. G. Wells') printed in the *Cornhill Magazine*, July 1945. The essays contain humorous reflections upon Wells's literary career.

BLEAK MARCH IN EPPING FOREST. First published in the *Pall Mall Gazette*, 16 March 1894, and reprinted in CPM: a description of a visit paid to Epping Forest on a wintry day by Wells and his wife.

BOOK OF CURSES, THE. First published in the *Pall Mall Gazette*, 9 June 1894 (under the title 'On Swearing') and reprinted in CPM: a humorous sketch of Professor Gargoyle, who deplores the decline of swearing.

BOOK OF ESSAYS DEDICATORY, THE. First published in the *Pall Mall*

Gazette, 14 February 1895 (under the title 'My Last Book') and reprinted in CPM: a humorous account of an idea for a book composed entirely of dedications.

BOON. *Boon, The Mind of the Race, The Wild Asses of the Devil, and The Last Trump:* a collection of humorous and satirical essays, published in 1915, although parts were written much earlier. The book purports to be a selection from the 'literary remains' of George Boon, a distinguished novelist, edited by his literary executor Reginald Bliss. In fact the entire volume is Wells's work, who acknowledged his authorship in a second edition published in 1920.

The book is important not only for its contribution to the debate with Henry James on the art of fiction and the role of the novel—the fourth chapter, 'Of Art, Of Literature, Of Mr. Henry James' is reprinted in *Henry James and H. G. Wells*, edited by Leon Edel and Gordon N. Ray (Rupert Hart-Davis, 1958)—but also for its insight into Wells's attitude to the First World War. The final chapter, 'The Story of the Last Trump', is reprinted in CSS.

Boon is also notable for the 26 sketches (or 'picshuas') which enliven its pages.

BROTHERS, THE. Novella, published in 1938. Two brothers, leaders of rival factions in a civil war, discover that they have far more in common than either had realised.

BRYNHILD. Novel, published in 1937. The story is analysed in detail in *Anatomies of Egotism: A Reading of the Last Novels of H. G. Wells*, by Robert Bloom (University of Nebraska Press, 1977).

BULLA, THE. *See* THE RECONCILIATION.

BULPINGTON OF BLUP, THE. Novel, published in 1932. Based in part upon Wells's friendship with Ford Madox Ford, *The Bulpington of Blup* is widely acknowledged to be one of the finest of the later novels. The story is analysed in detail in *Anatomies of Egotism: A Reading of the Last Novels of H. G. Wells* by Robert Bloom (University of Nebraska Press, 1977).

CAMFORD VISITATION, THE. Novella, published in 1937. The university town of Camford is visited by a voice from 'out of the deeps beyond space and time' which is highly critical of contemporary educational institutions.

CATASTROPHE, A. Short story, originally published in the *New Budget*, 4 April 1895, and reprinted in PS. A struggling shop-keeper is saved from bankruptcy by an unexpected legacy.

CERTAIN PERSONAL MATTERS. Sub-titled 'A Collection of Material, Mainly Autobiographical', this volume of humorous essays was published in 1897. It consists of 39 essays and articles originally printed in the *Pall Mall Gazette* and other journals, and includes some of Wells's earliest surviving journalism. (*See especially* THE MAN OF THE YEAR MILLION, THE EXTINCTION OF MAN, *and* ON THE ART OF STAYING AT THE SEASIDE.)

CHRISTINA ALBERTA'S FATHER. Novel, published in 1925. Albert Preemby, a humble clerk, becomes convinced that he is a reincarnation of Sargon, King of Sumeria, sent back to earth to bring about world unification.

CHRONIC ARGONAUTS, THE. The earliest surviving draft of *The Time Machine*. 'The Chronic Argonauts' was first printed in instalments in the *Science Schools Journal* in April, May and June, 1888, and is reprinted in its entirety in *The Early H. G. Wells*, by Bernard Bergonzi (Manchester University Press, 1961). For a discussion of the complex bibliographical history of *The Time Machine* see Bergonzi, *The Early H. G. Wells*, ch. 2, and Geoffrey West, *H. G. Wells: A Sketch for a Portrait* (Howe, 1930) Appendix I.

COAL SCUTTLE, THE. First published in the *Pall Mall Gazette*, 1893, and reprinted in CPM. Describes Euphemia's experiments with receptacles for storing coal.

COMPLETE SHORT STORIES OF H. G. WELLS, THE. This collection of 63 short stories includes all the tales in SB, PS, TST, TD and CB. It also includes *The Time Machine* and several short stories not previously published in volume form: 'My First Aeroplane', 'Little Mother up The Morderberg', and 'The Grisly Folk'. Another item, 'The Story of the Last Trump', is taken from *Boon*.

The *Complete Short Stories*, however, does not include the following:

'Statement of Archibald Ferguson, B.A.'; 'A Misunderstood Artist'; 'The Man with a Nose'; 'The Presence by the Fire'; 'The Rajah's Treasure'; 'Le Mari Terrible'; 'Mr. Marshall's Doppelganger'; 'A Perfect Gentleman on Wheels'; 'The Thing in No. 7'; 'The Thumb Mark'; 'The Loyalty of Esau Common'; 'Master Anthony and the Zeppelin'; 'The Wild Asses of the Devil'; 'The Queer Story of Brownlow's Newspaper'; 'Answer to Prayer'; 'The New Faust'.

CONCERNING A CERTAIN LADY. First published in *Black and White*, 29 September 1894, and reprinted in CPM: describes a certain ill-mannered lady in a blue serge suit and a black hat who continually annoys and impedes the narrator.

CONCERNING CHESS. First published in the *Pall Mall Gazette*, 12 February 1895, and reprinted in CPM: criticises the passion for playing chess as 'one of the most unaccountable in the world'.

CONE, THE. Short story, originally published in *Unicorn*, 18 September 1895, and reprinted in PS, CB and DW. The story, set in the Potteries, was written in 1888 when Wells was staying at Stoke on Trent whilst convalescing after a serious illness. (*See* EXPERIMENT IN AUTOBIOGRAPHY, pp. 306–10.)

COUNTRY OF THE BLIND, THE. Short story, originally published in the *Strand Magazine*, April 1904, and reprinted in CB and DW. The story is a parable on the theme of the sighted man accidentally discovering a valley populated by a blind people.

A revised version of 'The Country of the Blind' was published by the Golden Cockerel Press in 1939 and reprinted in *Masterpieces of Science Fiction*, edited by S. Moscowitz (World Publishing Company, USA, 1967). *See also the following entry.*

COUNTRY OF THE BLIND AND OTHER STORIES, THE. A collection of 'all the short stories by me that I care for anyone to read again', published in 1911. The volume contains 33 stories, 28 of which are reprinted from previous collections, whilst five are printed in book form for the first time—'A Vision of Judgement', 'The Empire of the Ants', 'The Door in the Wall', 'The Country of the Blind' and 'The Beautiful Suit'. Wells contributed a specially written preface which discusses his approach to the short story as a literary genre.

CROQUET PLAYER, THE. Novella, published in 1936. This story is a satire written in the form of an allegory. In its symbolism it has close affinities with *The Island of Doctor Moreau* and *Mr. Blettsworthy on Rampole Island.*

CRYSTAL EGG, THE. Short story, first published in the *New Review*, 1897. Included in TST and CB. A piece of crystal in the shape of an egg is discovered to be a communication device left on earth by inhabitants of the planet Mars.

DEAL IN OSTRICHES, A. Short story, first published in the *Pall Mall Gazette*, 1894. Included in SB. An ostrich is alleged to have swallowed a diamond, but the story is revealed to be a hoax.

DESERT DAISY, THE. *The Desert Daisy*, a reproduction in facsimile of a narrative written by Wells during the period 1878–80, was published by the University of Illinois, USA, in 1957.

DIAMOND MAKER, THE. Short story, first published in the *Pall Mall Budget*, 1894. Included in SB and DW. The narrator meets a man who claims to know a method of manufacturing artificial diamonds.

DOOR IN THE WALL, THE. Short story, first published in the *Daily Chronicle*, 14 July 1906. Included in CB and DW. Lionel Wallace, a prominent politician, describes a door he entered as a child and which led to an enchanted garden. He is haunted by the garden for the rest of his life and longs to revisit it.

The influence of the story upon later writers may be seen, for example, in James Hilton's novel *Lost Horizon* and in John Fowles's *Daniel Martin* (see especially the chapter entitled 'The Sacred Combe').

DOOR IN THE WALL AND OTHER STORIES, THE. A volume of eight short stories, all taken from previously published collections, published in 1911.

DREAM, THE. Novel, published in 1924. *The Dream* tells the life story of Harry Mortimer Smith, a poor boy who rises from humble beginnings to a position of some eminence within a popular publishing enterprise. The novel is notable for its account of the narrator's childhood, which parallels Wells's in certain particulars, and for the portrait of Joseph Wells as the narrator's father.

DREAM OF ARMAGEDDON, A. Short story, first published in *Black and White*, 1901. Included in TD, CB and DW. The narrator meets a solicitor on a train journey who relates a dream of world war in a future age.

DUNSTONE'S DEAR LADY. First published in the *Pall Mall Gazette*, 1894, and reprinted in CPM: a facetious account of a quiet, refined girl who gradually becomes more assertive and finally dominates the life of her husband, Dunstone, who still speaks of her fondly as his 'dainty little lady'.

EARLY WRITINGS IN SCIENCE AND SCIENCE FICTION. A collection of Wells's early science journalism, edited by R. M. Philmus and D. Y. Hughes, published in 1975 by California University Press. In addition to a wide range of non-fiction writings, the volume includes the following stories:

'A Talk with Gryllotalpa'; 'The Time Machine' (*National Observer* version); 'The Time Machine' (extracts from the *New Review* version); 'A Vision of the Past'.

EMPIRE OF THE ANTS, THE. Short story, first published in the *Strand Magazine*, December, 1905, and reprinted in CB. The story describes a plague of highly organised and intelligent ants which may ultimately present a threat to humanity. 'The Empire of the Ants' is essentially an elaboration of an idea advanced in his pessimistic essay 'The Extinction of Man' (*q.v.*).

EUPHEMIA'S NEW ENTERTAINMENT. First published in the *Pall Mall Gazette*, 9 May 1894, and reprinted (with an illustration) in CPM: describes the pleasures of clay modelling as a leisure-time amusement.

EXTINCTION OF MAN, THE. First published in the *Pall Mall Gazette*,

25 September 1894, and reprinted in CPM. This essay, one of Wells's early exercises in pessimism, reminds the reader of possible threats to his complacency, ranging from an invasion of creatures from the sea (elaborated in 'The Sea Raiders') to a plague of ants (elaborated in 'The Empire of the Ants') to the prospect of a new disease. 'In the case of every other predominant animal the world has ever seen . . . the hour of its complete ascendancy has been the eve of its entire overthrow.'

FILMER. Short story, first published in the *Graphic*, 1901, and reprinted in TD. Filmer, the inventor of the first successful flying machine, commits suicide before the machine is tested, but in spite of his fears the flight is a success. (Cf. 'The Argonauts of the Air', and 'Soaring' in *Tono-Bungay*.)

FIRST MEN IN THE MOON, THE. Scientific romance, published in 1901. Cavor, a scientist, discovers an anti-gravity substance with which he constructs a sphere and, together with a companion, journeys to the moon.

FLOWERING OF THE STRANGE ORCHID, THE. Short story, originally published in the *Pall Mall Budget*, 2 August 1894. Included in SB and CB. Winter-Wedderburn, a collector of orchids, purchases an unidentified species which eventually grows aerial rootlets: these attach themselves to his body and suck his blood. In rescuing him, the hot-house windows are smashed and the orchid collection, including the strange variety is destroyed.

FLYING MAN, THE. Short story, originally published in the *Pall Mall Gazette*, 4 January 1895, and reprinted in SB. A soldier trapped on a ledge makes an escape with the aid of an improvised parachute: this gives rise to a legend of a 'flying man'.

FOOD OF THE GODS, THE. Scientific romance, published in 1904. Originally entitled *The Food of the Gods and How it came to Earth*, the book is a satire on the limitations of local and national boundaries. Cf. Wells's Fabian lecture, 'The Question of Scientific Administrative Areas in Relation to Municipal Undertakings' (reprinted as an Appendix to *Mankind in the Making*). See also the preface to *The Scientific Romances of H. G. Wells*.

FOR FREEDOM OF SPELLING. First published in the *Pall Mall Gazette*, 21 October 1893, and reprinted in CPM: argues against the conventional insistence on standardised spelling, and states the case for total freedom.

FROM AN OBSERVATORY. First published in the *Saturday Review*, 1 December 1894, and reprinted in CPM. Wells points out that if the moon were brighter or the earth's atmosphere thicker 'we should never dream of the great stellar universe in which our little solar system swims. . . .'

GREAT CHANGE, THE. First published in the *Pall Mall Gazette*, 1894, and reprinted in SCU: discusses the great change brought about by marriage—'human metamorphosis'.

GRISLY FOLK, THE. Short story, originally published in the *Storyteller Magazine*, April 1921, under the title 'The Grisly Folk and Their War with Men'. An imaginative account of the first encounters between Neanderthal men and true men.

HAMMERPOND PARK BURGLARY, THE. Short story, published in the *Pall Mall Budget*, 1894, and reprinted in SB. A professional burglar plans to steal the wedding presents from Hammerpond House. The burglary is interrupted by local amateurs but is ultimately successful.

HAPPY TURNING, THE: A DREAM OF LIFE. A collection of essays, published in 1945, in which Wells describes his dreams and the personages he encounters in dreamland. For a discussion of *The Happy Turning* within the context of his final writings see *The Last Books of H. G. Wells* edited by G. P. Wells (London, H. G. Wells Society, 1968).

HENLEY HOUSE MAGAZINE. Wells was editor of the magazine while assistant master at Henley House School, Kilburn, from 1889 to 1891. During this period he contributed five short articles: 'Cricket'; 'Holiday Science'; 'The North Sea'; 'That Problem!'; 'Entre Nous'.

HISTORY OF MR. POLLY, THE. Novel, published in 1910. *The History of Mr. Polly* relates the biography of Alfred Polly, a dyspeptic shopkeeper, who escapes from his humdrum existence to find happiness as general factotum at a country inn. A critical edition of *The History of Mr. Polly* edited with an introduction by Gordon N. Ray, was published by the Houghton Mifflin Company, USA, in 1960. This edition contains two appendices: two versions of the final page of the novel, reproduced in facsimile from the original manuscript; and a passage deleted by Wells from Chapter 4.

HOLY TERROR, THE. Novel, published in 1939. *The Holy Terror* is a parable of a movement for world reconstruction which goes awry when its leader becomes obsessed by personal aggrandisement.

HOOPDRIVER'S HOLIDAY. A dramatised version of *The Wheels of Chance*, written in 1904. *Hoopdriver's Holiday*, edited with notes and an introduction by Michael Timko, was published in 1964 by English Literature in Transition, Purdue University, USA.

HOUSE HUNTING AS AN OUTDOOR AMUSEMENT. First published in the *Pall Mall Gazette*, 24 September 1894, and reprinted in CPM: describes the pleasures of house-hunting, not with the intention of acquiring a house, but simply as a source of amusement.

HOUSE OF DI SORNO, THE. First published in the *Pall Mall Gazette*, 21 August 1894, and reprinted in CPM. Sub-titled 'A Manuscript Found in a Box', the essay describes the accidental discovery of a romance written by the narrator's wife at the age of sixteen.

HOW I DIED. First published in the *Pall Mall Gazette*, 1895, and reprinted in CPM. Describes Wells's convalescence following a serious illness; his realisation that he is not, after all, going to die; and the regaining of his will to live (cf. *Experiment in Autobiography*, p. 310).

IN A LITERARY HOUSEHOLD. First published in the *Pall Mall Gazette*, 17 October 1894, and reprinted in CPM: describes the literary household as it is in reality and contrasts this with its fictional portrayal.

INCIDENTAL THOUGHTS ON A BALD HEAD. First published in the *Pall Mall Gazette*, 1 March 1895 (under the title 'Thoughts on a Bald Head') and reprinted in CPM: reflections on baldness and on the replacement of natural losses with artificial substitutes.

IN THE ABYSS. Short story, originally published in *Pearson's Magazine*, August 1896, and reprinted in PS. Describes a descent to the ocean bed in a sphere, and an encounter with an undersea civilisation.

IN THE AVU OBSERVATORY. Short story, originally published in the *Pall Mall Budget*, 9 August 1894, and reprinted in SB and CB. Describes an observatory in Borneo and an attack upon an assistant by an unidentified bat-like creature.

IN THE DAYS OF THE COMET. Novel, published in 1906. The story is essentially an elaboration of the short story 'The Star'. The opening chapters are notable for their portrait of Wells's mother, and for their insight into life in the Potteries.

IN THE MODERN VEIN: AN UNSYMPATHETIC LOVE STORY. Short story, originally published (under the title 'A Bardlet's Romance') in *Truth*, 8 March 1894. Aubrey Vair, a minor poet, becomes infatuated with a girl he meets at a tennis party, but she rejects him when he refuses to leave his wife.

INVISIBLE MAN, THE. Scientific romance, published in 1897. Griffin, a scientist, discovers the secret of invisibility and embarks on a reign of terror, culminating in his own death.

ISLAND OF DOCTOR MOREAU, THE. Scientific romance, published in 1896. The story is a satire written in the form of an allegory. In its symbolism it has close affinities with *Mr. Blettsworthy on Rampole Island* and *The Croquet Player*.

JILTING OF JANE, THE. Short story, first published *circa* 1894. Included in PS and CB. In the preface to the latter collection, Wells states: '"The Jilting of Jane" . . . is the only tolerable fragment of fiction I find surviving from my pre-Lewis Hind Period.' (Lewis Hind was editor of the *Pall Mall Budget* and gave Wells much encouragement as a short story writer.)

JIMMY GOGGLES THE GOD. Short story, originally published in the *Graphic*, December 1898, and reprinted in TD and CB. A party of white men is attacked by natives off the coast of Papua but one man, the narrator, is wearing a diving helmet and is received by the natives as a god from the sea.

JOAN AND PETER. Novel, published in 1918. Sub-titled 'The Story of an Education', the novel relates the schooling and adolescence of Joan Debenham and Peter Stubland.

JOYS OF BEING ENGAGED, THE. First published in the *Pall Mall Gazette*, 1893, and reprinted in SCU. The uncle discourses upon the advantages of being permanently engaged: 'Every man should be engaged, I think, to at least one woman. It is the homage we owe to womankind, and a duty to our souls.'

KING WHO WAS A KING, THE. Film scenario published in 1929. No film based on *The King who was a King* has been produced. Wells regarded it as a 'prentice effort' preparatory to the writing of *Things to Come*.

KIPPS: THE STORY OF A SIMPLE SOUL. Novel, published in 1905. The first draft of this story, *The Wealth of Mr. Waddy* (*q.v.*), was published in a critical edition in 1969.

LA BELLE DAME SANS MERCI. First published in the *Pall Mall Gazette*, October 1894, and reprinted in SCU. The uncle complains eloquently about a neighbour who practises the piano daily and mutilates classical compositions.

LADY FRANKLAND'S COMPANION. Novel, written *circa* 1887 and subsequently destroyed. The book is discussed in *Experiment in Autobiography*, pp. 304-11.

LAND IRONCLADS, THE. Short story, originally published in the *Strand Magazine*, December 1903, and reprinted in CSS. The story, a striking anticipation of the tank (which did not come into practical use until 1916) is discussed in *Experiment in Autobiography*, pp. 683-4, and in 'The Betterave Papers' (*q.v.*), p. 361.

LANGUAGE OF FLOWERS, THE. First published in the *Pall Mall Gazette*, 25 June 1894, and reprinted in CPM: a description of a book by Thomas Miller on the language of flowers.

LITERARY REGIMEN, THE. First published in the *Pall Mall Gazette*, 13 June 1894, and reprinted in CPM: argues that there is an inevitable connection between diet and thought, and suggests the regimen necessary to the literary man.

LITTLE MOTHER UP THE MÖRDERBERG. Short story, originally published in the *Strand Magazine*, April 1910, and reprinted in CSS: a humorous account of an ascent of the Morderberg by the narrator and his mother.

LITTLE WARS: A GAME FOR BOYS. A companion volume to *Floor Games* (*q.v.*), *Little Wars*, published in 1913, elaborates a number of ideas for war games played with wooden bricks and toy soldiers. *See also The New Machiavelli*, Chapter 2, §1.

LORD OF THE DYNAMOS, THE. Short story, first published in the *Pall Mall Budget*, 6 September 1894, and reprinted in SB and CB: a stoker employed at the Camberwell electric railway worships a large dynamo as a deity and kills his superior, Holroyd, in a religious frenzy.

LOST INHERITANCE, THE. Short story, first published *circa* 1896 and reprinted in PS: a rich uncle leaves his will hidden inside the pages of a book, but this is not discovered until years after his death, by which time it is too late to comply with his wishes.

LOVE AND MR. LEWISHAM. Novel, published in 1900. Sub-titled 'The Story of a Very Young Couple', *Love and Mr. Lewisham* is memorable for its account of Wells's student days at Midhurst ('Whortley') and the Normal School of Science, London.

LOYALTY OF ESAU COMMON, THE. Short story, originally published in the *Contemporary Review*, February, 1902. Not included in CSS.

The story was intended 'to open a series of kindly but instructive stories about the British Army. This project was abandoned. The fragment remains the picture of a point of view.'

MAGIC SHOP, THE. Short story, originally published in the *Strand Magazine*, June 1903, and reprinted in TD and CB: the narrator and his small son, Gip, visit a magic shop in which the illusions are disturbingly real.

MAN OF THE YEAR MILLION, THE. First published in the *Pall Mall Gazette*, 6 November 1893, and reprinted in a revised form as 'Of a Book Unwritten' (*q.v.*). Reprinted in CPM.

MAN WHO COULD WORK MIRACLES, THE. Short story, first published in the *Illustrated London News*, July 1898, with the subtitle 'A Pantoum in Prose', and reprinted in TST and CB: a man is suddenly endowed with the power to work miracles, with disastrous consequences. The story was elaborated by Wells in the film scenario *Man Who Could Work Miracles* (*q.v.*).

MAN WHO COULD WORK MIRACLES. Film scenario published in 1936. The film of the same title, based on this scenario, was produced by London Films in 1935. The story is essentially an elaboration of the short story 'The Man Who Could Work Miracles'.

MAN WITH A NOSE, THE. Short story, first published in the *Pall Mall Gazette*, 1894, and reprinted in SCU: reflections on an unshapely nose.

MARI TERRIBLE, LE. Short story, published in *Thirty Strange Stories* but not included in CSS: the narrator, Bellows, describes a conversation with a flirtatious wife.

MARRIAGE. Novel, published in 1912. Trafford and his wife Marjorie, dissatisfied with the emptiness of life in Edwardian London, leave England for Labrador in order to think out afresh their attitude to life.

MASTER ANTHONY AND THE ZEPPELIN. Short story, first published in *Princess Marie-Jose's Children's Book* (Cassell, 1916). Not included in CSS. The story, illustrated with 'picshuas', concerns a small boy who reforms a Zeppelin by teaching it to lay eggs.

MEANWHILE. Novel, published in 1927. This story, set at the time of the General Strike, is notable for its series of illustrations ('picshuas') which enliven the text.

MEN LIKE GODS. Romance, published in 1923. A group of earthlings are transported through a 'kink in space' to a planet at a far advanced stage of civilisation.

MIND OF THE RACE, THE. *See* BOON.

MISS WINCHELSEA'S HEART. Short story, first published in the *Queen*, October 1898, and reprinted in TD and CB: Miss Winchelsea becomes romantically involved with a young man whilst on holiday in Rome, but rejects his proposal of marriage on discovering that his surname is Snooks.

MR. BLETTSWORTHY ON RAMPOLE ISLAND. Novel, published in 1928. This story is a satire written in the form of an allegory. In its symbolism it has close affinities with *The Island of Doctor Moreau* and *The Croquet Player*.

MR. BRISHER'S TREASURE. Short story, originally published in the *Strand Magazine*, April 1899, and reprinted in TD: a box of half-crowns is discovered buried in a garden, but the coins are later found to be counterfeit.

MR. BRITLING SEES IT THROUGH. Novel, published in 1916. *Mr. Britling* (Wells truncated the title for the Atlantic Edition) relates the impact of the First World War upon a sensitive mind.

MR. LEDBETTER'S VACATION. Short story, first published in the *Strand Magazine*, October 1898, and reprinted in TD. A schoolmaster burgles a house whilst on vacation, and becomes involved in a strange adventure.

MR. MARSHALL'S DOPPELGANGER. Short story, first published in *Gentlewoman*, August 1897. Not included in CSS. The credulous vicar of Sussexville sees what is apparently the doppelganger (double) of Marshall, one of the villagers: but the real explanation is rather more mundane.

MR. SKELMERSDALE IN FAIRYLAND. Short story, first published in the *Strand Magazine*, 1901, and reprinted in TD: a young man falls asleep one midsummer's night on Aldington Knoll and wakes to find himself in fairyland.

MISUNDERSTOOD ARTIST, A. Short story, first published in the *Pall Mall Gazette*, October 1894, and reprinted in SCU: a poet and a cook meet in a railway carriage and discuss their respective approaches to art.

MODE IN MONUMENTS, THE. First published in the *Pall Mall Gazette*, 6 March 1894, and reprinted (with the subtitle 'Stray Thoughts in Highgate Cemetery') in CPM: a protest against the ugliness and commercialism of modern gravestones.

MOONLIGHT FABLE, A. *See* THE BEAUTIFUL SUIT.

MOTH, THE. Short story, originally published in the *Pall Mall Gazette*, 28 March 1895 (under the title 'A Moth—Genus Novo') and reprinted in SB and CB. Hapley is obsessed by thoughts of his late enemy, Professor Pawkins. He pursues a moth bearing a singular resemblance to Pawkins and breaks his leg while doing so. While confined to his bed the moth torments him until he becomes insane.

MY FIRST AEROPLANE. Short story, originally published in the *Strand Magazine*, January 1910, and reprinted (with the sub-title 'Alauda Magna') in CSS: a spirited account of a first aeroplane flight.

MY LAST BOOK. *See* THE BOOK OF ESSAYS DEDICATORY.

NEW ACCELERATOR, THE. Short story, first published in the *Strand Magazine*, December 1901, and reprinted in TD and CB: Professor Gibberne discovers a drug which accelerates the speed of the body thousands of times beyond normal.

NEW FAUST, THE. Short story, first published in *Nash's Pall Mall*, December 1936. Not included in CSS. Subtitled 'A Film Story', 'The New Faust' is a reworking of the basic idea of 'The Story of the Late Mr. Elvesham' (*q.v.*)

NEW MACHIAVELLI, THE. Novel, published in 1911. The opening chapters of *The New Machiavelli* are notable for their description of Bromley at the time of the author's childhood.

OBJECTIONS TO SOCIAL MUSIC. *See* ON SOCIAL MUSIC.

OBLITERATED MAN, THE. *See* THE SAD STORY OF A DRAMATIC CRITIC.

OF A BOOK UNWRITTEN. A revised version of 'The Man of the Year Million' (*q.v.*) The article was originally written in 1887, undergoing a series of revisions before its inclusion in CPM. In its account of man in the remote future it anticipates certain features of the Martians in *The War of the Worlds*. The article and its important place in Wells's early literary output is discussed in Bergonzi, *The Early H. G. Wells* (Manchester University Press, 1961).

OF BLADES AND BLADERY. Essay first published in *Pall Mall Gazette* (*circa* 1894) and included in CPM: contains practical advice to the would-be blade (i.e. man about town).

OF CLEVERNESS. First published in the *National Observer*, 9 March 1895, and reprinted in CPM (with the subtitle 'Apropos of One Crichton'): doubts the value of cleverness, as exemplified by his friend Crichton, and pleads for a return to dullness.

OF CONVERSATION. First published in the *Pall Mall Gazette*, 11 October 1894, and reprinted in CPM: a protest against the necessity for polite conversation.

OF CONVERSATION AND THE ANATOMY OF FASHION. First published in the *Pall Mall Gazette*, 1894, and reprinted in SCU: a discussion on the contrast between fashionable and vulgar conversation.

ON A TRICYCLE. First published in the *Pall Mall Gazette*, 1894, and reprinted in SCU: the uncle praises the merits of tricycles by comparison with bicycles.

ON SCHOOLING AND THE PHASES OF MR. SANDSOME. First published in the *New Budget*, 11 April 1895, and reprinted in CPM: describes the private school which the narrator attended as a boy. The sketch is apparently based on Thomas Morley, the headmaster of Morley's Commercial Academy, Bromley, which Wells attended as a child. (See West, Geoffrey, *H. G. Wells: A Sketch for a Portrait*, pp. 22–30.)

ON SOCIAL MUSIC. First published in the *Pall Mall Gazette*, 1894 (under the title 'Objections to Social Music') and reprinted in SCU: criticises the formality of the Victorian musical evening.

ON SWEARING. *See* THE BOOK OF CURSES.

ON THE ART OF STAYING AT THE SEASIDE. One of the earliest surviving examples of Wells's humorous journalism. First published in the *Pall Mall Gazette*, 1893, and reprinted in CPM: reflections on the art of deriving the maximum enjoyment from a seaside holiday. For an account of the genesis of the article see Wells, *Experiment in Autobiography*, pp. 370–4.

ON THE CHOICE OF A WIFE. First published in the *Pall Mall Gazette*, 1895, and reprinted in CPM: advice to young men on the wise choice of a wife.

OUT BANSTEAD WAY. *See* THE AMATEUR NATURE LOVER.

PAINS OF MARRIAGE, THE. First published in the *Pall Mall Gazette*, 1894, and reprinted in SCU: protests against the formality of conventional wedding customs.

PARKES MUSEUM, THE. First published in the *Pall Mall Gazette*, 24 March 1894, and reprinted in CPM: an account of a visit made by the narrator and Euphemia to a museum of sanitary science.

PASSIONATE FRIENDS, THE. Novel, published in 1913. One of a series of novels upon sexual problems, *The Passionate Friends* examines the question: 'Is friendship possible between men and women?'

PEARL OF LOVE, THE. Short story, first published in the *Strand Magazine*, 1925, and reprinted in CSS: an Indian prince builds an elaborate temple as a memorial to his dead queen, but in his desire for ornateness the original purpose of the building is lost.

PERFECT GENTLEMAN ON WHEELS, A. Short story, originally published in *Woman at Home*, April 1897, (with the subtitle 'The Humours of Cycling'). Not included in CSS. A young man tries to impress a lady cyclist by offering to repair her bicycle, but it becomes apparent that his mechanical skills are severely limited.

PLATTNER STORY, THE. Short story, originally published in the *New Review*, April 1896, and reprinted in PS and CB. Plattner, a school teacher, causes an explosion during a chemistry experiment and is projected into another world.

PLATTNER STORY AND OTHERS, THE. A collection of seventeen short stories published in 1897.

PLEASURE OF QUARRELLING, THE. Essay included in CPM: discusses the pleasures and techniques of quarrelling.

POET AND THE EMPORIUM, THE. First published in the *New Budget*, 6 June 1895, and reprinted in CPM: a poet describes his furniture-buying experiences.

POLLOCK AND THE PORROH MAN. Short story, first published in the *New Budget*, 23 May 1895, and reprinted in PS. A witch-doctor is murdered in Sierra Leone, but his patterned head haunts the murderer until the latter commits suicide to escape from it.

POSE NOVEL, THE. First published in the *Pall Mall Gazette*, 21 May 1894, and reprinted in CPM: reflections on a pretentious novel burned by the author when he realises its lack of literary merit. It is possible that the essay refers to *Lady Frankland's Companion* (*q.v.*), a novel written by Wells at the age of 21 and subsequently destroyed.

PRESENCE BY THE FIRE, THE. Short story, originally published in the *Penny Illustrated Paper*, 14 August 1897. Not included in CSS. A man is convinced he can see the features of his dead wife whilst musing in his study and is comforted by her presence, but eventually realises that the apparition is merely a trick of light and shadow.

PURPLE PILEUS, THE. Short story, first published in *Black and White*, Christmas 1896, and reprinted in PS and CB. A henpecked man eats a purple fungus and becomes intoxicated; the experience transforms his life.

QUEER STORY OF BROWNLOW'S NEWSPAPER, THE. Short story, first published in the *Strand Magazine*, 1932. Not included in CSS. On 10 November 1931, Brownlow receives a newspaper dated forty years hence. The story is discussed in the preface to *The Shape of Things to Come*.

RAJAH'S TREASURE, THE. Short story, first published in *Pearson's Magazine*, July 1896, and reprinted in *Thirty Strange Stories*. Not included in CSS. A rajah possesses a mysterious treasure for which he is murdered by his heir: it transpires that the treasure is a hoard of whisky.

   The story was later rewritten by Wells in the style of Henry James, and appears as part of Chapter 4 of *Boon* under the title 'The Spoils of Mr. Blandish'.

RECONCILIATION, THE. Short story, originally published (under the title 'The Bulla') in the *Weekly Sun Literary Supplement*, 1 December 1895, and reprinted in *Thirty Strange Stories*. Two men attempt a reconciliation after years of enmity: they become drunk and fight, and one attacks and kills the other with a whale's ear-bone.

RED ROOM, THE. Short story, first published in the *Idler*, March 1896, and reprinted in PS and CB. The narrator agrees to spend the night in the haunted Red Room of Lorraine Castle; after a series of unnerving experiences he realises that the room is haunted not by a physical presence but by fear itself.

REMARKABLE CASE OF DAVIDSON'S EYES, THE. Short story, first published in the *Pall Mall Budget*, 28 March 1895, and reprinted in SB and CB. Davidson, stooping between the poles of an electromagnet during a thunderstorm, becomes temporarily blind to the world about him and sees only an island beach. As he moves about his daily tasks he appears to himself to be moving about the island, which he describes clearly; his awareness of his actual surroundings returns slowly as that of the island recedes. (Cf. 'The Plattner Story' and *Men Like Gods*. The idea of a 'kink in space' is discussed in Appendix II of *The Conquest of Time*.)

RESEARCH MAGNIFICENT, THE. Novel, published in 1915. *The Research Magnificent* describes the life and loves of William Benham, and his quest for a 'natural aristocracy'.

SAD STORY OF A DRAMATIC CRITIC, THE. Short story, first published in *New Budget*, 15 August 1895, and reprinted in PS. A shy man becomes drama critic for a London paper but gradually his personality is submerged beneath theatrical gestures and extravagant speech.

SARGON, KING OF KINGS. *See* CHRISTINA ALBERTA'S FATHER.

SCIENCE SCHOOLS JOURNAL. Wells founded the *Science Schools Journal* while a student at South Kensington and was its first editor. During the period December 1886 to October 1893 he contributed the following articles and short stories:

'Socrates'; 'Mammon'; 'A Talk with Gryllotalpa'; 'Protylian Vapourings'; 'A Tale of the Twentieth Century'; 'A Vision of the Past'; 'The Chronic Argonauts'; 'The Devotee of Art'; 'Walcote'; 'The Lamias'; 'Something Good from Birmingham'; 'On Capital Punishment'; 'The Lay of the Sausage Machine'; 'Specimen Day'; 'The Beginning of the Journal'.

Of this material, the following is included as an appendix to *The Early H. G. Wells* by Bernard Bergonzi (Manchester University Press, 1961):

'The Chronic Argonauts' and 'A Tale of the Twentieth Century'.

The following items are included in *H. G. Wells: Early Writings in Science and Science Fiction*:

'A Talk with Gryllotalpa' and 'A Vision of the Past'.

SCIENTIFIC ROMANCES OF H. G. WELLS, THE. A collection of eight scientific romances published in 1933. This omnibus volume contains the following stories:

The Time Machine; *The Island of Doctor Moreau*; *The Invisible Man*; *The War of the Worlds*; *The First Men in the Moon*; *The Food of the Gods*; *In the Days of the Comet*; *Men Like Gods*.

The Scientific Romances also contains a specially written introduction by Wells.

SEA LADY, THE. Romance, published in 1902. A mermaid comes ashore at Sandgate and becomes emotionally involved with several human beings.

SEA RAIDERS, THE. Short story, first published in the *Weekly Sun Literary Supplement*, 6 December 1896, and reprinted in PS and CB: a circumstantial account of a raid on the south coast of England by a species of octopus-like creatures. 'The Sea Raiders' is essentially an elaboration of an idea advanced in his pessimistic essay 'The Extinction of Man' (*q.v.*)

SECRET PLACES OF THE HEART, THE. Novel, published in 1922. During a motoring holiday in south-west England, Sir Richmond Hardy reflects on current world problems and on his complex emotional life.

SELECT CONVERSATIONS WITH AN UNCLE (NOW EXTINCT) AND TWO OTHER REMINISCENCES. A collection of light humorous essays published in 1895. The character of the uncle appears to be loosely based on Wells's 'uncle' Alfred Williams, for whom Wells worked for a short period as a pupil-teacher at Wookey village school. In addition to the twelve conversations the volume includes two 'reminiscences'—'A Misunderstood Artist' and 'The Man with a Nose'.

SHAPE OF THINGS TO COME, THE. Scientific romance published in 1933. The story is cast in the form of a 'history of the future' from 1933 to 2105.

SHOPMAN, THE. First published in the *Pall Mall Gazette*, 23 November 1894, and reprinted in CPM: a light-hearted account of a visit to a draper's shop.

SLEEPER AWAKES, THE. Scientific romance, published in 1899 (under the title *When The Sleeper Wakes*) and reissued in a revised form in 1910. The story, which has close affinities with 'A Story of the Days to Come', is essentially a vision of London in the year 2100.

SLIP UNDER THE MICROSCOPE, A. Short story, originally published in the *Yellow Book*, January 1896, and reprinted in PS and CB: a student commits an error of judgment whilst sitting an examination and is subsequently disqualified. The story poses a number of interesting ethical problems.

SOUL OF A BISHOP, THE. Novel, published in 1917. An anglican bishop experiences a series of visions which lead him to renounce orthodox Christianity.

STAR, THE. Short story, first published in the *Graphic*, Christmas 1897, and reprinted in TST, CB and DW. Describes the invasion of the solar system by a comet from space.

STAR BEGOTTEN. Scientific romance published in 1937. Earth is bombarded by thought rays emanating from the planet Mars.

STATEMENT OF ARCHIBALD FERGUSON, B.A. Short story, written in 1887 whilst Wells was a schoolmaster at Holt, Wales. Not included in CSS. Cited by Michael S. Howard in *Jonathan Cape, Publisher* (Cape, 1971 and Penguin, 1977). Cf. also *Experiment in Autobiography*, pp. 293–4.

STOLEN BACILLUS, THE. First published in the *Pall Mall Budget*, 21 June 1894, and reprinted in SB and CB. An anarchist steals a tube under the impression that it contains cholera bacteria, but it transpires that the bacterium is harmless.

STOLEN BACILLUS AND OTHER INCIDENTS, THE. A collection of fifteen short stories published in 1895.

STOLEN BODY, THE. Short story, first published in the *Strand Magazine*, November 1898, and reprinted in TD. An elderly man conducts a series of experiments with a friend to test the possibility of 'projecting an apparition of oneself by force of will through space'.

STORIES OF MEN AND WOMEN IN LOVE. A collection of four novels, published in 1933. This omnibus volume contains the following stories:

> *Love and Mr. Lewisham*; *The Passionate Friends*; *The Wife of Sir Isaac Harman*; *The Secret Places of the Heart*.

> *Stories of Men and Women in Love* also contains a specially written preface by Wells.

STORY OF THE DAYS TO COME, A. Short story, first published in the *Pall Mall Magazine*, 1897, and reprinted in TST. The story describes Wells's vision of London in the 22nd century. Cf. *The Sleeper Awakes*.

STORY OF THE INEXPERIENCED GHOST, THE. Short story, first published in the *Strand Magazine*, March 1902, and reprinted in TD. Clayton relates a ghost story to a group of sceptical friends, but falls down dead whilst re-enacting a sequence of masonic passes.

STORY OF THE LAST TRUMP, THE. Short story, originally published as Chapter 10 of *Boon*. The trumpet of the Day of Judgement falls accidentally to earth and is blown—with astonishing results.

STORY OF THE LATE MR. ELVESHAM, THE. Short story, first published in the *Idler*, May 1896, and reprinted in PS and CB. Elvesham, an elderly philosopher, succeeds in transferring his brain and personality to the body of a younger man. The story is narrated by Eden, whose body Elvesham has usurped.

   In 1936 Wells wrote a film treatment of the story under the title *The New Faust* (q.v.)

STORY OF THE STONE AGE, A. Short story, first published in the *Idler*, May–September 1897, and reprinted in TST. An adventure story set in the remote past, in marked contrast to 'A Story of the Days to Come', written at the same time.

TALE OF THE TWENTIETH CENTURY, A. Short story, first published in the *Science Schools Journal*, May 1887, and reprinted in Bergonzi: *The Early H. G. Wells*. A farcical account of the application of perpetual motion to the London underground.

TALES OF SPACE AND TIME. A collection of five short stories published in 1899.

TALK WITH GRYLLOTALPA, A. Short story, first published in the *Science Schools Journal*, February 1887, and reprinted in Philmus and Hughes, *H. G. Wells: Early Writings in Science and Science Fiction*. An imaginary conversation with Gryllotalpa (the mole cricket) in which one's duty to one's neighbour is discussed.

TEMPTATION OF HARRINGAY, THE. Short story, first published in the *St. James's Gazette*, 9 February 1895, and reprinted in SB. Harringay, an artist, paints a man's head which comes to life and criticises his handiwork.

THEORY OF QUOTATION, THE. First published in the *Pall Mall Gazette*, 22 March 1894, and reprinted in CPM: argues against restrictions on quotation and states the case for freedom to plagiarise.

THEORY OF THE PERPETUAL DISCOMFORT OF HUMANITY, THE. First published in the *Pall Mall Gazette*, 1894, and reprinted in SCU. The uncle expounds a theory that humanity is doomed to permanent discomfort due to the time-lag between the realisation of the need for a reform and its eventual achievement. 'Ireland, when Home Rule comes home to it, will simply howl with indignation.'

THING IN NO. 7, THE. Short story, first published in the *Pall Mall Budget*, 25 October 1894. Not included in CSS. During a thunderstorm the narrator and his friends shelter in an empty house: there they discover the corpse of a thief who has been killed by lightning whilst stealing gas fittings.

THINGS TO COME. Film scenario, published in 1935. The film of the same title, based on this scenario, was produced by London Films in 1936. The story is essentially a dramatisation of material contained in Wells's 'history of the future', *The Shape of Things to Come*.

THIRTY STRANGE STORIES. A collection of thirty short stories published in the United States in 1897. The collection includes two stories not available in book form in Britain: 'Le Mari Terrible' and 'The Rajah's Treasure'.

THOUGHTS ON A BALD HEAD. *See* INCIDENTAL THOUGHTS ON A BALD HEAD.

THOUGHTS ON CHEAPNESS AND MY AUNT CHARLOTTE. First published in the *New Budget*, 17 May 1895, and reprinted in CPM: argues in favour of cheap, transitory possessions instead of articles which do not wear out.

THROUGH A MICROSCOPE. First published in the *Pall Mall Gazette*, 31

December 1894, and reprinted in CPM: an account of the curious life forms found in a single drop of water, and speculations upon their manner of existence.

THROUGH A WINDOW. Short story, originally published (under the title 'At a Window') in *Black and White*, 25 August 1894, and reprinted in SB: an account of the passing scene observed through a bedroom window by a convalescent man, culminating in a description of an exciting chase.

THUMB MARK, THE. Short story, first published in the *Pall Mall Budget*, 28 June 1894. Not included in CSS. An anarchist sets fire to a building but leaves a tell-tale clue to his identity in the form of a thumb print.

TIME MACHINE, THE. Scientific romance published in 1895. A scientist invents a machine which can travel through time and journeys to the year 802701. *See also* THE CHRONIC ARGONAUTS.

TONO-BUNGAY. Novel, published in 1909. One of the most ambitious of Wells's novels, *Tono-Bungay* tells the autobiography of the narrator, George Ponderevo, and the rise and fall of his uncle's financial empire.

TREASURE IN THE FOREST, THE. Short story, originally published in the *Pall Mall Budget*, 1894, and reprinted in SB and CB. Two treasure-seekers murder a Chinaman to gain possession of a chart but, on finding the treasure, are killed by the poisoned thorns which guard the hoard.

TRIUMPHS OF A TAXIDERMIST, THE. Short story, first published in the *Pall Mall Gazette*, 1894, and reprinted in SB: humorous reminiscences of a taxidermist.

TROUBLE OF LIFE, THE. First published in the *Pall Mall Gazette*, 2 August 1894, and reprinted in CPM: a farcical account of the bothers of everyday life—washing, shaving, answering letters, polite conversation.

TRUTH ABOUT PYECRAFT, THE. Short story, first published in the *Strand Magazine*, April 1903, and reprinted in TD and CB. Pyecraft, the fattest clubman in London, takes an Eastern medicine in order to lose weight, but becomes so light he floats up against the ceiling. His friend solves the problem by recommending lead underclothing.

TWELVE STORIES AND A DREAM, THE. A collection of thirteen short stories, published in 1903.

UNDER THE KNIFE. Short story, first published in the *New Review*, January 1896, and reprinted in PS and CB. The narrator, while undergoing an anaesthetic, has a dream in which he sees a vision of the universe as no more than a speck of light upon a ring worn on the hand of the creator.

UNDYING FIRE, THE. Novel, published in 1919. *The Undying Fire*, termed by Wells a 'dialogue novel', is a modern interpretation of the Book of Job.

UNSUSPECTED MASTERPIECE, AN. Essay, first published in the *Pall Mall Gazette*, 1 June 1894 (under the title 'Upon an Egg'), and reprinted in SCU. Reflections upon a stale egg.

UPON AN EGG. *See* AN UNSUSPECTED MASTERPIECE.

USE OF IDEALS, THE. First published in the *Pall Mall Gazette*, 1893, and reprinted in SCU: reflections on the role of idealism in everyday life.

VALLEY OF SPIDERS, THE. Short story, originally published in *Pearson's Magazine*, March 1903, and reprinted in TD and CB. Three men, riding in pursuit of a girl, find themselves in a valley where they are attacked by giant spiders floating through the air on gossamer webs.

VETERAN CRICKETER, THE. First published in the *Pall Mall Gazette*, 5 April 1894, and reprinted in CPM. A character sketch of an aged cricketer who reminisces about the days of his glory. Wells undoubtedly derived some of the material for this essay from the reminiscences of his father, Joseph Wells (1827–1910), who was for many years a professional cricketer.

VISION OF JUDGMENT, A. Short story, originally published in *Butterfly*, September 1899, and reprinted in CB: on the day of judgment all mankind is summoned into the presence of God and, after each individual has given an account of his life, all are shaken out of God's sleeve on to a different planet 'and all about me were the enlightened souls of men in new clean bodies'.

VISION OF THE PAST, A. Short story, first published in *The Science Schools Journal*, June 1887, and reprinted in Philmus and Hughes, *H. G. Wells: Early Writings in Science and Science Fiction*. While resting after a long walk a man dreams he is back in the age of reptilian monsters. The essay challenges the complacent assumption that man is the lord of creation.

WAR IN THE AIR, THE. Scientific romance, published in 1908. A world war fought with aerial weapons leads to global disaster and pestilence.

WAR OF THE WORLDS, THE. Scientific romance, published in 1898. Earth is invaded by Martians intent on global conquest.

WEALTH OF MR. WADDY, THE. The earliest surviving draft of the novel *Kipps*. *The Wealth of Mr. Waddy*, written in 1898–9, was published in 1969 by the Southern Illinois University Press, edited and with an introduction by Harris Wilson.

WHEELS OF CHANCE, THE. Novel, published in 1896. Subtitled 'A Holiday Adventure', *The Wheels of Chance* describes the two weeks' cycling holiday of a draper's assistant. *See also* HOOP-DRIVER'S HOLIDAY.

WHEN THE SLEEPER WAKES. *See* THE SLEEPER AWAKES.

WIFE OF SIR ISAAC HARMAN, THE. Novel, published in 1914. One of a series of novels upon sexual questions, *The Wife of Sir Isaac Harman* implicitly challenges the accepted moral attitudes of Edwardian England.

WILD ASSES OF THE DEVIL, THE. *See* BOON.

WONDERFUL VISIT, THE. Romance, published in 1895. An angel visits the earth and is highly critical of the contemporary social order.

WORLD OF WILLIAM CLISSOLD, THE. Novel, published in 1926. The book is a survey of Wells's mental world, seen through the eyes of his *alter ego* William Clissold, and a summary of his theory of world revolution.

WORLD SET FREE, THE. Scientific romance, published in 1914. *The World Set Free* is a remarkable forecast of nuclear warfare and subsequent world reconstruction.

WRITING OF ESSAYS, THE. First published in the *Pall Mall Gazette*, 2 February 1894, and reprinted in CPM: discusses the technique of essay writing and the influence of writing materials upon the style of essay produced.

YOU CAN'T BE TOO CAREFUL. Novel, published in 1941. The story describes the life and times of Edward Albert Tewler, a case-study in missed opportunities, and reflects upon the significance of 'Homo Tewler' for the future of mankind.

Part III

THE SHORT STORIES

The Short Stories

Wells published five collections of short stories: *The Stolen Bacillus and Other Incidents* (1895), *The Plattner Story and Others* (1897), *Tales of Space and Time* (1899), *Twelve Stories and a Dream* (1903) and *The Country of the Blind and Other Stories* (1911). Later these were collected together in a single compilation, *The Short Stories of H. G. Wells* (first published in 1927 and frequently reprinted) containing 63 stories in all.

He had graduated to writing short stories after a long apprenticeship of writing scientific articles for *The Saturday Review* and other journals and, following his breakdown in health, a series of humorous essays published in the *Pall Mall Gazette* during the years 1893–5. In the summer of 1894 he met C. Lewis Hind, then editor of the *Pall Mall Budget*, who invited him to contribute a series of 'single sitting stories'. Wells accepted this invitation readily. He recorded later:

> But I set myself, so encouraged, to the experiment of inventing moving and interesting things that could be given vividly in the little space of eight or ten such pages as this, and for a time I found it a very entertaining pursuit indeed. Mr. Hind's indicating finger had shown me an amusing possibility of the mind. I found that, taking almost anything as a starting-point and letting my thoughts play about it, there would presently come out of the darkness, in a manner quite inexplicable, some absurd or vivid little incident more or less relevant to that initial nucleus. Little men in canoes upon sunlit oceans would come floating out of nothingness, incubating the eggs of prehistoric monsters unawares; violent conflicts would break out amidst the flower-beds of suburban gardens; I would discover I was peering into remote and mysterious worlds ruled by an order logical indeed but other than our common sanity.[1]

The Stolen Bacillus contains fifteen stories, uneven in quality but strongly marked by those characteristics which were to earn for Wells a world-wide reputation in the ensuing decade—vivid descriptive powers, convincing narrative skill and, above all, an uncanny ability to translate unusual and inexplicable happenings into a commonplace environment. The collection includes a number of slight tales of the calibre of 'The Triumphs of a Taxidermist', which are little more than episodes, but it also contains several stories of undoubted literary power, most notably 'Aepyornis Island' and 'The Diamond Maker'. These contain clear intimations of Wells's powers as a storyteller.

'Aepyornis Island' is a variant on the desert island myth, of which *Robinson Crusoe* and *The Coral Island* are earlier examples. Wells imagines an explorer cast away on a remote atoll in the Indian Ocean hatching out the egg of an extinct bird, the aepyornis. It is written in a terse, economical style with a wealth of conversational vividness which adds colour and credibility to the narrative. Verisimilitude is lent to the story by the skilful use of detail:

> Presently the sun got high in the sky and began to beat down upon me. Lord! it pretty near made my brains boil. I tried dipping my head in the sea, but after a while my eye fell on the Cape *Argus*, and I lay down flat in the canoe and spread this over me. Wonderful things these newspapers! I never read one through thoroughly before, but it's odd what you get up to when you're alone, as I was. I suppose I read that blessed Cape *Argus* twenty times. The pitch in the canoe simply reeked with the heat and rose up into big blisters.

The atoll itself and the narrator's experiences on the island are described with a convincing use of detail (although Wells himself had not travelled outside England and Wales at the time of writing) and the moment when the death of the bird is recounted is written with extraordinary intensity. 'Aepyornis Island' can be read on several different levels—as a highly readable and entertaining yarn in the Kipling manner, as a parable on the theme of loneliness, or simply as another version of the desert island fable which has haunted English literature for centuries. What distinguishes Wells's vision is an engaging sense of wonder which holds the reader's attention and suspends disbelief.

'The Diamond Maker' begins with the assurance of a short story by Poe or Conan Doyle: 'Some business had detained me in Chancery Lane until nine in the evening, and thereafter, having some inkling of a headache, I was disinclined for entertainment or further work.' Reading it today it is difficult to realise that its author was a young man at the very outset of his literary career, so assured and convincing is his manner. In its essentials the story itself is slight enough—the narrator encounters by chance a down-and-out who claims to be a scientist in possession of the secret of making artificial diamonds. The interest of the tale lies partly in its technique—the account of how a chance meeting on the Thames Embankment led to a vision of unparalleled riches which haunted the imagination of the narrator—and partly in its introduction of the diamond maker, the man of science obsessed by dreams of power. The technique of the story is deceptively simple: the narrator describes how he came to be drawn in conversation with a ragged man he encounters by Waterloo Bridge and how, listening to the account of the man's experiences, he feels himself becoming more and more interested in the stranger. It is a device frequently employed by short story writers before and since, but in Wells's hands it has the effect of lending substance and credibility to the rather wild narrative unfolded to him by the tramp. At the beginning of the conversation, for example, the diamond maker produces 'a brown pebble' from a canvas bag and asks the narrator what he thinks it is. 'I took out my penknife and tried to scratch it—vainly. Leaning forward towards the gas-lamp, I tried the thing on my watch-glass, and scored a white line across that with the greatest ease.' It is impossible for the reader to doubt that, for a moment at least, the storyteller held in his hands a real man-made diamond: just as it is impossible for the reader to doubt that Mr. Thomas Marvel was pursued by an Invisible Man, or that the Time Machine really did travel through time. Wells's peculiar gift lay in his ability to make the improbable and fantastic seem believable in terms of everyday experience. Again and again the diamond maker is questioned and probed, but at the end Wells has convinced both himself and his readers that his apparently incredible narrative is true. The scientist himself, the half-deranged figure who is consumed with visions of domination over his fellow men, is a familiar figure in Wells's work. Nebogipfel in 'The Chronic Argonauts', Moreau in *The Island of Doctor Moreau* and Griffin in *The Invisible Man* are variants on a similar theme: each, in their different ways, testifies to his deep conviction that science has unlimited possibilities for both good and evil and that knowledge without moral responsibility corrupts and ultimately destroys its possessor.

The Plattner Story, a collection of seventeen stories, is not only a much more balanced compilation than *The Stolen Bacillus* but, in

its diversity of theme and treatment, illustrates much more effectively the full range of his talent. It includes two horror stories in
the Poe manner, 'The Red Room' and 'Pollock and the Porroh Man';
a remarkable anticipation of aviation, 'The Argonauts of the Air',
written eight years before the Wright brothers' first successful
flight; and a classic tale of the uncanny, 'The Story of the Late Mr.
Elvesham', frequently included in subsequent anthologies. There
are also, for good measure, a number of exercises in the genre he
was beginning to make all his own, and which our century has
termed 'science fiction': among these are such brilliant fantasies as
'In the Abyss', 'Under the Knife" and 'The Sea Raiders'. Of more
significance, perhaps, to the development of Wells as a novelist
and romancer are two stories which are both concerned with the
impact of unusual occurrences upon ordinary people, 'The Purple
Pileus' and 'A Catastrophe'. Neither story attracted much critical
attention at the time, yet each encapsulates in miniature form a
theme which was to dominate Wells both in his fiction and his
personal life—claustrophobia, and the urge to disentangle oneself
from frustrating or limiting circumstances.

Mr. Coombes, the central character of 'The Purple Pileus', is a
small shopman unhappily married to a loquacious and disloyal
wife. 'Bricklayers kick their wives to death,' he reflects, 'and dukes
betray theirs; but it is among the small clerks and shopkeepers
nowadays that it comes most often to a cutting of throats.' He
wanders out into the countryside to reflect upon his miserable
existence and, in a mood of curiosity, tastes a fragment of purple
fungi he sees growing by the wayside. He eats more until, intoxicated, he decides to head for home. There he wreaks havoc upon a
staid Victorian musical evening and scandalises his wife and her
guests by appearing drunk. The incident proves to be a turning
point in Coombes's life. His wife has a renewed respect for him
after this episode for, as he tells her: 'Now you know what I'm like
when I'm roused.' She abandons her extravagant ways and begins
to help Coombes more in the running of the business. No longer is
he meek and ineffective, but a man who has a reputation for
violence when goaded by intolerable pressures. Five years later he
passes the same patch of fungus to which he owes his reputation
but walks past with the simple comment: 'I dessay they're sent for
some wise purpose.' The story concludes with the words 'And that
was as much thanks as the purple pileus ever got for maddening
this absurd little man to the pitch of decisive action, *and so altering
the whole course of his life*' [my italics].

Winslow in 'A Catastrophe' is also a struggling shopkeeper,

faced with the prospect of almost immediate bankruptcy. His little drapery shop is not paying, and he is in debt to his wholesale dealers, Helter, Skelter & Grab. His situation is saved, not by his own resolute action but by an unexpected legacy which transforms his gloomy financial prospects and permits him, after days of despondency, to face the world with good cheer. It is a slight tale of only nine pages, yet it is marked by a restraint and shrewdness of observation worthy of a short story by Gissing. Wells vividly conveys a sense of Winslow's hopelessness:

> A shop assistant who has once set up for himself finds the utmost difficulty in getting into a situation again. He began to figure himself 'crib hunting' once more, going from this wholesale house to that, writing innumerable letters. How he hated writing letters! 'Sir,—Referring to your advertisement in the *Christian World*.' He beheld an infinite vista of discomfort and disappointment, ending—in a gulf.

Winslow regrets having married, 'with that infinite bitterness that only comes to the human heart in the small hours of the morning'. After a sleepless night he conveys the seriousness of the financial situation to his wife, who listens with sympathy and understanding. The news of the legacy comes in the form of a letter marked with a deep mourning edge. At once the shopkeeper has a mental image of what the bereavement will mean: 'The brutal cruelty of people dying! He saw it all in a flash—he always visualised his thoughts. Black trousers to get, black crepe, black gloves—none in stock—the railway fares, the shop closed for the day.' In fact the letter contains the news not only of the bereavement but of his wife's inheritance of seven cottages. It is this which transforms their lives and alters the whole perspective of their expectations. Despair is replaced by a resurgence of hope:

> The blow was a sudden and terrible one—but it behoves us to face such things bravely in this sad, unaccountable world. It was quite midday before either of them mentioned the cottages.

Both these stories may be regarded as first sketches of a situation Wells was to depict in fuller depth in *Kipps* and *Mr. Polly*: that of the 'little man' who, in seeking to escape from an intolerable or cramping environment, succeeds in changing the tenor of his life and achieving happiness in place of despair. In later years this was to become one of his most characteristic themes.

In *Tales of Space and Time* Wells collected together five stories which were originally published in various magazines during 1897-8. These are 'The Crystal Egg', 'The Star', 'A Story of the Stone Age', 'A Story of the Days to Come' and 'The Man Who Could Work Miracles'.

Of this group of stories by far the most well known is 'The Star'. It is frequently included in anthologies, and is by common consent an outstanding example of Wells's technique as a literary artist. Its theme—that of the narrowly averted collision between earth and a strange new planet from outside the solar system–is elaborated on a broader canvas in the novel *In the Days of the Comet* (1906), but in 'The Star' Wells made brilliant use of language and metaphor to achieve an effect of controlled suspense. Reading the story today one is struck again and again by the vivid use of imagery:

And everywhere the world was awake that night, and throughout Christendom a sombre murmur hung in the keen air over the countryside like the belling of bees in the heather, and this murmurous tumult grew to a clangour in the cities.

So the star, with the wan moon in its wake, marched across the Pacific, trailed the thunderstorms like the hem of a robe, and the growing tidal wave that toiled behind it, frothing and eager, poured over island and island and swept them clear of men.

Everywhere the waters were pouring off the land, leaving mud-silted ruins, and the earth littered like a storm-worn beach with all that had floated, and the dead bodies of the men and brutes, its children.

Wells attains the effect he desires, as in the opening pages of *The War of the Worlds* and *The Island of Doctor Moreau*, partly by a terse documentary style and partly by the deliberate manner in which he introduces recognisably ordinary human beings into the narrative. 'The Star', although concerned with events on a cosmic scale, is brought within the range of the reader's own experience by the skilful introduction of everyday characters—'lonely tramps faring through the wintry night', 'the schoolboy rising early for his examination work', 'pretty women, flushed and glittering', and so on. A similar technique is employed in 'The Man Who Could Work Miracles', a humorous story which Wells adapted for a film version in 1936. Here, as in *The Invisible Man*, an element of farcical comedy is added to the matter-of-fact description of extraordinary events. The whole story of George McWhirter Fotheringay and his inexplicable gift of working miracles is told with a high-spirited zest which anticipates the comic vitality of *Kipps* and *The History of Mr. Polly*. There can be no mistaking the enthusiasm with which Fotheringay's adventures are described: 'The small hours found Mr. Maydig and Mr. Fotheringay careering across the chilly market square under the still moon, in a sort of ecstasy of thaumaturgy, Mr. Maydig all flap and gesture, Mr. Fotheringay short and bristling, and no longer abashed at his greatness.' Here, as in so many of Wells's novels and stories, the unbelievable is rendered commonplace by the extraordinarily effective use of detail and engaging facility of language. It is no accident that the story is sub-titled 'A Pantoum in Prose'.

'A Story of the Stone Age' and 'A Story of the Days to Come' are less successful experiments in the novella form. Wells regarded them as 'two series of linked incidents',[2] and the two are indeed linked in the sense that they contrast attitudes to loyalty and emotional affinity between the remote past and the twenty-second century. 'A Story of the Days to Come', which describes a society closely akin to that of *The Sleeper Wakes*, is a powerful story marred by a curious ambiguity in the narration. It is never clear whether Wells approves or disapproves of the rigidly organised civilisation he describes—a civilisation which strongly resembles Aldous Huxley's anti-utopia *Brave New World*—and this deliberate ambiguity inevitably lessens the impact of his vision. Continually one has a sense of a number of vivid incidents—the roads constructed of Eadhamite, the exile of the young lovers in the open country, the description of the city ways, the labour serfs—which yet fail to gell into a coherent and consistent narrative. Wells was conscious of the defects in the story, for many years later he wrote that the society described within it

was essentially an exaggeration of contemporary tendencies: higher buildings, bigger towns, wickeder capitalists and labour more downtrodden than ever and more desperate. . . . It was our contemporary world in a state of highly inflamed distension. . . . I suppose that is the natural line for an imaginative writer to take, in an age of material progress and political sterility. Until he thinks better of it.[3]

Of far greater literary and imaginative power is the short story 'The Crystal Egg', one of Wells's most remarkable inventions. It begins in the restrained and careful manner he was beginning to make his own: 'There was, until a year ago, a little and very grimy-looking shop near Seven Dials, over which, in weather-worn yellow lettering, the name of "C. Cave, Naturalist and Dealer in Antiquities" was inscribed.' With considerable skill Wells builds up a picture of the Cave ménage—of Mr. Cave himself, the little old antique dealer, of his wife, 'a coarse-featured, corpulent woman', and of the intriguing discovery that the crystal egg, when viewed under certain light conditions, reveals details of the landscape of what can only be the planet Mars. The reader is given a vivid sense of Cave's loneliness, of his desire to confide the secret of the crystal to no one except his closest friend, and of his growing fascination with the perusal of the Martian terrain. It is with a real sense of loss and regret that one learns, at the conclusion of the story, of Cave's death and of the sale of the crystal to 'a tall, dark man in grey'. The reader has a tantalising glimpse of the crystal egg being, possibly, 'within a mile of me, decorating a drawing-room or serving as a paper-weight—its remarkable functions all unknown'. 'The Crystal Egg' embodies within its brief compass all those qualities which made Wells among the foremost storytellers of his time: convincing narrative, skilful and assured characterisation, accomplished use of scientific detail, and careful pacing of incident and dénouement.

Twelve Stories and a Dream comprises, as its title suggests, twelve tales (published during the years 1898–1903) together with 'A Dream of Armageddon', a sombre story of love and death told against a backcloth of a world war. The stories differ markedly in range and quality; perhaps the most characteristic, though for widely differing reasons, are 'Mr. Skelmersdale in Fairyland', 'The New Accelerator' and 'Miss Winchelsea's Heart'. Each illustrates different facets of Wells's strengths and weaknesses as a storyteller.

'Mr. Skelmersdale' is notable for its preoccupation with a theme which was to haunt his writings as a *leitmotiv* throughout his life—that of the man who is obsessed by a vision of a beautiful, elusive lady and who searches in vain for the promise the vision seems to embody. The theme recurs again in 'The Door in the Wall', in *The Sea Lady* and in numerous other writings; it underlies much of *Tono-Bungay* and *The New Machiavelli*; even as late as *Apropos of Dolores* (1938) the dream of the elusive, beckoning love goddess continued to haunt Wells's fiction. The Mr. Skelmersdale of the story, a village shopkeeper, falls asleep one night on Aldington Knoll and wakes to find himself in Fairyland. There he meets a beautiful Fairy Lady who talks to him of love. Realising too late his longing for her he becomes parted from her company, and at length loses sight of the fairy kingdom altogether. He returns to the world of everyday only to find that he is filled with an insatiable desire to return to the beautiful land within the Knoll. He tries on many subsequent occasions to fall asleep there and so return to Fairyland, but without success.

What distinguishes this story, apart from the obsessive quality of its theme, is the poetic beauty of its writing. The description of Aldington Knoll and of the summer night at the prelude of Skelmersdale's adventure is written with an intensity and clarity of vision which recalls the most memorable sequences in *The Time Machine* and *The First Men in the Moon*. Wells was exceptionally gifted at describing scenes of natural beauty; here he conveys to the reader a vivid sense of the Knoll and of the splendour of its setting. He conveys too a sense of Skelmersdale's unhappiness and his troubled mental state at the outset of the story. The account of Fairyland and of the elf kingdom in which the unhappy man was temporarily imprisoned is perhaps a little contrived, but there can be no doubting the feeling of wonder with which the fairy kingdom is described and the aura of unattainable beauty which surrounds the lady of his dream-like encounter. 'It is hard, it is impossible, to give in print the effect of her radiant sweetness shining through the jungle of poor Skelmersdale's rough and broken sentences. To me, at least, she shone clear amidst the muddle of his story like a glow-worm in a tangle of weeds.' The reader shares with the little shopkeeper the emotion of irreparable loss, the sense of almost physical anguish, which overwhelms him on his return to the village and his realisation that he will see the fairy lady no more. By contrast with Fairyland the world of humanity seems coarse and flat and uninspiring.

'The New Accelerator' is in complete contrast both in substance and style. It lacks altogether the poetic qualities, the atmosphere of haunting beauty, which irradiates 'Mr. Skelmersdale'; it belongs rather to the zestful, exuberant manner of the scientific romances. Professor Gibberne, a noted physiologist, discovers a drug which stimulates the nervous system many thousands of times faster than the normal pace. He and a friend (the narrator) both take a dose of the stimulant and, under its influence, walk along the Folkestone Leas to observe its remarkable effects. Since they are both moving 'a thousand times faster than the quickest conjuring trick that was ever done' the effect is to make it appear that all other people are moving in extreme slow motion. This provides the material for a novel and entertaining tale in which Wells delights in observing his fellows from an unfamiliar stance. There is a girl and a man smiling at one another, 'a leering smile that threatened to last for evermore'; a brass band playing incomprehensible music; a man struggling to refold his newspaper against the wind; an apparently immobile cyclist frozen in the act of overtaking a stationary charabanc; and so on. All are described with wry humour and a vivid sense of the absurd. The account of the sudden wearing off of the drug, of the abrupt return to the normal pace of everyday, is handled with assurance and conviction, as are the narrator's reflections on the ethical considerations arising from the experiment. The reader has a vivid sense of the novelty, of the extraordinary elation, of living for half an hour while the remainder of humanity lives through a second or so of normal time. The story is indeed a variant on the theme of time travelling: reflecting on Gibberne's discovery, the storyteller remarks that the Accelerator 'must necessarily work an entire revolution in civilised existence. It is the beginning of our escape from that Time Garment of which Carlyle speaks.' 'The New Accelerator' is in fact a not wholly successful attempt to fuse together the rumbustious humour of (say) *The Wealth of Mr. Waddy* with the scientific framework of the romances; but the tale bears vivid testimony to Wells's abundant zest for life and his infectious delight at the sheer joy of existence.

In March 1898, tired and ill from overwork, Wells arrived in Rome with his wife for a much-needed holiday. Here he had arranged to meet George Gissing, a writer who greatly admired Wells's work and who appreciated his friendship. Years later Wells recorded: "Miss Winchelsea's Heart' came into my head to tell my friend George Gissing on the Pincio one spring morning in 1898.' The plot of the story is simple enough: Miss Winchelsea, a refined school-mistress, meets a Mr. Snooks whilst on holiday. She is attracted towards him but declines him since she cannot face the prospect of being called 'Mrs. Snooks'. Later she learns that he has married her friend Fannie and changed his name, first to Senoks and then to Sevenoaks. Summarised thus baldly the story sounds slight, almost trite, but in Wells's hands it becomes a restrained and deliciously written satire on human pretentiousness.

There is, first, his shrewd awareness of Miss Winchelsea's innate snobbery:

> Her dress was a triumph of tactful discretion, sensible but not too 'touristy'—Miss Winchelsea had a great dread of being 'touristy'—and her Baedeker was carried in a cover of grey to hide its glaring red.

A young man travelling alone followed. He was not at all 'touristy' in his costume, Miss Winchelsea observed; his Gladstone bag was of good pleasant leather with labels reminiscent of Luxembourg and Ostend, and his boots, though brown, were not vulgar.

Then the whole story is suffused with delicate humour. One does not easily forget the mother of two daughters who boards the train in great excitement and who is driven at last 'to the muttered inventory of a basket of travelling requisites. Presently she looked up. "Lor!" she said, "I didn't bring *them*!" Both the daughters said "Oh, Ma!" but what "them" was did not appear.' Wells reserves most of his irony for the description of Miss Winchelsea's dismay on learning that the polite young man she has admired so much bears the surname 'Snooks':

She imagined the terrible rejoicings of certain girl friends, of certain grocer cousins from whom her growing refinement had long since estranged her. How they would make it sprawl across the envelope that would bring their sarcastic congratulations.

And so on for several pages of refined soul-searching. All in all this must be counted one of Wells's most successful attempts at the humorous short story, and provides interesting evidence of his growing self-confidence as a writer. It possesses in abundance those qualities which were to stand him in such good stead as a novelist in the years to come—a penetrating observation of human character and behaviour, a keen but never obtrusive sense of humour, and an ability to look upon human frailties with gentle irony and detachment. That Gissing enjoyed the story there can be no doubt. 'With no little chuckling I have read "Snooks"', he wrote. 'There is much of your right self in this, and I enjoy the end.'

The Country of the Blind and Other Stories was Wells's final selection: it consisted, he wrote, of a collection under one cover 'of all the short stories by me that I care for any one to read again'. The compilation includes 28 of the finest stories from previously published collections, together with five reprinted for the first time: 'A Vision of Judgment', 'The Empire of the Ants', 'The Door in the Wall', 'The Country of the Blind' and 'The Beautiful Suit'.

'The Country of the Blind' (1904) is by common consent one of Wells's most memorable short stories. It shares with *The Wonderful Visit* and *The Invisible Man* a concern with the fate of the outcast; it is, with them, a parable on intolerance, but it goes beyond them in its eloquent assertion of the invincibility of the human spirit.

Nunez, a mountaineer, enters by accident 'that mysterious mountain valley, cut off from the world of men, the Country of the Blind'. Here, in a remote valley in the Andes, he stumbles upon a community of people completely blind, their entire civilisation and way of life adapted harmoniously to a world without sight. Wells conveys with unforgettable vividness the contrast between the blind villagers, ignorant of the wonders of sunrise and sunset and the beauty of the physical universe, and Nunez, the man from the outside, the representative of a world of unimaginable things. But as a sighted man Nunez is an outsider, an alien. He attempts to assert his superiority over the blind people but quickly realises that they have developed acute senses of hearing and touch which help to compensate for their blindness. In a scene of almost unbearable tension Nunez is pursued by a group of men wielding spades and sticks, alert for the slightest sound of movement. (The scene, so vividly imagined and described, is strongly reminiscent of the death of Griffin in *The Invisible Man*.) He is taken prisoner and is obliged to submit to the rule of the community; he ceases to talk of sight and of the great world beyond the valley. Gradually Nunez falls in love with a native girl, Medina-saroté, but the village elders—convinced that he is an idiot—consent to the proposed marriage only on condition that he forfeits his sight. At first, overwhelmed with his emotion for the girl, he consents, but then realises that he cannot endure the prospect of a world eternally in darkness:

> He had fully meant to go to a lonely place where the meadows were beautiful with white narcissus, and there remain until the hour of his sacrifice should come, but as he went he lifted up his eyes and saw the morning, the morning like an angel in golden armour, marching down the steeps. . . .
>
> It seemed to him that before this splendour he, and this blind world in the valley, and his love, and all, were no more than a pit of sin.
>
> He did not turn aside as he had meant to do, but went on, and passed through the wall of the circumference and out upon the rocks, and his eyes were always upon the sunlit ice and snow.
>
> He saw their infinite beauty, and his imagination soared over them to the things beyond he was now to resign forever.

The final scene in the story describes Nunez slowly climbing out of the valley, forsaking Medina-saroté and all that she embodies in his determination to escape from the valley and return to the world of men.

That 'The Country of the Blind' is satirical, even parabolic, in intent, there seems little doubt. There is also no question that the story can be read on a number of different levels, rich as it is in symbolisms and nuances—of some of which Wells himself may have been unaware. In common with *The Time Machine* and *The Island of Doctor Moreau* one is continually aware of allegorical elements: the story has a transparent quality which renders the experience of reading it extraordinarily unsettling. Each generation will read into it the undertones which have meaning to its own age.

On its simplest level it is a homily on the theme of inhumanity: the sighted man in a blind world becomes a social outcast and is persecuted. Wells neatly inverts the saying 'In the Country of the Blind, the one eyed man is King' and demonstrates the truth that in a sightless world the gift of sight can bring in its train ostracism and danger. Read from a different angle, the story is a parable on conformity: Nunez is the rebel who refuses to conform with a rigid and narrow-minded social order. He seeks to disentangle himself from a situation which he finds intolerable, a course of behaviour which Wells in his own person invariably adopted and urged others to follow. My own reading supports these two interpretations but would add a third: that Nunez symbolises the free independence of the human psyche, the indomitable will to survive of the spirit. Faced with a choice between losing his eyesight (and, by implication, his ability to imagine a larger and freer world) and the prospect of escape, even at the risk of physical death, he chooses the latter. There is no doubt that for Wells this dilemma had direct relevance to the problems of daily life. Throughout his career he advocated the utmost freedom of thought and expression, and it was entirely characteristic of him that in September 1939, when war clouds were ominously gathering, he planned to deliver an address to the Annual Congress of the International P.E.N. entitled 'The Honour and Dignity of the Free Mind'.

'The Door in the Wall' (which, together with 'The Country of the Blind', is deservedly counted among his finest stories) marks a return to the central theme of 'Mr. Skelmersdale in Fairyland' and *The Sea Lady*—that of the man who is haunted by an elusive vision of lost beauty. Lionel Wallace, the central figure, is a much more substantial character than Skelmersdale; he is a prominent politician on the brink of a Cabinet appointment. But he is a man obsessed, haunted by the tormenting memory 'of a beauty and a happiness that filled his heart with insatiable longings, that made all the interests and spectacle of wordly life seem dull and tedious and vain to him.' As a boy of five, Wallace had first stumbled across the door—a green door against a plain white wall. The door held a considerable attraction for him and, after some hesitation, he opened it 'and so, in a trice, he came into the garden that has haunted all his life'. Many years later Wallace describes to his friend Redmond the peculiar effect the wonderful garden had upon him as a child—its beauty, its exhilarating atmosphere, its indefinable quality of paradise. There he met kindly people who talked to him and played delightful games with him. There too he met a sombre woman who showed him a book containing an account of his own life, including his entry into the beautiful world beyond the green door. When he finds himself suddenly outside the white wall he is distraught with unhappiness and pleads in vain to be allowed to return. During the ensuing years Wallace sees the door again on no less than six different occasions but each time he passes by without entering, always for some pressing reason. At last he realises that the door symbolises for him escape from a life he has come to despise, and swears to himself that if ever he encounters it again he will enter without hesitation. He confesses to Redmond that his soul 'is full of inappeasable regrets'. At the end of the story Redmond explains that Wallace is now dead, having fallen through a door into a deep excavation near East Kensington Station. The narrative concludes with the reflection that Wallace 'had, in truth, an abnormal gift, and a sense, something—I know not what—that in the guise of wall and door offered him an outlet, a secret and peculiar passage of escape into another and altogether more beautiful world'.

'The Door in the Wall' is essentially a fantasia on a characteristically Wellsian theme—that of the man who believes he has found a way of escape from the commonplace world of everyday into a *different* life, a life of paradisal enchantment. Many of Wells's novels and romances touch upon this theme, which was clearly a powerfully recurring element in his imagination. (It is significant that the wall itself recurs as a mental image in *Tono-Bungay*: 'There stretches away south of us long garden slopes and white gravestones and the wide expanse of London, and somewhere in the picture is a red old wall, sun-warmed, and a great blaze of Michaelmas daisies set off with late golden sunflowers and a drift of mottled, blood-red, fallen leaves. *It was with me that day as though I had lifted my head suddenly out of dull and immediate things and looked at life altogether.*' [my italics]) The possibility of passing out of this life into a different and happier one was one which exercised Mr. Polly, for example, in his romantic day-dreams; it underlies much of *Men Like Gods*; in some form, implicit or explicit, it lies close to the surface of almost all his fiction. To anyone with any understanding of Wells's life and background 'The Door in the Wall' is a fascinating, indeed moving, piece of writing—for behind the obvious literary skill of the narrative is revealed a deeply divided personality: a man who, despite all the outward appearance of material happiness and success, was haunted by a vision of loveliness which continually eluded him.

After the publication of 'The Door in the Wall' in 1906 Wells's output of short stories virtually ceased: during the remaining 40 years of his life he wrote nine stories (the last to be written, 'Answer to Prayer', dates from 1937). Already by the time *The Country of the Blind and Other Stories* was published Wells had realised that

I was once an industrious writer of short stories, and that I am no longer anything of the kind. . . . I find it a little difficult to disentangle the causes that have restricted the flow of these inventions. It has happened, I remark, to others as well as to myself, and in spite of the kindliest encouragement to continue from editors and readers. There was a time when life bubbled with short stories; they were always coming to the surface of my mind, and it is no deliberate change of will that has thus restricted my production. It is rather, I think, a diversion of attention to more sustained and more exacting forms.

As a short story writer Wells has been described as 'the product of a union between Dickens and Poe'.[4] Certainly it is possible to detect the influence of both these writers upon his work, as also the influence of Kipling, Barrie and Gissing. Wells would have been the first to acknowledge his indebtedness to other writers, and as a novelist he made no secret of his lifelong admiration for Charles Dickens and Laurence Sterne. But in the last analysis his stories have a distinctive quality which gives them a flavour peculiar to himself: it lies in their ability to stimulate thought, to suggest new possibilities of action, to unfold novel horizons of human en-deavour. Each story, he insisted, 'is intended to be a thing by itself; and if it is not too ungrateful to kindly and enterprising publishers, I would confess I would much prefer to see each printed expensive-ly alone, and left in a little brown-paper cover to lie about a room against the needs of a quite casual curiosity'.[5] Any reader browsing through these stories in such a mood of curiosity would find a range diverse enough to suit his every mood. He would smile at the comic observation of 'The Truth About Pyecraft' or 'The Jilting of Jane', be enthralled by the horror of 'The Empire of the Ants' or 'The Sea Raiders', be diverted by the tension of 'A Slip Under the Microscope' or 'Under the Knife'. Above all he (or she) would find release from the limitations of the everyday world in the immense fertility of Wells's imagination.

The short stories, for all their manifold diversity, have one overriding factor in common: that they are *disturbing*. In their capacity to stimulate and inspire, to suggest unsuspected possibilities of both terror and happiness, to illuminate a thousand dark corners of human ignorance, lies their greatest strength. The stories will 'live' because they bear witness to man's limitless curiosity and sense of wonder.

Part IV

THE ROMANCES

The Romances

THE TIME MACHINE

The Time Machine was Wells's first full-length work of fiction. Since its original publication in book form in 1895 it has occupied an important place in his writings and is widely acknowledged to be among his finest literary and imaginative achievements.

Bernard Bergonzi[1] has demonstrated that the story in the form in which we know it today has a long and complex bibliographical history, and had perhaps a longer gestation than any of his later works. Beginning with the earliest draft under the title *The Chronic Argonauts* (serialised in the *Science Schools Journal*, April–June 1888) and concluding with the Heinemann edition (May 1895) which is now accepted as the final and definitive text, the book went through no fewer than seven different versions before Wells was satisfied. The Heinemann text is a reworking of a version written early in 1894 for W. E. Henley's *National Observer*, and largely rewritten during the summer of that year (at Tusculum Villa, 23 Eardley Road, Sevenoaks) for serialisation in the *New Review*, where it appeared under the title 'The Time Traveller's Story'. It is clear from the evidence cited by Bergonzi, by Geoffrey West and by Wells himself[2] that immense pains were taken over its writing, and that Wells realised his reputation would be made or broken by its publication. In the event the book was immediately recognised as a work of unusual imaginative power—W. T. Stead, writing in the *Review of Reviews*, wrote 'Mr. H. G. Wells, who is writing the serial in the *New Review*, is a man of genius'—and *The Time Machine* has continued to be in print, in both hardback and paperback editions, for more than eighty years. Today it has achieved the status of a classic.

Whilst critics have been unanimous in recognising the literary merits of the work, opinion is divided as to its meaning. Some commentators have seen the story as a fable, an allegorical myth rich in satirical undertones. Others see it as a romance on a par with Stevenson's *Treasure Island* or Haggard's *King Solomon's Mines*—a gripping tale of adventure which can be enjoyed by readers of all ages but need not be studied too closely for hidden symbolisms. My own reading supports the former view. It is, I think, clear from many internal indications that Wells had a satirical intention in mind when writing *The Time Machine*. Indeed, one could go further and argue that this is true of all the scientific romances—that he was in fact using science fiction as a device to attack many of the widely held and prevalent beliefs, attitudes and assumptions of his time. Viewed from this standpoint *The Time Machine* and *The War of the Worlds* are both warnings against the complacent assumption of the inevitability of progress; *The Invisible Man* is a parable illustrating the dangers inherent in the misuse of science; *The Sleeper Awakes* and *The First Men in the Moon* are anti-utopian satires on regimentation and the servile state; *The Food of the Gods* is an allegory upon the pettiness of local and national boundaries; and so on. Anthony West has argued that Wells came to hate the rigid hierarchical society symbolised in the closed world of Up Park, and that *The Time Machine* is a parody of the elitist order on which the 'Bladesover tradition' was based. Certainly the contrast and interplay between leisure and activity, between light and darkness, between 'above ground' culture and 'below ground' degradation, between the decadent Eloi on the one hand and the brutish Morlocks on the other, is a continually recurring theme throughout.

Consider, first, some of the more obvious satirical elements within the framework of the tale. There is, for example, the ambivalent attitude of the narrator towards the eating of meat. The reader is invited to feel disgust and horror at the cannibalism of the Morlocks, and yet at several points in the narrative the Time Traveller refers to his own partiality for meat:

'Save me some of that mutton. I'm starving for a bit of meat'.[3]

'Where's my mutton?' he said. 'What a treat it is to stick a fork into meat again!'[3]

'I heard your voices and the clatter of plates. I hesitated—I felt so sick and weak. Then I sniffed good wholesome meat, and opened the door on you.'[15]

Then the ventilating shafts which connect the underground

world of the Morlocks with the surface bear a striking resemblance to the ventilators of the underground kitchens which Wells must have seen as a child at Up Park. Indeed, the whole story can be regarded as an extended allegory on the theme of the exploitation of man by man. The Time Traveller realises the truth of the situation when he reflects: 'Man had been content to live in ease and delight upon the labours of his fellow-man, had taken Necessity as his watchword and excuse, and in the fullness of time Necessity had come home to him.'[10] Yet he himself is guilty of living in the same ease and delight:

> He reached out his hand for a cigar, and cut the end. 'But come into the smoking-room. It's too long a story to tell over greasy plates.' *And ringing the bell in passing* [my italics], he led the way into the adjoining room.

The narrator, in other words, is just as indifferent to his servants as are the Eloi to the labouring Morlocks: both are simply taken for granted.

The story, then, can be read on several different levels and is particularly rich in symbolism, of some of which Wells may have been unaware. Even the sphinx, which is the narrator's first sight of the world of 802701, can be read as a symbol for an enigma: it is as if the Time Traveller is posing the question to himself and the reader: 'What is this riddle? What is the meaning of this world?'

David Lodge, in *The Language of Fiction*, has described *The Time Machine* as 'one of the most desolating myths in modern literature'. It is certainly one of Wells's most pessimistic works, and almost rivals *The Island of Doctor Moreau* in its utter hopelessness of outlook. Written when its author was a young man in his twenties, one might have expected his first novel to be a work of youthful optimism. Wells, after all, had studied biology under the great T. H. Huxley and might have been supposed to take a more hopeful view of the human future. Instead, the work is one of almost unrelieved scepticism and holds out little prospect of happiness for mankind.

In retrospect it can be seen as an assault on the complacent assumptions of evolutionary theory. The closing years of the nineteenth century were years of widespread optimism—an optimism accentuated by the popular idea that, in the light of Darwin's teachings, the only vista opening out for man was one of progress. Wells is at pains to argue the reverse case: that nature is indifferent to homo sapiens and that the prospects for human advancement are at best uncertain and at worst doubtful. In asserting this he was being utterly consistent from his earliest writings to his last. In his essay 'The Extinction of Man' (1894) he had written:

> But since the Cephalapsis and the Coccosteus many a fine animal has increased and multiplied upon the earth, lorded it over land or sea without a rival, and passed at last into the night. Surely it is not so unreasonable to ask why man should be an exception to the rule. From the scientific standpoint at least any reason for such exception is hard to find.'

And in *The Fate of Homo Sapiens*, written in 1939, he made much the same point: 'There is no reason whatever to believe that the order of nature has any greater bias in favour of man than it had in favour of the icthyosaur or the pterodactyl.'

The epilogue to the story concludes with the reflection that the Time Traveller 'saw in the growing pile of civilisation only a foolish heaping that must inevitably fall back upon and destroy its makers in the end. If that is so, it remains for us to live as though it were not so.' In the final analysis, then, the mood which dominates *The Time Machine* is one of stoicism: life, for all its pains and disappointments, for all its injustice and unhappiness, is to be endured. In this short tale of 100 pages Wells created a myth which embodies many of the most characteristic themes of his fiction. At the same time he created a work of art which has taken its place among the finest of its genre in the language.

THE WONDERFUL VISIT

The Wonderful Visit is not a scientific romance in the same sense as *The Time Machine* and *The War of the Worlds*, but is rather a satirical fantasy in the vein of George MacDonald or Swift. Writing a few years after its publication, Wells remarked of it: 'I tried to suggest to people the littleness, the narrow horizon, of their ordinary lives by bringing into sharp contrast with typical characters a being who is free from the ordinary human limitations.'[3] This imaginary account of the visit of an angel to earth is partly a delicately written fantasia on human behaviour when confronted with a visitor from another world, and partly an allegory on the theme of intolerance.

The angel, as an intruder from outside, is treated with suspicion and contempt—just as the Time Traveller is regarded by the

Morlocks, or Nunez by the inhabitants of the country of the blind. He is different in manner and appearance from the villagers and so they cannot tolerate him, just as the people of Iping could not tolerate the Invisible Man. The device of the critical visitant who is ignorant of earthly institutions and has to have customs and conventions explained to him was one which enabled Wells to satirise late Victorian society in a more overt way than had been possible in *The Time Machine*. The latter is much the more skilfully written of the two works yet *The Wonderful Visit*, although almost unknown today, is still of interest for the evidence it affords of Wells's characteristic preoccupations at the outset of his literary career

There is, first, an abiding affection for the unchanging rural order he had known as a boy and a young man in the countryside of Kent and Sussex. Flowing through the novel as a continuous backcloth is a sensitively drawn evocation of English village life in the eighteen-nineties. The entire action takes place in and around the village of Siddermorton (South Harting and its surrounding area), and the descriptions of the community and its inhabitants are among the most memorable passages in the work. With a sure pen Wells draws a vivid picture of the angel's encounter with a group of hobbledehoys standing outside the blacksmith's forge: indeed the whole account of the angel's exploration of the village is written with the gusto and sharp observation he was later to employ in *The Invisible Man* and *The Food of the Gods*. The village characters are drawn with a warmth which belies the satirical intention. Sandy Bright 'coming down the road from Spinner's carrying a side of bacon he had taken in exchange for a clock'; Mrs. Gustick scolding her granddaughter; Mrs. Jehoram and Mrs. Mendham, the local gossips—these are sketched lightly enough but with unmistakeable affection for human foibles. Wells had had abundant opportunities to observe village life in and around South Harting during his visits to Up Park (where his mother was housekeeper) from 1880 onwards: to him, coming fresh from the suburban sprawl of Bromley, it must have seemed a microcosm of the English rural community. How sharp his observation was can be readily seen in this novel, which now has the added charm of a period piece.

Secondly, there is the gentle satire on contemporary English morals and institutions. This is not obtrusive and lacks the bitterness which is evident in some of the later novels, such as *You Can't Be Too Careful*. It is muted, controlled, almost whimsical in its vein of gently mocking criticism of the established order. Already in 1895 at the age of 29, it is plain that Wells intended to discuss social problems in his fiction and even to attack such ideas as the private ownership of land. Whilst the discussion of social issues is handled to greater effect in the more mature fiction, it is introduced here with remarkable assurance and ease for such a comparatively inexperienced writer.

Bearing in mind that at the time *The Wonderful Visit* was written Wells was still feeling his way as a creative writer, the novel is rich in minor characterisation. Among a range of subsidiary characters one might single out Lady Hammergallow, surely the very archetype of the feudal *grand dame* (and later drawn in fuller depth as Lady Drew in *Tono-Bungay*); the Respectable Tramp with his endearing notion that human beings are 'pithed'; the Vicar of Siddermorton, oddly moving in his confused attempts to explain to the angel the complexities of English social nuances. Less successful is the encounter with Sir John Gotch, a rather contrived anticipation of the socialist ideas Wells elaborated in his later fiction, whilst the angel's love affair with the maid Delia seems clumsy in retrospect. On the other hand Wells does succeed admirably in introducing dramatic moments into the novel, not least the unforgettable scene in which the angel, taught by the vicar to be excessively polite to ladies, relieves Lady Hammergallow's parlour maid of the tea-tray.

This rather slight novel has never attained the popularity of the other romances, possibly because of its apparent immaturity. On publication, however, it was well received by the critics. The *Saturday Review* commented: '... underlying the sweet or acid wit, or even the pure fun (for fun abounds), there is a vein of seriousness and sadness which, with the beautiful descriptive miniatures scattered here and there, justify us in calling the story a piece of literature.' Today this may seem extravagant praise, yet the reviewer was surely right to praise its wit and underlying seriousness of purpose. Wells, encouraged by the success of *The Time Machine* and *The Wonderful Visit*, next applied his energies to the task of completing *The Island of Doctor Moreau*.

THE ISLAND OF DOCTOR MOREAU

Wells rejected the view that man is inherently evil. To him, man was only inherently animal. His thinking on evil, sin and human nature can most instructively be examined through the medium of three satirical novels: *The Island of Doctor Moreau* (1896), *Mr.*

Blettsworthy on Rampole Island (1928), and *The Croquet Player* (1936). All three contain satirical and allegorical elements. Each needs to be read several times before the full meaning of the allegory is understood.

The Island of Doctor Moreau is a parable worthy of comparison with Swift and Voltaire. The satirical intention is not immediately apparent, and many readers have laid the book aside under the impression that they have read a gripping horror story and nothing more. That Wells had a more serious, didactic intent is shown by the fact that he originally proposed as its subtitle *A Satire* or *A Satirical Grotesque.*

The book, which is vividly written in the terse, documentary style of *The Time Machine* and *The War of the Worlds*, relates the story of Edward Prendick, a private gentleman who is the sole survivor of a collision at sea. He is rescued and subsequently finds himself an unwelcome guest on a small volcanic island in the Pacific. The island is inhabited by Moreau, a notorious vivisector, his assistant Montgomery, and the ungainly Beast Folk—who are in reality animals subtly humanised by Moreau's skill. Prendick has many opportunities for observing the Beast Folk. He perceives clearly that 'Each of these creatures, despite its human form, its rag of clothing, and the rough humanity of bodily form, had woven into it, into its movements, into the expression of its countenance, into its whole presence . . . the unmistakable mark of the beast.'[4]

Moreau, who has made a life-long study of physiology, is seeking to discover the limits of plasticity in living beings. By a process of vivisection he reshapes animals into a low kind of man.

His experiments are never a complete success, for the delicate reshaping of the brain eludes him, and his humanised beasts gradually increase in number and form themselves into a colony on the island. The Beast Folk evolve a travesty of human civilisation, including a parody of religion ('the Litany of the Law') and the fear of Hell ('the House of Pain'), monogamous marriage, and a strict code of behaviour and decorum. The attempt to educate them and maintain respect for law and decency is a continual struggle against animal traits and instincts, a constant battle against deep-seated emotions and cravings. The effort to build a rational life is only a mockery, a flimsy façade behind which the animal characteristics try to reassert themselves. Moreau claims he 'can see through it all, see into their very souls, and see there nothing but the souls of beasts, beasts that perish—anger, and the lusts to live and gratify themselves. Yet they're odd. Complex, like everything else alive. There is a kind of upward striving in them. . . .'[5]

In this story, Wells is gently nudging the shoulder of the reader
and asking him to see that the ostensible world of civilisation is in
truth Doctor Moreau's Island writ large. In the closing pages
Prendick succeeds in escaping and returns to England, but he
cannot bring himself to admit that there is any fundamental difference between the seeming men and women about him and the
Beast Folk. 'I feel as though the animal were surging up through
them; that presently the degradation of the Islanders will be played
over again on a larger scale.' He tries to reassure himself by
contrasting the evil Beast Folk with normal human beings, 'perfectly reasonable creatures, full of human desires and tender sol-
icitude, emancipated from instinct, and the slaves of no fantastic
Law'.[6] Once pointed out, the satire and sarcasm are plain for all to
see.

Some of the most savage satire is reserved for the parody of
organised religion:

> At that the others began to gibber in unison, also rising to their
> feet, spreading their hands, and swaying their bodies in rhythm
> with their chant.... All three began slowly to circle round,
> raising and stamping their feet and waving their arms; a kind of
> tune crept into their rhythmic recitation, and a refrain—'Aloola'
> or 'Baloola' it sounded like. Their eyes began to sparkle and their
> ugly faces to brighten with an expression of strange pleasure.[7]

It has to be remembered that much of Wells's childhood and
adolescence had been dominated by orthodox religion of a markedly narrow, Calvinistic mould. Again and again in his novels and
autobiography he refers to the stultifying influence of this religious
background, and it is not difficult to see why it is the theme for his
most biting irony or such a continually recurring motif in his work.

At the time of writing *Moreau* Wells had never travelled outside
England and Wales. In spite of its vivid description of tropical
scenery, therefore, the setting is purely imaginary and is a classic
example of the 'desert island' myth exemplified by such tales as
Treasure Island and *Swiss Family Robinson*. Some of the details of
the setting and background may have been derived from other
literary sources, in particular Poe's stories 'The Narrative of Arthur
Gordon Pym' and 'The Gold Bug', in addition to such obvious
examples as *Robinson Crusoe*.

It is significant that he chose to discuss the problem of evil
through the medium of fiction, using in each case the device of a
self-contained island or region as the setting for his fable. The

adoption of this technique meant that the issues could be viewed from outside, with a sense of detachment quite unattainable in the orthodox non-fiction essay. It is akin to the device of the critical visitants in *The Wonderful Visit* and *The Sea Lady*. Wells is, in a sense, looking at man dispassionately *from the outside*, with the relentless honesty of an extra-terrestrial observer, and is urging the reader to do likewise. This requires an effort of imagination beyond the mental range of most. The author's ruthless candour jolts the reader from his complacency and forces him to see man in his true light—with all his limitations and vast potential for good or evil.

What was his motive in writing this story? He is asking the reader, firstly, to recognise man for what he is: an animal—an animal removed from the ape and the ox by an immeasurable process of evolution and many centuries of moral training and education. Man was superficially a rational being but he possessed immense potential for evil if the animal within him was allowed to conquer the rational. The bestial trait manifested itself in violence and anger, and all education must necessarily be a modification and a sublimation of these primitive elements. Any retrogression towards his ancestral past was to be sedulously guarded against, for he was all too prone to revert to his animal nature and give way to treachery and hatred. These characteristics flashed out in storms of anger and fear, in ugly moods of violence and lust. For much of life they remained dormant, but they could burst out and consume the whole being with uncontrollable force.

Secondly, through his fable of the creatures on Doctor Moreau's island, Wells is drawing attention to the unhappiness and confusion of much of human life. Driven by fear and pain, tormented by intolerable desires, the Beast Monsters blunder through their squalid existence, fretted and constrained by rigid laws. The purposelessness and folly of their lives moved and distressed Prendick, just as Wells was bored and exasperated by the blind stupidity of man's existence. 'I must confess I lost faith in the sanity of the world when I saw it suffering the painful disorder of this island.'[8]

THE INVISIBLE MAN

It is perhaps difficult for a twentieth-century reader to recapture the sense of excitement which must have been experienced by those who read *The Invisible Man* for the first time on its publication as a serial in *Pearson's Weekly* in the summer of 1897 and as a book in the autumn of that year. To a contemporary reader, encountering Wells's works in the order of their publication, it must have been immediately apparent that here was a work of unusual imaginative power. For *The Invisible Man* is a much more assured piece of storytelling than either *The Wonderful Visit* (1895) or *The Wheels of Chance* (1896), and marks a considerable advance in narrative skill. One has only to consider the opening paragraph to recognise at once the hand of a literary artist thoroughly acquainted with his medium:

'The stranger came early in February, one wintry day, through a biting wind and a driving snow, the last snowfall of the year, over the down, walking as it seemed from Bramblehurst railway station, and carrying a little black portmanteau in his thickly gloved hand. He was wrapped up from head to foot, and the brim of his soft felt hat hid every inch of his face but the shiny tip of his nose; the snow had piled itself against his shoulders and chest, and added a white crest to the burden he carried. He staggered into the Coach and Horses, more dead than alive as it seemed, and flung his portmanteau down.'

To compare these introductory sentences—so circumstantial and realistic— with the openings of his previous full-length fictions, even including *The Time Machine*, is to appreciate afresh Wells's deftness as a writer and to understand why his friends George Gissing and Arnold Bennett praised the book so highly.[9]

Almost all the early romances are set in a specific and identifiable locality. *The Time Machine,* for example, albeit describing events which occur in the remote future, is set in and around Richmond and throughout the narrative the reader is continually reminded of familiar landmarks in the valley of the Thames. *The Wonderful Visit* is set in the village of Siddermorton (South Harting), and here again the location of the angel's visitation in a typically English village strengthens the verisimilitude of the story. The exciting series of encounters with the Martians recounted in *The War of the Worlds* are confined for the most part to a precisely identified stretch of Surrey countryside, and most of the drama occurs in the area bounded by Woking and Kingston on Thames. *The Invisible Man*, in common with these, is based on an actual and quintessentially English setting: and one which Wells must have known well from his days as a student at Midhurst. The village of Iping, situated some three miles from

Midhurst and sixty miles from London on the edge of the Sussex Downs, is the setting for one of his most remarkable parables. (The village also figures in *The Wonderful Visit* and in *Love and Mr. Lewisham*, in the latter as 'Immering'.) Picturesquely placed on the River Rother and bounded by an extensive common, Iping clearly symbolised for Wells the characteristic, unchanging rural community: its very normality makes a striking contrast to the tumultuous events which destroy its Whit Monday calm.

The chapters describing the arrival of the Invisible Man and the reaction of the villagers to his strangeness are so sharply observed and convincing in their accumulation of detail—the wintry cold on the day of his appearance, the unpacking of the thousand and one bottles, the burglary at the vicarage, the mêlée in the Coach and Horses—that the reader's initial disbelief in the concept of invisibility is quickly dispelled. So sure is Wells's touch that it is impossible to doubt the reality of the Invisible Man; just as, in his hands, it is impossible to doubt the existence of a Time Machine or of Cavorite. No one has surpassed his ability to dispel scepticism by placing extraordinary occurrences in an everyday setting.

Griffin's subsequent explanation to his friend Kemp of the principles of invisibility and his account of his experiments and ultimate success has all the vividness and nightmare quality of a Poe short story. Wells was above all an accomplished story teller, and these chapters contain some of his most consistently entertaining writing. Naked, hungry and bitterly cold, Griffin becomes increasingly a hunted and isolated figure: a loner at war with society. Disillusionment follows rapidly:

'The more I thought it over, Kemp, the more I realised what a helpless absurdity an Invisible Man was,—in a cold and dirty climate and a crowded civilised city. Before I made this mad experiment I had dreamt of a thousand advantages. That afternoon it seemed all disappointment. . . . And for this I had become a wrapped-up mystery, a swathed and bandaged caricature of a man!'

It is arguable that the structure of *The Invisible Man* is somewhat lopsided, beginning as it does with the arrival of Griffin already invisible, followed after a series of incidents by a detailed explanation of how the transformation was achieved, then a final group of chapters which take up the story from the point where Griffin leaves Iping. At first sight this rather unusual device seems clumsy—later Wells was to employ a similar structural method in

The History of Mr. Polly—but on second reading it undoubtedly makes for a tauter narrative and more evenly paced flow of incident than would otherwise have been possible. The final 'Epilogue' (which seems to have been added after publication of the first edition) rounds off the story with a satisfying sense of completeness. The picture of Mr. Thomas Marvel, incidentally one of Wells's most Dickensian creations, musing over Griffin's notebooks whilst smoking a clay pipe is beautifully done; Wells achieves his effects with an economy and humour he rarely excelled.

The Invisible Man, for all the comic vitality of its opening scenes and the climactic nature of its ending, is in reality a profoundly serious parable about human behaviour. What is demonstrated in this short allegory is the truism that without social morality men are less than human: that power without moral control is dangerous and irresponsible. The sympathy of the reader is in fact with Griffin for much of the action of the novel: it is only when he runs amok and embarks on a reign of terror that he forfeits our understanding and becomes an outcast, an enemy to be hunted down and cast out of the fold. Indeed, the final sequence in which the Invisible Man is kicked and beaten to death by a mob intent on retribution recalls the scene in 'The Country of the Blind' when Nunez is surrounded by blind men intent on capture. In each case it is the *otherness*, the departure from the accepted norms of behaviour, which leads to persecution: invisibility in the one instance, sightedness in the other. Today the book has achieved the status of a science fiction classic and its fame—thanks in part to the film version directed by James Whale which Wells much admired—shows no sign of abating. He confessed wryly in his autobiography that 'to many young people nowadays I am just the author of *The Invisible Man*'.

THE WAR OF THE WORLDS

In 1896, whilst *The War of the Worlds* was being written, Wells wrote to his friend Elizabeth Healey: 'I'm doing the dearest little serial for Pearson's new magazine, in which I completely wreck and destroy Woking—killing my neighbours in painful and eccentric ways—then proceed via Kingston and Richmond to London, which I sack, selecting South Kensingon for feats of peculiar atrocity.' He was at this time living at Lynton, Maybury Road,

Woking and during his cycling explorations in the area he amused himself by noting down places to be destroyed by the Martians. The story is written in the vivid documentary style he had employed with such effectiveness in *The Time Machine* and *The Island of Doctor Moreau*. In common with these it is written in the first person, a device which gives immediacy to the narrative and a convincing atmosphere of verisimilitude.

Wells's great skill in *The War of the Worlds* lies in the convincing way he is able to describe startling and novel events happening to perfectly ordinary people. The description of 'The Exodus from London', for example, is an extraordinarily vivid imaginative account of mass hysteria and panic produced by fear of the unknown—and a remarkable anticipation of scenes of crowd behaviour in cities such as Petrograd and Moscow during the Russian Revolution. Wells was one of the earliest writers to describe mass panic in the face of universal disaster: a theme which has become almost a stock-in-trade of twentieth-century science fiction. But it is the essential *ordinariness* of his characters which lingers in the mind long after the book is finished:

> In Woking the shops had closed when the tragedy happened, and a number of people, shop-people and so forth, attracted by the stories they had heard, were walking over Horsell Bridge and along the road between the hedges that run out at last upon the common. You may imagine the young people brushed up after the labours of the day, and making this novelty, as they would make any novelty, the excuse for walking together and enjoying a trivial flirtation. You may figure to yourself the hum of voices along the road in the gloaming. . . .

The introduction of an actual location, Horsell Bridge and the Chobham Road, strengthens the narrative by an additional element of reality. Indeed the fast-moving action of the story can be fully appreciated only by reference to a map of the area around Woking. It is by any standards a novel dealing with huge themes, a novel on the cosmic scale; at the same time one is constantly reminded that the events described with such conviction occur in England, in the peaceful setting of the Surrey countryside. (When a pirated version of the novel, set in the United States, was serialised in the *Boston Post* in 1897, he sent a strong letter of protest, objecting to 'this manipulation of my work in order to fit it into the requirements of the local geography'. Similarly, the attempt by Orson Welles in

1938 to transplant the story to America displeased him greatly. 'I am deeply concerned at the effect of the broadcast,' he cabled. 'Totally unwarranted liberties were taken with my book.') Continually, then, one is aware that the author is describing recognisable English people faced with an unparalleled threat of death and destruction: *this*, one feels, is the way in which human beings would behave in the face of this kind of situation. Moreover the constantly reiterated topographical details—the circumstantial account of the narrator's journey from Leatherhead via Ockham, Ripley and Pyrford is an excellent example of the technique—serve to fix the narrative against an identifiable background.

The story is an interesting example of Wells's predilection for scenes of destruction and violence: a predilection which he frankly admits in his autobiography.[10] There is no mistaking the relish of his letter to Elizabeth Healey, or the enthusiasm with which he wrote such passages as: 'I must confess the sight of all this armament, all this preparation, greatly excited me. My imagination became belligerent, and defeated the invaders in a dozen striking ways; something of my schoolboy dreams of battle and heroism came back.' There can be no question that spirited descriptions of warfare and destruction appealed to some deep-seated emotion within him. As a boy he had often dreamed of military skirmishes in and around Martin's Hill at Bromley, and his evident enthusiasm for scenes of warfare can be clearly seen in such works as *The War in the Air* and *Little Wars*.

In the last analysis *The War of the Worlds* will survive because of its outstanding literary qualities. Since its first appearence in book form in 1898 it has never ceased to be in print in a variety of editions and its popularity shows no sign of abating. The *pacing* of the narrative—the skilful way in which, following the sombre opening paragraphs, suspense and excitement is built up during the unscrewing of the cylinder; the vivid description of the destruction of Weybridge and Shepperton; the unforgettable, nightmare vision of dead and abandoned London—all these linger in the memory. Like all great myths it possesses that quality of timelessness which permits it to be read and enjoyed long into adult life, even when first read as a child. That Wells had a more serious intention than simply an exciting tale of interplanetary warfare is evident from the epilogue. Here the narrator comments: 'It may be that in the larger design of the universe this invasion from Mars is not without its ultimate benefit for men; it has robbed us of that serene confidence in the future which is the most fruitful source of decadence, the gifts to human science it has brought are enormous,

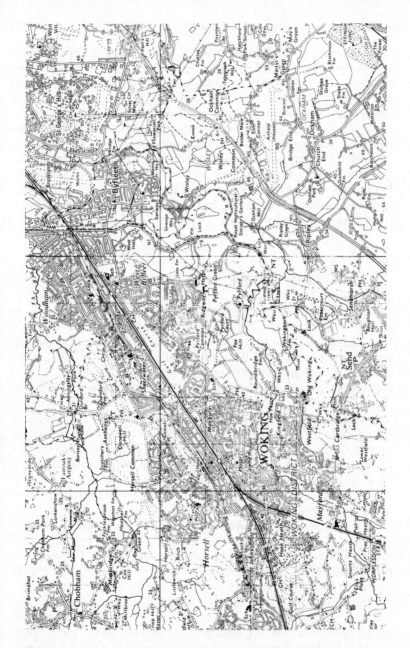

Map showing the area around Horsell Common, Woking, the site of the first Martian landings in *The War of the Worlds*. During the writing of this story Wells was living at Woking (Lynton, Station Road) and 'wheeled about the district marking down suitable places and people for destruction by my Martians'

and it has done much to promote the conception of the common-weal of mankind.' And in his essay 'What I Believe' Wells noted that both *The Invisible Man* and *The War of the Worlds* illustrated the dangers of power without moral control, the development of the intelligence at the expense of humanitarian considerations. This story, then, like his earliest imaginative work *The Time Machine*, is allegorical in intent and emphasises two fundamental themes: a salutary warning against the complacency of optimism, and an insistence that scientific progress without human sympathy is negative and ultimately self-destructive. These preoccupations were to be stated in a variety of forms in the romances which flowed from his pen in the succeeding years.

WHEN THE SLEEPER WAKES

Throughout the winter of 1897–8 Wells was simultaneously at work on two totally dissimilar works of fiction: *Love and Mr. Lewisham*, a realistic novel based in large measure on his experiences as a student at Midhurst and in London, and *When the Sleeper Wakes*, a fantastic romance set in the year 2100. He was also working at a number of short stories and worried by ominous signs of ill health. He was anxious to complete one or other of his full-length novels before holidaying in Rome with his wife and his friend George Gissing, but some instinct warned him against hastening the conclusion of *Love and Mr. Lewisham*. This was not in fact completed until January 1899, but he had to admit later that he 'scamped the finish' of *When the Sleeper Wakes* in his anxiety to press on with his next project.[11] The work bears all the hallmarks of hasty writing; so much so that Wells, conscious of its defects, produced a revised version in 1910 under the title *The Sleeper Awakes*. The revision is slightly shorter than the original, but does not differ substantially from his original conception. He remained dissatisfied with it and described it later as 'one of the most ambitious and least satisfactory of my works'.[12]

What immediately strikes one on reading the novel today is Wells's foresight in describing inventions and developments which were then either unknown or in embryonic form. Television, broadcasting, aeroplanes, phonetic spelling, urban walkways—all these are described in convincing detail. It is difficult to realise that the book was written even before the Wright brothers had made their first flight in a heavier-than-air machine.

The concept of enormously hypertrophied cities and an immense growth of urbanisation has also proved to be more accurate than Wells thought at the time. Already by 1900 (in *Anticipations*) he had come to doubt this thesis, but the steady growth of cities such as London and Birmingham in the latter half of the twentieth century has done much to confirm his earlier forecast. Wells regarded it as the first of a series of books which he termed 'fantasias of possibility'; each of these, he wrote, 'takes some great creative tendency, or group of tendencies, and develops its possible consequences in the future'.[13] It is perhaps less satisfying than any of his other fantasias of possibility, partly at least because, ambitious though it is, one continually has a sense of unrealised possibilities. The basic idea is interesting and potent but it fails to rise to the expectations one has of it. It is a bold but flawed attempt at sociological speculation in fictional form.

The significance of *When the Sleeper Wakes*, for all its imperfections, lies in its anticipation of many of the concepts employed by subsequent science fiction writers—usually without acknowledgement. Zamyatin's *We* (1924), Huxley's *Brave New World* (1932) and Orwell's *Nineteen Eighty Four* (1949) all derive, consciously or unconsciously, from Wells's vision of a regimented totalitarian state. In its emphasis on uniformity and dehumanisation, on mechanisation and lack of individual privacy, *The Sleeper* is in fact an anti-Utopia—it is, in common with *The Time Machine*, a dystopia—and one of the earliest to come from Wells's pen. It is important in that it was one of the first novels of any imaginative merit to question the complacent assumption of progress so widely held at the end of the Victorian age. The prevalent view was that scientific advancement must inevitably mean social progress and a widening of human freedom. Instead, Graham awakes after a slumber of 200 years to find an England ruled by a despotic minority, an England in which individuality is sacrificed to regimentation and the growth of a corporate state. Viewed in relation to other utopian novels of the period, Bulwer Lytton's *The Coming Race*, Edward Bellamy's *Looking Backward* and William Morris's *News from Nowhere*, Wells's vision is revealing in that it presupposes degradation and soulless uniformity in place of social advancement. Indeed, the rigidly controlled Labour Company workers in their identical uniforms of blue canvas are a clear anticipation of the 'proles' in Orwell's dystopia. Jack London also borrowed heavily from Wells in writing *The Iron Heel* (1907).

There can be little doubt that Wells found the labour of planning and writing the book a heavy one: all the evidence from his

autobiography, and letters written at the time, point to travail and
continual revision. To Gissing he confided: 'I'm having awful
times with my beggar. He won't shape. The fact of it is its gotten just
at the top of my powers or a little beyond em! So I'm midway
between a noble performance and a noble disaster.' And to Bennett:
'*The Sleeper* has a broken back and a swollen rump. *You* don't
know.'[14] It manifestly lacks the literary and artistic qualities of *The
Time Machine* and its successors and, largely for this reason, it has
never attained the popularity of his other scientific romances. It
stands as a testimony to the deeply rooted pessimism of the early
Wells, and as an intriguing glimpse of an imaginative writer's
nightmare conception of a future society.

THE FIRST MEN IN THE MOON

The idea of describing an imaginary journey to the moon had been
attempted by many writers before *The First Men in the Moon*
appeared in 1901. As long ago as the second century Lucian in
Icaromenippus had exploited the idea, and a quotation from his
romance appears on the title page of the first edition. In 1835 Edgar
Allan Poe, in *The Unparalleled Adventure of One Hans Pfaall*,
gave an account of a flight to the moon and back in a balloon. And
in 1865 Jules Verne returned to the theme in *From the Earth to the
Moon* (and again in a sequel, *Round the Moon*). What is new and
original in Wells's story is first the fact that the journey to the moon
is undertaken not by caricature figures but by well-drawn and
convincing individuals; second, the idea of the anti-gravity device,
'Cavorite', which makes possible the construction of the sphere;
third, the detailed and circumstantial descriptions of the lunar
landscape; and finally the satirical account of the Selenite civilisation. It is these elements, combined with an assured narrative style,
which have won for *The First Men in the Moon* a permanent place
in the literature of science fiction as a classic of the imagination.

   As with *The Time Machine* and *The War of the Worlds*, Wells
devotes several pages of the introductory chapter to establishing a
firm and recognisable setting: in this case Lympne, on the Kentish
coast. The background is described with an attention to detail
which serves to fix the local topography as familiar and solid:

   That outlook on the marsh was, indeed, one of the finest views
   I have ever seen. I suppose Dungeness was fifteen miles away; it

lay like a raft on the sea, and further westward were the hills by Hastings under the setting sun. Sometimes they hung close and clear, sometimes they were faded and low, and often the drift of the weather took them clean out of sight. And all the nearer parts of the marsh were laced and lit by ditches and canals.

This opening sequence is clearly intended as a backcloth for the appearance of the scientist Cavor, a complex figure who has some of the characteristics of Edward Ponderevo. For all Cavor's grandiose plans for the construction of an interplanetary sphere, he overlooks that quirkiness, that unpredictable quality which lies at the root of human affairs and of all Wells's fiction:

But it chanced that, unknown to Cavor, dissension had arisen about the furnace tending. Gibbs, who had previously seen to this, had suddenly attempted to shift it to the man who had been a gardener, on the score that coal was soil, being dug, and therefore could not possibly fall within the province of a joiner; the man who had been a jobbing gardener alleged, however, that coal was a metallic or ore-like substance, let alone that he was a cook. But Spargus insisted on Gibbs doing the coaling, seeing that he was a joiner and that coal is notoriously fossil wood.

These touches of humour, so shrewd in their observation, so Dickensian in their quality, distinguish Wells's work from such a writer as Jules Verne. Moreover they demonstrate the increasing confidence with which he was fusing together the realistic, documentary style of the scientific romance and the discursive, expository manner of the novel. *The First Men in the Moon* is by common consent one of the finest of the romances because it succeeds so convincingly in combining imaginative writing of a high order with the humour of the social novels. Indeed, on careful reading it can be seen that the entire work is rich in humorous detail: Cavor in his dirty cricket cap and cycling knickerbockers, Bedford lunching on beef and beer in a public house near Elham and startling the landlord by remarking apropos of the weather, 'A man who leaves the world when days of this sort are about is a fool!', the curious little boy 'with a penetrating sniff' who meddles with the sphere on its return to earth – touches such as these illuminate the story throughout and enhance the descriptive framework with a pattern of social comment which is apt and satisfying.

The account of the journey into space is written with unemotional tautness which yet succeeds in conveying to the reader the sense of awe which the narrator, Bedford, undoubtedly feels. Since the first actual moon landing by an Apollo spacecraft in 1969 something of the wonder and fascination of Wells's vision has inevitably been lost, but this does not diminish his achievement. What is so remarkable for a story written in 1900—before even flying machines had been invented—is the uncannily accurate anticipation of the methodology of space flight, including lift-off, weightlessness, zero gravity, radio communication with earth, re-entry and splashdown.

With the repetitions of the Apollo landings during the past decade the terminology of space travel has become so familiar as to be taken for granted, but when Wells was writing all these factors lay far in the future. Astonishing also is his prescience in describing the sense of detachment to which Neil Armstrong and others have testified (see especially the chapter entitled 'Mr. Bedford in Infinite Space'); the experience of seeing earth from the outside has brought to all who have undergone it the ability to view themselves and others with greater charity and without illusions: 'Do you know, I had a sort of idea that really I was something quite outside not only the world, but all worlds, and out of space and time, and that this poor Bedford was just a peephole through which I looked at life.'

The description of the lunar morning is universally accepted as one of his most unforgettable pieces of writing—as fine, in its own way, as the Time Traveller's vision of the end of the world. The quality of the writing is such that the scenes described remain in the memory long after the book has been read. (The present writer can testify that the moment when Cavor tests the lunar atmosphere by thrusting a piece of lit paper through the manhole of the sphere is still vivid in his memory after 30 years.) Equally memorable is the moment when Bedford, alone on the moon, finds the sphere which he thought to have been lost beyond hope of recovery. The elation of this discovery, with all that it means to Bedford, and the travail of his ultimately successful attempt to reach the sphere, is communicated with a vividness and feeling Wells rarely excelled.

Wells rounded off *The First Men in the Moon* with a series of chapters describing 'the natural history of the Selenites', which are clearly satirical in intent. Whether these sections were intended as part of his original design or conceived as an afterthought is not clear. (Bedford, at the commencement of Chapter 22, suggests the latter.) What is evident from this vision of Selenite civilisation is that Wells is using the opportunity to satirise human affairs—in particular the trend to over-specialisation which he disliked so intensely in the Webbs' and which he had previously allegorised in the Morlocks, and the tendency to exaggerate the intellect at the expense of human sympathy. The description of the Selenites, which owes much to his account of the Martians and of the 'Man of the Year Million', should be closely studied for an understanding of his thinking at this time and for the further evidence it offers of Wells's ambivalence. For it is by no means certain from these passages where his own sympathies lie: is the Selenite world depicted as a nightmare, a dystopia, or as a society to be emulated? My own reading supports the first view, but the chapters in question are capable of more than one interpretation.

This romance can be seen as the last of the 'true' scientific romances, or it can be regarded as marking a transition between the imaginative power of *The Invisible Man* and the more overtly ideological fantasias yet to come. Critics are divided on its final place in the canon but not on its overall excellence. It seems destined to be one of that handful of works which will carry his name and reputation into the twenty-first century and beyond.

THE SEA LADY

The idea of *The Sea Lady* came to Wells one day in 1900 while lying on the beach at Sandgate. Never well received by the critics or the reading public (the first edition was not exhausted until many years after its publication in book form in 1902), this rather slight tale appears at first sight to be merely a variation on the theme of *The Wonderful Visit*, with a mermaid as the critical visitant in place of an angel. Its importance lies not so much in the quality of its writing, which is admittedly undistinguished, but rather in its symbolic undertones; for *The Sea Lady* is in essence a fantasia on a theme which was to dominate Wells's fiction for several decades—'the harsh incompatibility of wide public interests with the high, swift rush of imaginative passion'.[15]

He acknowledged in later years that two of the central characters—Chatteris, a rising politician, and his fiancée Adeline Glendower—are frankly derived from Mrs. Humphrey Ward's novel *Marcella*, and indeed the device of a Marcella-like heroine is employed in a number of his novels. The story takes place against the background of Sandgate and Folkestone (the Randolph Buntings appear to be based on the Pophams, Wells's congenial neighbours when living at Arnold House) but this familiar setting serves as the backcloth to a fantasy rich in allegorical meanings.

The scene in which the Sea Lady makes her first appearance, after being rescued from drowning whilst apparently suffering an attack of cramp, contains echoes not only of Weena being rescued by The Time Traveller but also of Rowena being saved from drowning in *Mr. Blettsworthy on Rampole Island*. Drowning appears to have been for Wells a powerful symbolic image, for it plays a significant part in a number of his novels including *Joan and Peter* and *The History of Mr. Polly*. Again, the final scene, in which Chatteris is drawn down into the sea 'until the soft waters closed above him, down into a gentle ecstasy of death', recalls the ending of the short story 'The Door in the Wall' in which the politician Lionel Wallace falls to his death down a deep pit. This womb-like image, symbolising both withdrawal from the ostensible world and renewal, clearly exercised for Wells a strong imaginative appeal.

Although *The Sea Lady* bears the signs of having been written quickly and without undue care, it contains interesting indications of Wells's inner uncertainty at this time and his divided artistic and temperamental loyalties. It is difficult not to see in Melville's soliloquy upon Chatteris, for example, the author thinking aloud about himself:

'Think again of the many honest souls who aspire to the service of their kind, and are so hemmed about the preoccupied that they may not give it! And then this pitiful creature comes, with his mental gifts, his gifts of position and opportunity, the stimulus of great ideas, and a wife, who is not only rich and beautiful—she *is* beautiful!—but also the best of all possible helpers for him.—And he turns away. It isn't good enough. It takes no hold upon his imagination, if you please. It isn't beautiful enough for him, and that's the plain truth of the matter.'

Years later in *Boon* he gave vent to the same mood of discontent:

Sometimes—in the morning sometimes—he would be irritable and have quarrels with his shaving things, and there were extraordinary moods when it would seem to him that living quite beautifully in a pleasant villa and being well-off and famous, and writing books that were always good-humoured and grammatical and a little distinguished in an inoffensive way, was about as boring and intolerable a life as any creature with a soul to be damned could possible pursue.

Clearly Wells was prone at times to moods of profound dissatisfaction, phases when he was overwhelmed by claustrophobia and a desire to escape from familiar sights and sounds. It was in such a mood that he decided to sell Spade House and, later, to spend his winters in the South of France.[16] In the dilemma confronting Chatteris—that of the choice between public duty in the pursuit of his political career or romantic passion, symbolised by the mermaid—there is a foretaste of a theme he was to explore in greater depth in *The New Machiavelli* ten years later. A feeling of claustrophobia, of a 'fugitive impulse', hangs over both novels. It is as if Wells, unable to resolve satisfactorily the tensions within his own life, sublimated them in the form of fictional romance.

The Sea Lady is also revealing in that it illustrates that conflict between classical and romantic elements which underlies so much of his work. Towards the end of the novel, when Melville seeks to dissuade Chatteris from his pursuit of the mermaid, Chatteris replies:

'But why—why should the mask of death be beautiful? After all. . . . We get our duty by good hard reasoning. Why should reason and justice carry everything? Perhaps, after all, there are things beyond our reason; perhaps, after all, Desire has a claim on us?'

Wells's scientific training disposed him inevitably towards rational solutions to human problems, towards reason and justice and a dispassionate regard for the truth; his artistic predilections, on the other hand, drove him with equal force towards an imaginative and emotional response. This was the central dilemma of his life, perfectly symbolised in this brief cautionary tale.

Deep in his innermost being he harboured romantic longings which he confessed to few. That these came to the fore in his fiction he acknowledged many years afterwards—in words which are as telling as they are poignant:

There is an element of confession in the tale but it is a confession in motley. And love, instead of leading to any settling down, breaks things up. But the defeat of the disinterested career is just as complete. Chatteris, the lover, plunges not into domesticity but into the sea, glittering under a full moon. A craving for some lovelier experience than life had yet given me is the burden in this second phase. Not only Catherine Wells but I too could long at times for impossible magic islands.[17]

THE FOOD OF THE GODS

The Food of the Gods and How it Came to Earth—to give it its original title—was written at a time when Wells was becoming increasingly interested in social questions. He became a member of the Fabian Society in February 1903 and marked his debut by reading to the Society a paper entitled 'The Question of Scientific Administrative Areas in Relation to Municipal Undertakings'[18] in which he developed at length his view that local government areas were far too small for modern conditions. *The Food of the Gods*, which is a satire on the limitations of local and national boundaries, is essentially an allegorical fantasia on the central theme of his Fabian lecture: that the immense change of scale in human affairs rendered contemporary political arrangements impracticable.

The story contains much admirable characterisation, particularly in the opening chapters, and the Skinners—the decrepit couple who manage the experimental farm at Hickleybrow—are among Wells's most memorable creations.

The account of the coming of the food, Herakleophorbia, and its impact on the rural peace of Kentish villages, is likewise very competently done, recalling in its eye for detail and verisimilitude the opening sequences of *The Wonderful Visit* and *The Invisible Man*. Rarely did Wells achieve more vivid writing than in the description of the giant wasps and rats. These passages, written with such gusto, recall the spirited fighting scenes in *The War of the Worlds*, the unforgettable description of morning on the lunar surface, and the discovery of the strange man's invisibility in the Coach and Horses at Iping. His skill in pacing dramatic effects is again exploited to the full in the exciting account of the rats pursuing and attacking the Podbourne doctor driving in his buggy, and the plague of giant wasps causing panic and confusion. These creatures are described with such vividness that the readers' credulity is totally at one with the narrator.

An aspect of the story which has received comparatively little attention is the insight it provides into the ambivalence which lay at the heart of Wells's makeup. *The Food of the Gods* is not only notable for its gripping description of giant animals and plants but for its exquisite pen pictures of the English countryside. Here, for example, is the village of Cheasing Eyebright:

The village was looking its very best just then, under that

western light. It lay down along the valley beneath the beech-woods of the Hanger, a beading of thatched and red-tiled cottages—cottages with trellised porches and pyracanthus-lined faces, that clustered closer and closer as the road dropped from the yew trees by the church towards the bridge. The vicarage peeped not too ostentatiously between the trees beyond the inn, an early Georgian front ripened by time, and the spire of the church rose happily in the depression made by the valley in the outline of the hills. A winding stream, a thin intermittency of sky blue and foam, glittered amidst a thick margin of reeds and loosestrife and overhanging willows, along the centre of a sinuous pennant of meadow. The whole prospect had that curiously English quality of ripened cultivation—that look of still completeness—that apes perfection, under the sunset warmth.[19]

As a vignette of pastoral England it would be difficult to fault such a description. In its way it is quite perfect: it might almost be lifted from a novel by Gissing or Bennett. But it illustrates not only his extraordinary ease of manner in conveying a word picture of an undisturbed village but also the deep contradictions in his attitude already apparent in such works as *When the Sleeper Wakes*. Do his sympathies lie with the peaceful village communities portrayed so idyllically in this and other paragraphs, or do they lie with the new forces of change and progress symbolised by the giant children? Was he at heart looking forward to a new world of rapid transformation and dislocation, or backward to the unchanging rural order he had witnessed as a boy at Up Park? It was this fundamental dichotomy in his own mind—a desire on the one hand for sweeping social and political reforms, and on the other for a stable, identifiable local community—that lay at the root of his discontent and which he never satisfactorily resolved.

In the second half of the book, with its laboured account of the growth of the giant children, the allegory is less convincing and Wells seems to lose the thread of his story. His obsession with the idea of bigness *per se* comes to the fore. 'It was bigness insurgent. In spite of prejudice, in spite of law and regulation, in spite of all that obstinate conservatism that lies at the base of the formal order of mankind, the Food of the Gods, once it had been set going, pursued its subtle and invincible progress.' Wells at this time was greatly exercised by the novelty of parenthood (his sons, George Philip and Frank, were born in 1901 and 1903 respectively) and the enthusiasm for nursery education which had characterised *Mankind in the Making* is also abundantly evident in the account of the upbringing of young Redwood and the Cossar children. What had begun as an apparently straightforward scientific romance becomes in the second part an increasingly clumsy and overt parable on the theme of human pettiness. It is as if the story has a broken back; the disparity between the two parts is uncomfortably noticeable and deprives the book of the artistic unity of its predecessors. It may be that *The Food of the Gods* was too hastily written; it may be that Wells was too preoccupied with the purely sociological problems he was dealing with to take the necessary pains with structure and plot. Whatever the explanation the book remains an unsatisfactory hybrid. It is a valiant attempt to fuse together the imaginative approach of the romance with the prophetic style of *Anticipations*. The attempt fails, but not without moments of rare comedy: the pullets descending on Hickleybrow and the eccentric behaviour of Miss Durgan, Mr. Skinner and his lugubrious lisp, the burning of the experimental farm, the arrival of the wasp inside the British Museum reading room. For these and similar moments the novel will continue to be read and enjoyed, regardless of its imperfections.

IN THE DAYS OF THE COMET

In the Days of the Comet (1906) could be classified as either a novel or a romance, for it has some of the characteristics of both. The whole of the first Book, comprising the opening five chapters, is cast as a novel in the conventional sense and anticipates the sociological manner of *Tono-Bungay*. These opening sequences are notable for their sensitive portrayal of Wells's mother as Mrs. Leadford, and for their insight into life in the Potteries.

The reader is struck again and again by the parallels between Wells's own experience and that of the narrator, Willie Leadford. Leadford is passionately in love with Nettie Stuart, and in the description of Nettie and of his emotional attachment to her there are unmistakable echoes of Wells's love affair with his cousin Isobel. In the description of the narrator's close friend Parload (whose favourite subject is physiography) there are several hints that the character Wells actually had in mind was his friend from his student days, R. A. (later Sir Richard) Gregory. But it is in the portrait of Leadford's mother that we are given one of the finest fictional sketches of Sarah Wells as she must have appeared during her careworn years at Bromley. The description of the underground kitchen, his mother's fierce religious views, the drabness of his physical surroundings, the continual financial worry—all this has the ring of truth and tallies with what is known of Wells's childhood. It is interesting to note also that the seventeen-mile walk from Southsea to Up Park which the author had undertaken when apprenticed to a draper appears in the novel in the guise of the walk from Clayton to Checkshill Towers. The account of that 'long tramp' (in Book One, Chapter 2, 2) should be studied carefully and compared with the account of the same walk in *Tono-Bungay* (Book One, Chapter 2, 3).

In the Days of the Comet is the only one of Wells's novels which is set entirely in the Potteries (although part of *The New Machiavelli* and the short story 'The Cone' are located in the Five Towns), and the early chapters do succeed in conveying the sombre dust-laden *feel* of the district. As a young man convalescing after one of his recurrent haemorrhages, Wells had spent three months staying with a friend at Etruria, and the area undoubtedly made a deep impression upon him. Writing to Arnold Bennett (October 1897) he confided 'I felt dimly then and rather less dimly today vast possibilities there. Think of Trentham, white Newcastle, and that Burslem Hanley ridge jostling one another—the difference in the lives and "circles of thought" there must be!'

The descriptions of the characteristic industrial landscape of the Five Towns are perhaps more reminiscent of Lawrence than Bennett in their intimacy and implied criticism. Wells is particularly skilful in conveying the sense of *hopelessness* at a time of industrial unrest, and the manner in which complex economic issues become oversimplified during a period of crisis. (Cf. George Gissing's interesting short story, 'The Firebrand'.)

The remaining six chapters of the novel, describing the approach of the comet and the beneficial effects of the 'green vapours' which accompany it, differ markedly in form from Book One. It is almost as if Wells was torn between writing a social novel and a futuristic romance, and could not satisfactorily resolve the dilemma. Indeed the closing chapters contain some of the weakest sections of the whole work and the account of the meeting with Melmount, the Prime Minister, lacks plausibility.

In the closing pages Wells came nearer than ever before to an open advocacy of free love. The novel was violently attacked by a number of reviewers, and Wells was placed so much on the defensive as to deny any such intention. He admitted in his autobiography, however, that in making these denials he was being less than honest with his readers or himself.

The narrator is the embodiment of a problem soon to become increasingly familiar in Wells's fiction: that of the man who is genuinely devoted to his wife but is at the same time passionately in love with another woman. It is an issue presented time and again—indeed there are few of Wells's novels written after 1900 in which the problem does not appear in some form—yet never satisfactorily resolved. The author demonstrates that simple stereotyped solutions will not work when applied to particular personalities. Willie Leadford loved two women, but loved each for rather different motives. 'In the old days love was a cruel proprietary thing. But now Anna could let Nettie live in the world of my mind, as freely as a rose will suffer the presence of white lilies. If I could hear notes that were not in her compass, she was glad, because she loved me, that I should listen to other music than hers.' Conventional morality would have dictated the suppression of the second love. It would either have pretended it did not exist, or necessitated a furtive affair. But Wells's inclinations were for freedom and openness in these matters, and an end to evasions and hypocrisies.

The closing sequences provide further evidence of his apparent inability to separate his private life from his fiction. Not only is there a moving account of the death of his mother (which had occurred on 12 June 1905 while the book was in draft) but there is a description of a love affair with a young woman called Anna Reeves. The close similarity between this name and Amber Reeves, Wells's friend in real life, would not have been lost on his contemporaries.[20]

In summary then, *In the Days of the Comet* is not wholly consistent as a work of creative imagination although it remains a novel of abundant energy and interest. The book could have been, on the one hand, a realistic story of working-class life—after the manner of Lawrence's *Sons and Lovers* or Bennett's *A Man from the North*. As such, had it fulfilled the promise of the opening chapters, it would undoubtedly occupy an important place in the canon as a precursor of *Tono-Bungay* and *The New Machiavelli*. Conversely, it could have been conceived as a utopian fantasia after the manner of *Men Like Gods* or *A Modern Utopia*. As it is, however, the book is an uneasy hybrid of two quite different literary genres and for this reason it lacks the artistic unity of Wells's finest work.

He himself regarded it as the last of the scientific romances. Seen in the perspective of the whole of his fictional output we can now see that it can properly be regarded as a rough first draft of *The

Dream. Whereas in the earlier work he fell short of the intention he had set out to achieve, in *The Dream*, as will be seen, he succeeded in fusing together futuristic speculation and sociological commentary in a coherent work of art.

THE WAR IN THE AIR

The War in the Air was written in 1907, serialised in the *Pall Mall Magazine* commencing in January 1908, and published in book form later in that year. This was *before* any extensive use of the flying machine—Bleriot did not cross the Channel until July 1909—and the story is thus not only a remarkable forecast of the use of airships in warfare but also a striking anticipation of the way in which techniques of war would be changed by the introduction of the aeroplane for military purposes. Wells regarded it as a 'fantasia of possibility' and as one of a series of books, including *When the Sleeper Wakes* and *The World Set Free*, which imagined the development of a tendency or group of tendencies in human affairs.[21]

The full title of the book is *The War in the Air and Particularly how Mr. Bert Smallways Fared while it Lasted.* The title is significant, for throughout the story there is a continuous interaction between the two contrasted elements: on the one hand, the account of a world gradually drifting into a catastrophic global war and, on the other, the humorous adventures of a typically Wellsian hero, Bert Smallways. The interplay between these two strands is very skilfully achieved, so that throughout the escapades of Smallways and his companions one is aware that appearing behind and through the narrative is a backcloth of increasingly ominous world events.

The introductory chapter, 'Of Progress and the Smallways Family', is written with the assurance and eye for detail of a major novelist. The picture of Bun Hill (Bromley) and the impact of change upon a community which was once 'an idyllic Kentish village' anticipates the masterly account of the same process in *The New Machiavelli* and, whilst brief, is a brilliant piece of descriptive writing. The whole of this opening section—the description of the bicycle shop in which Bert is an assistant; Bert's father, Old Smallways; the 'beano' on Whit Sunday; the flight across the North Sea in the balloon—recalls the early chapters of *Kipps* in its shrewd observation of human behaviour and engaging touches of humour. Bert Smallways is indeed a markedly Kipps-like figure: 'Bert Smallways was a vulgar little creature, the sort of pert, limited soul that the old civilisation of the early twentieth century produced by the million in every country of the world. He had lived all his life in narrow streets, and between mean houses he could not look over, and in a narrow circle of ideas from which there was no escape.' Much of the skill of *The War in the Air* lies in the way Wells is able to demonstrate that events of world-wide importance can happen to such an apparently insignificant figure.

The substance of the story, an extraordinarily sustained account of aerial warfare fought on a global scale, is a curious hybrid between a straightforward scientific romance in the vein of *The War of the Worlds* and a sociological novel after the manner of Jack London. His biographers Norman and Jeanne Mackenzie describe the book as 'an extraordinary concoction' and certainly there are moments when Wells seems undecided whether he is writing an exciting adventure tale or a serious piece of analysis warning against the dangers of militarism. It is a testimony to his abilities as a creative writer that he succeeds so well in fusing together the two genres in a continuously readable and well-constructed narrative. In spite of all the remarkable adventures in which he is unwittingly involved, Bert remains to the last a typically irreverent Cockney, a Hoopdriver grown none the wiser or less gullible.

What immediately impresses the reader today is the vivid forecast, in the concluding chapters 'The Great Collapse' and 'The Epilogue', of world-wide disaster as the result of war. This description of the total collapse of civilisation, so uncannily prescient of the aftermath of a nuclear holocaust, must have made astonishing reading in 1908. Later writers—most notably Jack London in *The Scarlet Plague* (1915) and John Wyndham in *The Day of the Triffids* (1951)—have employed a similar descriptive approach, but Wells must have been one of the earliest writers to depict with such unnerving conviction the ending of civilised communities. There is no disguising the hopelessness of his ultimate vision:

'The great nations and empires have become but names in the mouths of men. Everywhere there are ruins and unburied dead, and shrunken, yellow-faced survivors in a mortal apathy. Here there are robbers, here vigilance committees, and here guerilla bands ruling patches of exhausted territory, strange federations and brotherhoods form and dissolve, and religious fanaticisms begotten of despair gleam in famine-bright eyes. It is a universal dissolution.'

This vision of a ravaged planet, so chilling in its nightmare clarity, is further evidence of Wells's deep-rooted pessimism in the face of a global disaster. This time there is no renaissance, no minority of Open Conspirators to bring about world unification in the aftermath of war. The reader is left in no doubt that the decay of civilisation is irreparable. In this sense the book is a more realistic fantasy than, say, *The World Set Free*, which presupposes an enlightened group of monarchs who impose world government. Written at a time when English military and naval power was at its height and the idea of world war seemed remote, one might have supposed Wells would conclude the romance on a note of optimism. Instead, the work ends with a horrifying description of universal social collapse: a picture of a world laid waste by war, famine, brigandage and disease. It is an astonishing prognosis emanating from a writer normally condemned as the apostle of the inevitability of progress.

THE WORLD SET FREE

During the summer of 1913 Wells wrote to his friend A. T. Simmons: 'I've suddenly broken out into one of the good old scientific romances again, and I want to know quite the latest about the atomic theory and sources of energy.' The 'good old scientific romance' on which he was engaged was *The World Set Free: A Story of Mankind*, written on a sudden impulse whilst holidaying in the Swiss Alps. This remarkable book, at once prescient and naïve, embodies many of his most characteristic themes and in its scenario of world war followed by enlightened reconstruction anticipates much of the substance of *The Shape of Things to Come*.

In the latter work Wells used the device of a partially deciphered manuscript, the 'dream book' of Dr. Philip Raven. In *The World Set Free* he adopts the pretence of quoting long extracts from Frederick Barnet's *Wanderjahre*, an autobiographical novel published in 1970. These extracts, describing in considerable detail a war between the European powers breaking out in the year 1956, are among his most impressive sociological forecasts. Reading the book today it is difficult to realise that it was written before the First World War, before the discovery of artificial radioactivity, before the potentialities of the aeroplane as a military weapon had been fully realised. Wells could not have foreseen that 'artificial radium' would be produced by Irene and Frederic Joliot-Curie, the daughter and son in law of Madame Curie, but he was uncannily accurate in forecasting that this discovery would be made in 1933. Fascinating also in the light of Hiroshima and Nagasaki is his forecast of atomic warfare, astonishing in its eerie anticipation of reality, and his prognosis of the stalemate in warfare brought about by nuclear weapons.

The weakest section of the book is undoubtedly the account of the sudden outbreak of sanity and enlightenment on the part of the world's politicians, led by 'God's Englishman', King Egbert. The idea that planetary reconstruction could only be achieved through the initiative of an intelligent and exceptional minority was always with him: it was his King Charles's Head. Again and again in his writings we find this emphasis on a world renaissance brought to fruition by and through an elite: in the New Republicans of *Anticipations*, the Samurai of *A Modern Utopia*, the Open Conspirators of *The World of William Clissold* and the 'Modern State' movement of *The World Set Free* and *The Shape of Things to Come*. In his sociological works—most notably in *Anticipations*—Wells presented a reasoned and carefully worked out statement of his theory of world revolution, but the attempts to illustrate his ideas in fictional form were not always successful. King Egbert and his enlightened colleagues appear to a modern reader as impossibly facile, although it has to be remembered that something akin to the same atmosphere of optimism accompanied the activities of President Wilson in 1919 (and President Kennedy in our own time). The transition from world war to reconstruction is unconvincing, and this is perhaps the greatest defect in a story which is in so many respects a forward-looking and even inspiring document.

One of the most fascinating figures in the story is Marcus Karenin (oddly reminiscent of Lenin, whom Wells did not meet until 1920), whose deathbed valediction has a strong bearing on Wells's own last days. At the end of his life, diseased and ailing, Karenin confides to a friend:

> 'I do not see why life should be judged by its last trailing thread of vitality. I know it for the splendid thing it is. . . . I know it well enough not to confuse it with its husks. Remember that, Gardener, if presently my heart fails me and I despair, and if I go through a little phase of pain and ingratitude and dark forgetfulness before the end. Don't believe what I may say at the last. If the fabric is good enough the selvage doesn't matter.'

In the light of the pessimism of *'42 To '44* and *Mind at the End of its Tether* this is a remarkable passage: it is almost as if he has anticipated his own final phase and is counselling the reader not to pay too much regard to a mood of despair. Karenin, a supreme example of a Wellsian alter ego, expounds before his death a moving summary of his philosophy, including a forecast of space travel and a reminder that the planet earth will not forever be man's prison.

Writing in 1921, Wells described the story as 'the latest in a series of three fantasias of possibility, stories which all turn on the possible developments in the future of some contemporary force or group of forces. . . . The dream of *The World Set Free*, a dream of highly educated and highly favoured leading and ruling men, voluntarily setting themselves to the task of reshaping the world, has thus far remained a dream.' His central thesis, then as later, was that developments in transport and communications had rendered independent sovereign states outmoded and dangerous, and that sooner or later conflict was inevitable in the absence of global political machinery. It is a thesis which today requires no advocacy: but in 1913 it was still considered bold and novel. This is also the dominating idea of another 'fantasia of possibility', *The War in the Air*, and one he was to return to on an even wider canvas twenty years later.

MEN LIKE GODS

Between the writing of *The World Set Free* and the publication of *Men Like Gods* there was a gap of ten years, a decade in which Wells was intensely preoccupied with the huge issues of the war and reconstruction. The writing of *Men Like Gods* in 1921–2 marks a return not only to the romance as a literary genre but to his earliest imaginative reveries. When reading Plato's *Republic* as a boy at Up Park Wells's mind had been filled with 'the amazing and heartening suggestion that the whole fabric of law, custom and worship, which seemed so invincibly established, might be cast into the melting pot and made anew'.[22] From that time onward the idea of a complete recasting of human life was never far from him and he delighted in presenting novel ways of living to his readers. In 'Another Basis for Life' (1894) he even speculated on the possibility of a totally different atomic basis for living matter, and time and again—in *Anticipations, In the Days of the Comet, The World Set Free* and a score of later works—contrasted the world which could be with the squalid world he knew. The contrast was attempted principally to act as a stimulus towards social change. In certain moods life in the first half of the twentieth century impressed him as almost intolerable. Clothes, houses, schools, laws, institutions and conventions—all these were ugly and wretched. Many, finding existence unbearable, sought refuge in alcohol, in drug addiction, in religious devotion or reverie; he sought spiritual release in the idea of the impermanence and insignificance of contemporary rules and customs. 'Most of my activities,' he confessed, 'have been to get my soul and something of my body out of the customs, outlook, boredoms and contaminations of the current phase of life.'[23] Like Lionel Wallace in his short story 'The Door in the Wall', he was haunted by visions of a world fairer beyond imagining, a world like a great garden in which love and kindness triumphed over every human folly. This vision irradiated his life and, finally, rendered meaningful all his beliefs and actions.

In *A Modern Utopia* (1905) he had imagined an ideal world attained as the result of a quite deliberate effort of will. He envisaged a ruling minority, the Samurai, which had arisen as a militant, crusading Order aiming at the realisation of a unified, collectivist world-state and the assimilation of all pre-existing political bodies; it had achieved a world economically and politically unified. This was a dream for which Wells yearned with an aching nostalgia, yet it was not presented as a millennial vision impossible of attainment. It has an unmistakable feel of reality about it. The book is set, in fact, in the foreseeable future, well within the bounds of present possibilities but tantalisingly beyond our furthest reach. In this respect *A Modern Utopia* is a major departure from almost all previous essays in Utopian speculation. Wells supposes no miraculous change in human nature nor a return to an imaginary 'golden age' of pastoral simplicity. There are still criminals and drunkards, there is still unhappiness and disease, discontent and industrial grime. Unlike Morris's *News from Nowhere* it is not an escapist Utopia.

Men Like Gods, in contrast, is an attempt to see much further into the future, to discern the framework and delineate the outlines of a Utopian society in an advanced stage of development. It is a much slighter work which fails to emulate the artistry of its predecessor. Its abiding interest lies in its flashes of Wellsian vitality: the lampooning of Winston Churchill as Rupert Catskill, the moving account of a new Jesus of Nazareth, the 'Teacher of Teachers' who had swayed Utopian thought with his gospel of human brotherhood, the portrait of a world restless with the urge to achieve and create. There are also memorable portraits of Arthur Balfour (Cecil Burleigh) and Edward Marsh (Freddy Mush).

Anthony West has pointed out[24] that *Men Like Gods* is in reality a totally pessimistic book, since the ideal society described is so manifestly beyond human reach. It is as if Wells is acknowledging the impossibility of achieving such a world within a measurable time span and so postulates a different dimension of both time and space. (The idea of a 'kink in space' is also discussed in the short stories 'The Plattner Story' and 'The Remarkable Case of Davidson's Eyes'.) The book is primarily of interest today for the insight it affords into Wells's undoubted visionary gifts.

In spite of his ebullient friendships he was in fact one of the most detached and introspective writers this century has seen. He possessed the ability to withdraw himself from the ostensible world and to appraise it with the cold, dispassionate gaze of an intelligence from an alien planet. This cosmic vision can be traced throughout his work, beginning with *The Time Machine* and the short stories and culminating in *The World of William Clissold* and the final novels. It can also be seen in his sense of detachment, in his propensity to refer to himself in the third person and to write about himself in his own novels as if viewing his literary reputation from outside.[25]

It is most evident in the early romances, in the grim parable of *The War of the Worlds* and such short stories as 'Under the Knife' and 'The Star'. There is an unforgettable passage in *The War of the Worlds*, haunting in its vividness, in which he lays bare his mood:

'At times I suffer from the strangest sense of detachment from myself and the world about me; I seem to watch it all from the outside, from somewhere inconceivably remote, out of time, out of space, out of the stress and tragedy of it all.'[26]

Wells in fact, as *William Clissold* made plain, possessed an unusual sense of externality not uncommon among men of exceptional poetic insight. He did not accept the world of fact as final and concrete; to him it was something much vaguer, more transluscent, a magic crystal into which he peered and from which, paradoxically, he longed to escape. He was convinced that the outlines of the present world were not fixed and hard, that there were other planes of living quite unknown to man and that the superficial boundaries of our everyday life could dissolve into strange and unsuspected dimensions. This was a theme he returned to in the short stories, in *Men Like Gods* and again in *William Clissold*. He also experienced the sensation of seeing all life in miniature, of seeing men as ants and houses and cities as minute, although in these visions it was the universe about him which shrank: he himself did not seem to shrink to scale. This sense of being an unseen observer, of being suspended in the unknown depths of space, was an extremely powerful element in his imagination. This detachment from the limitations of the ego and the merger of his personality with cosmic forces was utterly characteristic of the man.

Seen in these terms *Men Like Gods* is an entirely characteristic work which, in common with *The Time Machine* and his other mythopoetic visions, holds out little prospect of hope for humanity. It is a fable intended to stimulate thought and to criticise contemporary institutions rather than to suggest any practicable solutions for man's impasse.

THE KING WHO WAS A KING

Throughout his literary career Wells was acutely interested in the possibilities of translating his imaginative ideas into dramatic or visual form. As early as 1895, together with Robert W. Paul, he lodged a patent application for a film version of *The Time Machine* which 'anticipated most of the stock methods and devices of the screen drama'.[27] During 1901–2 he and Arnold Bennett planned to collaborate over the writing of a play, 'The Crime', and although this project never came to fruition he went on to produce a dramatised version of *The Wheels of Chance* under the title *Hoopdriver's Holiday*, written in the years 1903–4. In collaboration with St. John Ervine he also prepared a dramatisation of *The Wonderful Visit* (February 1921), staged at the St. Martin's Theatre, London. With the arrival of sound films in the late nineteen-twenties he turned his attention to the cinema as a means of conveying his ideas to a wider audience. (In 1928 he had written three short film comedies, 'Bluebottles', 'The Tonic' and 'Daydreams', which were screened successfully; these, according to their director Ivor Montagu, 'were extracted from H.G. early one morning in a flat in Paris while he was still in his dressing gown'.)

The original version of the book which later became *The King who was a King* was a film synopsis written in 1926 and entitled 'The Peace of the World'. Wells did not recall until later that he had previously used that title for a collection of First World War articles; dissatisfied with the synopsis, he continued to brood over the idea until at last he rewrote it completely in the form of a detailed scenario. *The King who was a King: The Book of a Film* was published by Ernest Benn in 1929.

It is prefaced by a long and extremely interesting introductory chapter in which he outlines his approach to the film as an art form. 'Behind the first cheap triumphs of the film today,' he wrote, 'rises the possibility of a spectacle—music—drama, greater, more beautiful and intellectually deeper and richer than any artistic form humanity has hitherto achieved.' Clearly Wells at this time was deeply impressed with the latent potentialities of the motion picture as a means of translating a story into a powerful symbolic medium and was feeling his way towards a spectacular and entertaining presentation of his political ideas. The question he poses at the outset is this: 'Can form, story and music be brought together to present the conditions and issues of the abolition of war in a beautiful, vigorous and moving work of art, which will be well within the grasp and understanding of the ordinary film audience?'

The scenario itself is deliberately cast in a symbolic form, the hero and his antagonist representing respectively Man the Maker and Man the Destroyer, whilst the heroine, Princess Helen, stands for Woman the Protector and Sustainer. In consciously framing the story in this form, even to the extent of setting the action in the entirely imaginary states of Clavery and Agravia, Wells unwittingly weakened its effectiveness. Indeed the book is open to the charge that it depicts events which are wholly removed from normal life: the symbolism is such that at times the story ceases to be convincing and becomes instead a melodrama, a masque, in which each character represents not himself but an abstraction. Two years earlier he had strongly criticised Fritz Lang's film 'Metropolis' on the grounds of its lack of originality and general naïveté, but his own attempt to discuss the complex issues of war and peace in cinematic form is vitiated by the same intrinsic weaknesses. It is as if the ingredients of *When the Sleeper Wakes* have become entangled with those of a Ruritanian romance: the result is a hybrid, a pastiche where every incident, every confrontation, is merely stage scenery conveying wider meanings. Geoffrey West said of it: 'Its characters are not men and women, but heroes and villains, Makers and Destroyers, puppets wholly symbolic; certainly unity of action and idea is achieved, but at the expense of humanity.'

No film version of *The King who was a King* was in practice ever made. Wells himself anticipated as much on the final page of the book when he added wryly: 'But at the present time . . . I doubt if my film about him [Paul Zelinka] will get itself made, and even if it is made whether it will be booked with any rapture for ordinary popular exhibition.' The scenario in fact suffers from defects of which he must have been aware, for he wrote later that he regarded it as a 'prentice effort' preparatory to the writing of *Things to Come*. In the writing of it he learned a number of techniques which bore fruit seven years later in his two scenarios for London Films,[28] and he emerged from the experiment with a much clearer conception of the limitations and possibilities of the cinema screen as a medium for education. Although Wells never altogether lost his interest in the film as a propaganda medium—in 1945 he was projecting a new film for Alexander Korda, a reworking of *Things to Come*—his later successes were much more in the vein of *The Croquet Player* and *The Brothers* than that of film stories. In these satirical and allegorical works he finally mastered the technique of expressing his ideas in symbolic form; in them he returned to the source of his greatest strength.

THE AUTOCRACY OF MR. PARHAM

The Autocracy of Mr. Parham, written in 1929, is a satirical fantasia in which Wells lampooned a number of leading political figures of the day. There are thinly disguised caricatures of Max Beaverbrook (Sir Bussy Woodcock), Ramsay Macdonald (Ramsy McDougal), Mussolini (Paramuzzi), and other personalities of the time—portrayals made all the more explicit by the amusing illustrations by David Low which adorn the book.

In form it follows the conventions of science fiction rather than a novel (Wells himself classified it as a 'fantastic and imaginative romance') and borrows a number of ideas he had employed in previous fictions: the spiritualist seance (*Love and Mr. Lewisham*), possession by another spirit (*Christina Alberta's Father*) and the fantastic dream (*The Dream* and *Mr. Blettsworthy*). Mr. Parham, 'a lifelong student and exponent of history and philosophy', dreams he is possessed by the spirit of a Martian warlord, and as Lord Paramount of England embarks at once upon a holy war. He is possessed by unlimited power:

And then he perceived that imperceptibly and incomprehensibly, the Master Spirit had incorporated him. He realised that an immense power of will had taken possession of him, that he lived in a new vigour, that he was still himself and yet something enormously more powerful, that his mind was full and clear and certain as it had never been before.

Wells had never been attracted by the Great Man theory of history and in the succeeding chapters, before Parham awakens from his dream, he evokes a series of increasingly elaborate visions—including a lively anticipation of the Second World War—designed to demonstrate the shallowness and shortsightedness of military dictatorship. It was a theme which he had handled in more masterly fashion in tract form—such essays as 'The Probable Future of Mankind' and 'The Way to World Peace'[29] stated the case for world disarmament and an end to national sovereignty with a cogency and reasonableness which could not be bettered—and the attempt to restate the argument in fictional guise lacks conviction. It fails, just as *The King who was a King* fails, because Wells forgets he is writing a novel and writes instead a political extravaganza, a charade which is alternately entertaining and wooden. He himself thought highly of the book and remarked that he laughed aloud when writing it. Unquestionably it has all the ingredients of a successful exercise in satire but somehow the ingredients do not gell to produce a coherent whole. Perhaps it smacks too much of a fantasia composed of diverse elements from many of his earlier novels; whatever the reason, the book was not favourably reviewed and soon went out of print.

Although *Mr. Parham* was praised by Geoffrey West ('This is Wells's best story, as such, since 1914. The attitude, the ideas, the message remain, but their sting is where it should be, in the tale.') later scholarship has tended to be less enthusiastic. Measured against his other experiments in satirical form it seems clumsy and contrived; it lacks the biting sarcasm which makes *Mr. Blettsworthy*, for example, such a memorable excursion into the realms of allegory and, Sir Bussy Woodcock apart, its characterisation is weak. All in all it has to be counted, in my own view, as one of his least vital novels. Yet, as always with Wells, it is redeemed by flashes of his puckish humour: the party at the Savoy when Mr. Parham becomes entangled in polite conversation with Lady Glassglade; his amorous encounter with Miss Gaby Greuze; the deliciously written scene in the House of Commons; the touching moment on the last page when Parham is bid a reluctant farewell. It is in moments such as these that we are compelled to forgive Wells his literary lapses and acknowledge the diversity and power of his genius.

THE SHAPE OF THINGS TO COME

'In this newly built Spade House I began a book *Anticipations* which can be considered as the keystone to the main arch of my work. That arch rises naturally from my first creative imaginations, "The Man of the Year Million" (written first in 1887) and "The Chronic Argonauts" (in the *Science Schools Journal*, 1888), and it leads on by a logical development to *The Shape of Things to Come* (1933)....'[30] This book, which Wells acknowledged was 'as deliberate and laborious a piece of work as anything I have ever done', is one of his most ambitious works. Cast in the form of a history of the world from 1929 to 2105, *The Shape of Things to Come* sets out to describe his matured theory of world renaissance through an open conspiracy of enlightened revolutionaries. In it he made use of a number of ideas he had previously introduced both in his fiction and in his sociological writings; it is his most comprehensive statement of world revolution.

For many years he had been fascinated by time and by time theories: *The Time Machine* bears witness to his preoccupation with the idea of journeying into the future, as does *When the Sleeper Wakes* and numerous other books and short stories. 'I am extravagantly obsessed by the thing that might be, and impatient with the present,' he wrote; 'I want to go ahead of Father Time with a scythe of my own.'[31] J. W. Dunne's *An Experiment with Time* was published in 1927 and Wells reviewed it enthusiastically. He found Dunne's theories fresh and stimulating and, partly under their influence, wrote an amusing short story, 'The Queer Story of Brownlow's Newspaper', which imagines a citizen of 1931 receiving a newspaper dated forty years hence. In *The Shape of Things to Come* he postulates the idea of a dream book, a Short History of the Future, which is read by Dr. Philip Raven, a League of Nations official, and written down by him. The manuscript of the book is supposed to have come into Wells's hands after Raven's death.

Deliberately written in the factual, unemotional style of his own *Short History of the World*, the book begins by summarising world events during the years 1914–33, then proceeds to describe the series of cataclysmic events which follow, culminating in world war—imagined by Wells as breaking out in 1940 and continuing until 1949. The war is succeeded by a long phase of social collapse, aggravated by famine and disease, leading to an apocalyptic vision of the world in ruins. The final third of the narrative describes the gradual rebuilding of civilisation under the leadership of a minority of technical revolutionaries and the final achievement of a unified world order. The central thesis of the book—that there would be a disastrous world war followed by planetary reconstruction led and engineered by a minority of dedicated open conspirators—was one which he had described and speculated upon from *Anticipations* (1900) onwards. 'But as some supersaturated solution will crystallise out with the mere shaking of its beaker, so must the new order of men come into visibly organised existence through the concussions of war.'[32] The thesis had previously found expression in a number of his romances, most notably in *The World Set Free*, and whilst a considerable amount of fresh detail was added the essential shape of Wells's vision of the future remained unchanged. His prognosis of the main outlines of human history remained as it had at the beginning of the century:

> When the existing governments and ruling theories of life, the decaying religious and the decaying political forms of today, have sufficiently lost prestige through failure and catastrophe, then and then only will world wide reconstruction be possible. And it must needs be the work, first of all, of an aggressive order of religiously devoted men and women who will try out and establish and impose a new pattern of living upon our race.

Wells lavished great pains on its writing and undoubtedly set great store upon it as a diagnosis of the crisis confronting twentieth-century man. He brought to the task the visionary qualities of the historian combined with the narrative power of the novelist. The result, whilst not entirely consistent, is a document of compelling interest and forcefulness. *The World Set Free* is arguably a more cohesive work from the point of view of structure and narration, but the later work lacks the naïveté of the earlier romance: it is a fully matured vision of the shape of the future. Its enduring value lies not so much in its ideas (these, as we have seen, were familiar elements in his work) nor even in its ambitious scope (its massive architecture is rivalled only by *The Outline of History*) but in the skilful way in which imaginative forecasting of the future is blended with sociological analysis. It is open to question whether Wells's motive in writing it was to arouse fear of the dangers of war or to instil in his readers a receptiveness towards the idea of world government. What is not in doubt is that the vivid account of the 'last war cyclone' must have gripped and alarmed many thousands of readers in 1933 and helped to prepare the English intelligentsia for the realities of the Second World War.

The book is probably the most well known, if only by reputation, of all his fiction. The title has become part of the common stock of memorable phrases and is included in numerous books of quotations. Together with the film *Things to Come* it has probably done more to spread an awareness of his ideas than any other work of fiction.

THINGS TO COME

The film *Things to Come*, based on Wells's specially written scenario derived in turn from materials in his *Shape of Things to Come*, was produced by Alexander Korda for London Films in 1934–6. The scenario, a short book of 140 pages, begins with the outbreak of war in 1940 and, after describing the world-wide collapse which follows, concludes in the year 2036 with a vision of a reconstructed civilisation.

The film has now achieved the status of a classic, some critics regarding it as one of the ten greatest films ever made. What is so novel about *Things to Come*, quite apart from the ambitious scope of the basic concept, is the total integration of the scenario and the background music. Arthur Bliss was commissioned to write the music and produced a brilliantly stirring score which delighted Wells. There are few more memorable moments in the history of the film than the sequence where automatic machines rebuild a world devastated by war, to the accompaniment of Bliss's hauntingly unforgettable music. But on the whole Wells was dissatisfied with the film. He felt it compressed his ideas to much, that the attempt to reduce his vision of the future to a manageable scale failed to do justice to the wide sweep of his design or to the force of his argument for world unification. Moreover the film unwittingly gave the impression that he was *advocating* a technological utopia instead of simply *predicting* such a development as the probable course of human destiny. That he would in practice have had scant regard for a community based upon scientific advancement at the expense of humanitarian considerations is implicit in all his work from *The Time Machine* onwards. It is this imbalance, this apparent emphasis on material progress to the detriment of man's aesthetic and creative potentialities, which is perhaps the film's gravest weakness. Unquestionably, however, it remains a powerful and visually exciting document, remarkable alike for its anticipation of aerial warfare and of the social collapse and brigandage war brings in its train. The final sequence, in which a spaceship is launched to the moon against the background of a mob determined to prevent the launching, is a fittingly dramatic climax to the story and also recalls the closing scene of *The Food of the Gods* when Cossar and Redwood stand outside the pit made by the Giants and see the great machinery in course of construction. Both sequences are symbolic of the choice confronting mankind: to turn inwards upon ourselves and cease intellectual curiosity, or to opt deliberately for a prospect of ever-expanding mental horizons. The image which remains in the mind at the conclusion of the film is that of Passworthy and Cabal gazing up at the stars, and Cabal's voice appealing to his friend to recognise this fundamental truth:

'Rest enough for the individual man. Too much of it and too soon and we call it death. But for Man no rest and no ending. He must go on—conquest beyond conquest. This little planet and its winds and ways, and all the laws of mind and matter that restrain him. Then the planets about him, and at last out across immensity to the stars. And when he has conquered all the deeps of space and all the mysteries of time—still he will be beginning.'

Things to Come deservedly has an honoured place in the history of science fiction, not only for its cinematic effects and blending of prophecy with social realism but also because it was one of the first films to attempt the translation of a serious sociological argument into a satisfying visual presentation. That the film has worn so well in spite of its manifest imperfections is a tribute to its underlying vitality.

THE CROQUET PLAYER

The Croquet Player marks a return to the allegorical mood of *The Island of Doctor Moreau* and *Mr. Blettsworthy on Rampole Island*, but here the problem of evil is discussed from a rather different angle. It was written in 1936, at a time when Wells was deeply distressed by the horror of the Spanish Civil War and the widespread growth of tyranny in Germany, Italy and elsewhere. This short but profoundly disturbing and impressive tale is saturated with the mood of disillusionment associated with that period.

Mr. Frobisher (the croquet player of the title), a squeamish, effeminate young man who combines the naïveté of Arnold

Blettsworthy with the shallowness of Theodore Bulpington, encounters a certain Dr. Finchatton who relates to him the story of the
malignant, brooding fear which is haunting the fen districts of
Cainsmarsh. He conveys a vivid sense of an evil presence, a spirit of
violence and anger which hangs over Cainsmarsh and pervades its
whole atmosphere. This spirit broods 'below the surface. An unhappy, wicked spirit that creeps into us all. . . . Something that
might still be urgent to hurt and torment and frighten. Something
profoundly suspicious and easily angered.'[33] As the story unfolds it
becomes clear that this contagion is very deeply embedded in the
population; it is an irrational, endemic sickness which breaks out
in violence and hatred. Dr. Finchatton is alarmed at 'the deep
fountains of cruelty in the human make-up'.[34] He visits a local
museum and is shown the skull of a Neanderthal man. The curator
reminds him that the cave-man was the ancestor of *Homo sapiens*,
that for countless generations he had stalked the earth and that his
brutishness and primitive fears were in the blood of modern man.
These savageries could return—were indeed returning now in
many parts of the world. There were ominous signs of a recrudes-
cence of the ancestral ape. The animal fears and lusts were raging
anew in a world powerless to restrain them.

The book moves to a sombre climax with Finchatton's psychia-
trist, Dr. Norbert, warning Frobisher that the resurrection of evil in
man, if unchecked, could become a world epidemic, endangering
the very future of the species. The thin veil of civilisation had been
momentarily drawn aside, revealing the animal lurking in all men.
'Man is still what he was. Invincibly bestial, envious, malicious,
greedy.'[35] He had not changed essentially in a hundred thousand
years. In the time-scale of history he was an ape only yesterday. The
choice before mankind was either to be driven to degradation and
death or to make an unprecedented mental effort and enlarge the
human mind to the scale of universal history and cosmopolis.

The Island of Doctor Moreau, Rampole Island, Cainsmarsh: these
are the settings for Wells's parables of man's folly. The three books
have many similarities, for the element of symbolism and allegory
is common to each. Each has a transparent quality, a continual
reminder of the bestial elements lying only just beneath the surface
of ostensible reality.[36]

Wells's argument throughout is threefold: first, that man was
inherently animal, that many primitive characteristics lingered
within him and that he was dangerously prone to sudden outbursts
of irrational cruelty and fear. History could not be a continuous
upward progression; there would be temporary lapses and periodic

waves of violence. These outbreaks of ancestral emotion were inevitable, given man's animal origins and slow evolution.

Second, these animal traits had not been implanted in his nature consequent upon his 'fall' from a supposed perfect state. Such a state of perfection was completely imaginary. They were the lingering vestiges of his animal past—no more and no less.

Third, much of the confusion and frustration of human life was preventable. Ignorance, fear, superstition, hasty and irrational habits of mind—all these things were curable and within man's power to banish. They could not be ended, however, without a titanic effort of intellect and will: a task demanding the undivided concentration of man's intelligence.

The Croquet Player is a wholly distinguished piece of writing which is surprisingly little known today. It achieves its effects through its undoubted literary qualities: a skilful building up of atmosphere and tension, economy and precision of language, and careful pacing of incident. Above all, the work is notable for its merits as *a story*—which is indeed the subtitle Wells gave to it. The tale provides impressive evidence that his gifts as a storyteller were as yet undimmed and that he was still capable of writing stories worthy of standing beside *The Time Machine*. On its publication the *Observer* commented: 'It has all those maturities of style, wisdom and vision which reveal the master. Only Mr. Wells would have chosen this theme, and none but he could have handled it thus.'

MAN WHO COULD WORK MIRACLES

The film *Man Who Could Work Miracles* was produced by London Films in 1935. It was based on a specially written scenario, published under the same title, and derived in turn from the short story 'The Man Who Could Work Miracles' which originally appeared in 1898. The scenario broadly follows the short story in its general conception and shape but differs from it in a number of interesting particulars. Whereas the original story (subtitled 'A Pantoum in Prose') is concerned with events happening on a relatively minor scale, the film is necessarily planned to a more ambitious design as the hero's miracles become increasingly spectacular. The principal new elements added by Wells are, first, a prologue and an epilogue which set the film within a symbolic frame of reference and, second, the ascription to George McWhirter Fotheringay of a megalomaniac desire to become master of the world.

The prologue and epilogue, which are strongly reminiscent of the 'Prologue in Heaven' in *The Undying Fire*, were seen by Wells as an essential part of the whole. 'The Frame could be stripped off and the film would still remain a coherent imaginative story, but the Frame is necessary to broaden out the reference and make *Man Who Could Work Miracles* a proper companion piece to *Things to Come*.' These sequences, in which the 'elemental powers'—the Observer, the Indifference, and the Giver of Power—discuss human nature and whether or not man is innately base, are among the most fascinating in the book and reveal his gift for symbolism on a cosmic scale. The Giver of Power (also referred to as The Player) wishes to extend power to one sample human being but his faith in human potentialities is not shared by the other two spirits. He decides to proceed with his experiment in spite of their scepticism, whilst admitting that there are limits to his dispensation. 'There is a limit to the Power I can give. So the Master has decreed. There is a bit of gritty stuff at the heart of every individual, no Power can touch. The Soul—the Individuality—that ultimate mystery only the Master can control. Their Wills—such as they are—are Free.' This recalls the admission by Moreau that, in seeking to transform animals into human beings, there are certain forces beyond his power to change: 'And least satisfactory of all is something that I cannot touch, somewhere—I cannot determine where—in the seat of the emotions. Cravings, instincts, desires that harm humanity, a strange hidden reservoir to burst suddenly and inundate the whole being of the creature with anger, hate, or fear.'

After performing a series of miracles of steadily expanding complexity and impressiveness Fotheringay becomes convinced he can impose his will on the politicians and become effective dictator of the world. In a melodramatic sequence he convenes a gathering of all the ruling men and women of earth and admonishes them on their shortcomings. They need time for further thought before acceding to his demands for an ending of war and the inauguration of a new era of economic plenty. Fotheringay declines to give them more time and attempts to stop the sunset by arresting the rotation of the earth; everything moveable is flung violently off the earth's surface. He realises that the only way in which he can restore normality is to return everything to as it was at the outset of his adventure and to forego his ability to perform miracles. The film ends, as does the short story, with Fotheringay realising somewhat reluctantly that he no longer possesses the power to effect change—either in his own personal life or in the world at large.

Without the Frame the film would be a pessimistic one, for it appears to convey the idea that man is irredeemably consumed with ignoble motives. That this is not the intention is clearly shown by the penultimate sequence in which the elemental powers converse once again:

> The Indifference: 'They know nothing. He said "Forget it". And what has your experiment shown, Brother? What did you get out of that sample man? Egotism and elementary lust. A little vindictive indignation. That's all the creatures have—or will have for ever. What can you make of them?'
> The Player: 'They were apes only yesterday. Give them time.'
> The Indifference: 'Once an ape—always an ape.'
> The Player: 'You say they are all just egotism and lust. No. There was something in every one of those creatures more than that. Like a little grain of gold glittering in sand, lost in the sand. A flash of indignation when they think things are false and wrong. That's God-like. Dirt is never indignant. That's why they interest me.'

What Wells had conceived in 1898 as an entertaining yarn, lacking any overt didactic element, becomes as a film scenario a much more openly propagandist piece of writing. However, whilst lacking the literary qualities which the original story undoubtedly possessed, the film treatment contains many touches of both humour and drama which demonstrate that Wells at the age of seventy could still produce forceful and imaginative writing.

STAR BEGOTTEN

During 1936 and 1937 Wells wrote three novellas which he termed 'long short stories'—*The Croquet Player*, *The Camford Visitation* and *Star Begotten*. A note facing the title page of *World Brain* (a collection of essays published in 1938) draws the reader's attention to these stories, 'in which the same issues are viewed from a rather different angle'. It is clear, therefore, that Wells regarded the novellas, superficially so dissimilar, as linked by a common theme: the crisis confronting man in the mid-twentieth century.

Star Begotten, which is sub-titled 'A Biological Fantasia', is dedicated to Winston Churchill: a dedication which at first strikes one as infelicitous but which on reflection is most appropriate once it becomes evident that the book is an ingenious fantasia on the idea of exceptional individuals and the impact of such individuals on the mass of humanity. The central idea of the book is the notion that for centuries earth has been bombarded by cosmic rays emanating from the planet Mars. Mars is envisioned as a world inhabited by infinitely wise beings who have been subjecting earth to an increasingly accurate bombardment of rays. Individuals possessed of unusual intellectual or artistic abilities—Leonardo da Vinci, Buddha, Confucius—are those who have been infected with the Martian rays. Once a person has been 'Martianised' he becomes imbued with exceptional qualities of vision and begins to seek out and recognise others who have been similarly infected. The substance of the book is an account of how this novel idea first affected the life of Mr. Joseph Davis and his wife Mary (the symbolical implications of their Christian names is surely not accidental) and Davis's circle of friends.

The introductory chapters are written with an ease and freshness astonishing for a writer of seventy and betray no sign of any flagging of Wells's powers as a storyteller. The account of the upbringing of Joseph Davis, his early religious ideas and wrestling with history, is admirably done, as is the portrayal of his wife and the description of their gradual estrangement on his approaching fatherhood. The device of casting the bulk of the chapters in the form of a dialogue between three interlocuters—Davis, Professor Ernest Keppel, and Doctor Holdman Stedding—is not so wholly successful, for what begins as a fascinating idea is almost lost in a welter of repetitive discussion in which the three men continually digress to speculate upon the future of mankind. In an intriguing passage towards the end of the dialogue Wells seems to indicate his own dislike for the film version of *Things to Come*:

> 'World peace is assumed, but the atmosphere of security simply makes them [the citizens of the future] rather aimless, fattish and out of training. They are collectively up to nothing—or they are off in a storm of collective hysteria to conquer the moon or some remote nonsense of that sort. Imaginative starvation. They have apparently made no advances whatever in subtlety, delicacy, simplicity. Rather the reverse. They never say a witty thing; they never do a charming act. The general effect is of very pink, rather absurdly dressed celluloid dolls living on tabloids in a glass lavatory.'[37]

Star Begotten is the longest of the three linked short stories and the one in which Wells permits himself to elaborate and discuss his

ideas to the fullest extent. Artistically it is perhaps the least
satisfying of the three and yet its literary qualities, particularly in
the opening sections, are undeniable. To compare the story with
The War of the Worlds, as some critics have been wont to do, is
misleading, since the apparent similarity of theme conceals fundamental differences of genre. The former is a classic example of a
scientific romance, an exercise of the imagination which relies on a
series of vividly narrated incidents to achieve its effects. *Star
Begotten* is by contrast a dialogue, an intellectual speculation, in
which a group of highly intelligent men discuss the implications of
the Martian cosmic rays for our world and attempt to visualise a
planet cleansed and beautified by a wise minority. In form it is
more akin to *The Undying Fire*; viewed in the context of his life's
work it can be seen to be a restatement of the idea of an elite, a
minority of exceptionally able men and women, who voluntarily
set themselves the task of reshaping and unifying the earth. This
idea, which had dominated Wells's thinking since 1900, forms a
leitmotiv in his work and is arguably his most permanent contribution to twentieth-century thought. 'That conception of an open
conspiracy of intellectuals and wilful people against existing institutions and existing limitations and boundaries is always with
me; it is my King Charles's head ... in that matter I have a
constitutional undying patience. That open conspiracy will come.
It is my faith. It is my form of political thought.'[38]

THE CAMFORD VISITATION

The device of the critical visitant is one which is frequently
employed in Wells's fiction. The angel in *The Wonderful Visit*, the
mermaid in *The Sea Lady*, the giant children in *The Food of the
Gods*—all these are intruders outside the range of normal human
experience who criticise and comment upon earthly institutions.
In *The Camford Visitation*, written at a time (1937) when he was
preoccupied with the idea of a world encyclopaedia and educational reform, the critical visitant is a voice devoid of bodily form.
In this short tale of 75 pages Wells summarises many of his current
preoccupations in the form of a parable which is noteworthy for its
careful building up of atmosphere and its lively and biting characterisations.

In form it belongs to a genre Wells termed the 'long-short story'
but which is more commonly referred to as the 'novella'. Other

novellas written at about this time are *The Croquet Player* and *Star
Begotten*, and all three stories are allegories from varying points of
view on the crisis confronting man in the mid-twentieth century.

In the opening chapters the sense of a presence slowly invading
the university town of Camford—'as a voice, as a slight but palpa-
ble pressure, mental rather than bodily, as a faint stir and draught
during a lecture, as a deeper shadow in the shadows that waited
and watched'—is skilfully suggested. With an economy of style
reminiscent of the short stories Wells describes the coming of the
voice to a representative selection of Camford personalities: the
Master of Holy Innocents College; Trumber, a lecturer in English
literature; Scott-Harrowby, Hooker Professor of Latent History; and
so on. In each case the inhuman voice asks searching questions
regarding their educational beliefs and practices, subjecting their
replies to a pitiless scrutiny. The voice then goes on to criticise
contemporary educational institutions and to urge the imperative
need for a renaissance of intellectual effort, for a reinvigoration of
schools and universities throughout the world and for a reappraisal
of the whole purpose of education.

In less skilful hands the book could have been simply a polemical tract. The interest of *The Camford Visitation* from a literary
standpoint lies precisely in its force of characterisation. Mr.
Trumber with his art-conscious pontifications on poetry and prose
and his 'little lemon-covered monthly magazine'; the Master of
Holy Innocents indulging in lofty table-talk with his dining room
guest; Scott-Harrowby sitting on a felled tree beside the Cramb,
smoking a pipe and conversing with the unseen presence; these
and others are drawn with a masterly pen.

In 1936 Wells was awarded the honorary degree of D.Lit. at a
ceremony held in the Great Hall of the Imperial Institute at South
Kensington, and it may well be that the academic atmosphere of the
occasion set in motion a train of thought which culminated in this
story. Certainly the final manifestation of the voice takes place on
Congregation Day during the presentation of honorary degrees.
The voice makes a last eloquent appeal to reason—concluding
with the words 'Half the stars in the sky are the burning rubbish of
worlds that might have been'—before ceasing to speak, never to be
heard again.

At the conclusion of the short story 'The Story of the Last Trump'
Wells observed that 'If a thing is sufficiently strange and great no
one will perceive it. Men will go on in their own ways though one
rose from the dead to tell them that the Kingdom of Heaven was at
hand. . . .' *The Camford Visitation* ends on the same note of inertia:

with the passing of time the university dons begin to question whether they had, after all, heard the voice, and to postulate alternative explanations—hallucination, a hoax, ventriloquism. Time is indeed 'the healing touch in history', and twelve months after the visitation very few are prepared to assert that they had beyond doubt heard the mysterious voice.

Whilst necessarily written on a less diffused canvas than the full-length sociological novels, *The Camford Visitation* is nevertheless an interesting experiment which will repay careful re-reading. The limitations imposed by the novella form preclude the ampler development of character and nuance rendered possible in the novel, and impose on the author the discipline of compactness. Within these constraints Wells succeeds to a marked degree in achieving the effect he desired. Although it lacks the sustained imaginative power of *The Croquet Player*, this 'long-short story' possesses intrinsic merits which place it alongside 'The Inexperienced Ghost' and 'The Remarkable Case of Davidson's Eyes' as a study in the inexplicable.

ALL ABOARD FOR ARARAT

All Aboard for Ararat belongs to a category in Wells's writings which might be termed 'theological speculation'. This category includes such short stories as 'A Vision of Judgment', 'Answer to Prayer' and 'The Last Trump', the novels *The Soul of a Bishop* and *The Undying Fire*, and the conversations with Jesus of Nazareth in *The Happy Turning*. Wells regarded theology as 'an arena for clean fun that should do no harm to any properly constituted person',[39] and in *All Aboard for Ararat* he returned to the genre with a fantasia on the story of Noah and the Ark. It is one of his gentlest and wisest allegories, and is at the same time a profound restatement of his theory of world revolution.

Noah Lammock, who in 1940 believes that 'madness had taken possession of the earth and that everything he valued in human life was being destroyed', meets the Lord God and becomes involved in a series of conversations with him. Together they discuss the crisis in human affairs and the possibility of preserving a summary of human knowledge and achievement which could survive the Second World War. God reminds Noah that the idea of salvaging representative examples of technology and literature for the enlightenment of future generations was implicit in such an early work as *The Time Machine* (in the derelict science museum) and in many of the later writings such as *World Brain*. Certainly the notion had played an important part in Wells's thought for many years. Even the phrase 'the salvaging of civilisation' was used as the title for a collection of lectures and newspaper articles published in 1921, and in the same work the idea of a 'Bible of Civilisation', incorporating all that is noblest in poetry and prose, was described.

God proceeds to discuss the potentialities of microphotography and the possibility of filming the contents of the British Library, the Bodleian Library and the Library of Congress as a precaution against their destruction. Throughout this conversation Wells is gently taking himself to task for having failed to think through the 'world encyclopaedia' idea with sufficient clarity (in 1936 he had lectured to the Royal Institution on 'The Idea of a World Encyclopaedia') and for having skated over some of the difficulties inherent in such an ambitious concept.

Noah then goes for a meditative walk, in the course of which he thinks aloud (and incidentally talks to an attentive vole) on the problem of manning the Ark with a crew of sufficient calibre and intelligence. 'My Ark cannot be a wide popular movement. Nor can it be a movement among people in power and authority. Ordinary people won't understand a new world they have never seen.' The conversation with the vole is described with admirable whimsicality and recalls the scene in *Apropos of Dolores* in which Stephen Wilbeck soliloquises with a donkey. In the course of his reflections Noah ranges over possible sources of recruitment for the Ark and speculates on the reasons why previous revolutionary movements, including Christianity, had failed. The whole sequence ('Blue Prints for the New Ark') is brilliantly conceived and includes much profound philosophising on revolutionary theory and human behaviour.

What is notable about both this book and *The Happy Turning* is the way in which Wells describes conversations with the divinity without a trace of irreverence. Although as a young man he had rejected orthodox Christianity, more especially in the narrow, dogmatic form exemplified by his mother, he never lost his ability to write about theological matters with sensitivity and care. These religious speculations must have caused distress to those readers who imagined him to be a militant atheist—see, for example, the essay 'Gethsemane' in his collection of journalism *Guide to the New World*—and provide interesting evidence of his ambivalent posture towards conventional belief.

All his life Wells was at heart an elitist. His view of the means for achieving social amelioration changed with the passing of the years but throughout his long career as novelist, romancer and journalist he did not waver from his basic belief that enduring reforms could only be achieved through the efforts of an active and dedicated minority. *All Aboard for Ararat* is in a sense a distillation of years of writing and reflection on revolutionary theory. Although incomplete—it breaks off tantalisingly in mid-narrative on page 106—it is a thought-provoking and even moving testimony to his faith in mankind at a time when it must have been difficult to maintain hope in the face of a world holocaust. And in his insistence on absolute freedom of speech and publication he was again returning to first principles: '. . . everywhere our liberating education must go, like the water of a gold washer releasing the gold. The Ark of today has to become the world of tomorrow.'

THE HAPPY TURNING

The Happy Turning was written in 1944 and published in February 1945. It is therefore contemporary with the unhappy *Mind at the End of its Tether*, but although Wells's last two books were written at about the same time they are, in both mood and content, in the sharpest contrast. Whereas *Mind at the End of its Tether* holds out little, if any, hope for the future of mankind, *The Happy Turning* is suffused with cheerful optimism and ends on a note of forward-looking stoicism.

Sub-titled 'A Dream of Life', the book has the form of a collection of essays in which Wells describes his dreams and the range of personalities and experiences he encounters in dreamland. It was written at 13 Hanover Terrace, Regents Park, against a background of war and ill-health, and in the opening pages Wells seeks to convey to the reader some idea of his mental and physical atmosphere at this time. The first two sections also contain a number of autobiographical references which show that, at the age of 78, he could still clearly recall childhood episodes and dreams. There are references to his youthful astigmatism, to his Uncle Williams who described 'some frightful spiders that scratched and crawled' and his subsequent nightmare (this episode probably occurred at Wookey when Wells was fourteen), and to his mother's attempt to conceal a picture of hell in an old prayer-book.

Wells records that 'The companion I find most congenial in the

Beyond is Jesus of Nazareth', and in a series of chapters he describes his conversations with Jesus. These sections—in which Jesus discusses his disciples, his parables, the miracles, and his approach to revolution—are among the most delightful in the book, imbued with whimsical humour and lacking any hint of irreverence. The reader has been prepared for these sections by the observation:

> ... theology has always seemed to me an arena for clean fun that should do no harm to any properly constituted person. . . . From first to last I have invented a considerable amount of excellent blasphemy. *All Aboard for Ararat* is the last of a long series of drawings and writings, many of which have never seen and probably never will see the light of print.[40]

In a section headed 'A Hymn of Hate against Sycamores' Wells recounts his attempts at gardening, and how his efforts are frustrated by the 'vast lumping sycamore that grows in the deserted garden next door to me'. He expresses his hatred for sycamores in a long quotation from the 28th chapter of Deuteronomy. He is, of course, not simply expressing his detestation of sycamore trees *per se* but also of the trees as a symbol of all that is ugly and squalid in life.

The final section, 'The Divine Timelessness of Beautiful Things', is a serene reflection upon beauty and its central importance to human happiness. Wells contemplates the beauty found in Shakespeare, in drama, poetry and fiction, concluding with the thought that 'every new realisation, every fresh discovery, has for those who make it, a quality of beauty, transitory indeed but otherwise as clear and pure as that enduring Beauty we cherish for ever, an ephemeral beauty for one man or for a group of mortals, sufficient to make a life's devotion to the service of truth worthwhile.'

To the student of Wells's writings *The Happy Turning* is of interest not only for the insight it gives into his state of mind during his closing years but also for its relationship to his most deeply felt imaginative concerns. There is abundant evidence in his work that he was acutely dissatisfied with the world as it is and longed to enter an altogether different and lovelier world (cf. for example the short story 'The Door in the Wall'; such romances as *Men Like Gods* and *A Modern Utopia*; the concluding section of *A Year of Prophesying*; and Book One, §2 of *The World of William Clissold*). *The Happy Turning* is clearly linked to these earlier writings and provides further evidence of his tendency to seek escape from the

life of everyday in imaginative reverie.[41] It is interesting, for
example, to consider the similarities between such passages as
the following:

> At times I suffer from the strangest sense of detachment from
> myself and the world about me; I seem to watch it all from the
> outside, from somewhere inconceivably remote, out of time, out
> of space, out of the stress and tragedy of it all. (*The War of the
> Worlds*, Book One, §7)

> There are times when I feel as though it was less the sphere that
> enclosed me and made my all, than a sort of magic crystal into
> which I peered and saw myself living. I have, as it were, a sense of
> externality and a feeling that perhaps it might be possible,
> though I cannot imagine how it could be possible, to turn away
> and look at something else quite different from this common-
> sense world—another world. (*The World of William Clissold*,
> Book One, §2)

> Then very haltingly at first, but afterwards more easily, he
> began to tell of the thing that was hidden in his life, the haunting
> memory of a beauty and a happiness that filled his heart with
> insatiable longings, that made all the interests and spectacle of
> worldly life seem dull and tedious and vain to him. ('The Door in
> the Wall', §1)

> I dream I am at my front door starting out for the accustomed
> round. I go out and suddenly realise there is a possible turning I
> have overlooked. Odd I have never taken it, but there it is! And in
> a trice I am walking more briskly than I ever walked before, up
> hill and down dale, in scenes of happiness such as I have never
> hoped to see again. (*The Happy Turning*, §1)

It is this sense of wonder, this sense that it might be possible to
enter totally different and altogether happier worlds, that is such a
recurring theme in his work. This cosmic vision can be traced
throughout his fiction, beginning with *The Time Machine* and the
short stories and culminating in *The World of William Clissold*
and the final novels. It can also be seen in his sense of detachment,
in his propensity to refer to himself in the third person and to write
about himself in his own novels as if viewing his literary reputation
from outside. It is most evident in the early romances, in the grim
parable of *The War of the Worlds* and such short stories as 'Under

the Knife' and 'The Star'. This was a theme he returned to in 'The Plattner Story', 'The Remarkable Case of Davidson's Eyes', in *Men Like Gods* and again in *William Clissold*.

He also experienced the sensation of seeing all life in miniature, of seeing men as ants and houses and cities as minute, although in these visions it was the universe about him which shrank: he himself did not seem to shrink to scale. This sense of being an unseen observer, of being suspended in the unknown depths of space, was an extremely powerful element in his imagination. It was as if he was H. G. Wells and yet simultaneously he was outside his own body, an onlooker: 'fundamentally I am outside life, receiving experiences'.[42]

And inseparably linked with this withdrawal from the individual self was the wide sweep of his mind, his concern with the full conspectus of history and with the broad fundamentals of philosophy and science. This detachment from the limitations of the ego, and the merger of his personality with cosmic forces, was utterly characteristic of the man:

> If I find any difference between my mind and the minds of most of the people I meet, it is that my perception of time is rather more detached than is usual from the dimensions of the individual life . . . that the race process as a whole has come home to me with unusual vividness, and that future things and our relationship to future things have an abnormal reality for me.[43]

From 'The Rediscovery of the Unique' to *The Conquest of Time* he was fascinated by the relationship of the human mind to physical reality. Few writers, indeed, have imparted so skilfully their sense of wonder and of the littleness of man embarking on the illimitable ocean of knowledge. For him the riddle of the space-time continuum was a fascinating one, leading inevitably to a realisation of man's limited intellectual powers. The ultimate truth of things was inconceivable and perhaps unknowable to beings with finite minds: it must remain an immense, tantalising enigma. Within this frame of wonder life upon this planet flowed on to its destiny, a tiny oasis of activity in the vast, inhospitable emptiness of space. Within the confines of that oasis there was interest beyond measure, use for the utmost achievements of which man was capable. But there still returned at times the urge to gaze at those brooding immensities, to speculate on the nature of the universe and the uttermost problems of metaphysics.

In his own philosophy of life he did not advance far beyond

Schopenhauer's phrase *Die Welt als Wille and Vorstellung*. Life, he recognised, breathed a driving force, a purpose, a will to live. Life, moreover, was not haphazard, it was not an aimless confusion. The universe was subject to an inexorable law; a law independent of the human will and even perhaps irrelevant to it. The world could be understood, it was explicable, given only a mind of sufficient range and depth to comprehend.

It was his greatest gift to envision all life as one unfolding process, to recognise that alone among living things man reckoned with his destiny. All other forms of life passively submitted to the forces that created them; man alone sought to harness nature to his service and control the shape and interaction of his environment. In this struggle his most powerful weapon was his reasoning faculty and his skill at adaptation; he was engaged in a Promethean fight for survival against an indifferent cosmos. *The Happy Turning*, indeed, stands out from the pessimistic writings which surround it as a shining testimony to his faith in human betterment. It is a very short book, not entirely even in mood, yet of abiding fascination to the student of his philosophy.

Part V

THE NOVELS

The Novels

THE WHEELS OF CHANCE

Whilst living at Woking in 1895–6 Wells recorded that 'I learnt to ride my bicycle upon sandy tracks with none but God to help me; he chastened me considerably in the process, and after a fall one day I wrote down a description of the state of my legs which became the opening chapter of *The Wheels of Chance*. I rode wherever Mr. Hoopdriver rode in that story.'[1] This novel, which records a cycling holiday along the South Coast at the height of the boom of the 1890s, has now acquired a certain nostalgic charm—heightened by the delightful illustrations by J. Ayton Symington which adorn the first edition. Sub-titled 'A Holiday Adventure', it is one of Wells's most lighthearted excursions in the field of romance.

The early chapters, although somewhat marred by an excessive amount of authorial intervention (a trait Wells displayed in his early fiction but which disappeared as he gained greater confidence) draw on his experiences as a draper's apprentice and convey a vivid picture of life in a drapery emporium in late Victorian England. Later he was to paint the scene on a much broader canvas in *Kipps*, but in the description of Antrobus & Co. of Putney we have his first recollections of life from the standpoint of a shopman and written whilst the *feel* of the shop was still clear and distinct in his memory. There is a lively account of Hoopdriver setting forth on his annual holiday and a vivid sense of the exhilaration felt by this rather Pollyesque figure at the prospect of two weeks of freedom.

The novel is interspersed with a considerable amount of topographical detail as Hoopdriver travels through Sussex and Hampshire, stopping at many attractive villages *en route*, including a sojourn at Midhurst—a town which Wells knew intimately from his days as a chemist's apprentice and as a student at the grammar school. At Midhurst Hoopdriver stays with the same 'neat, bright-eyed little old lady' with whom Wells lodged in his student days and to whom he paid a warm tribute in his autobiography.[2] The villages and the English countryside are described with insight and affection, offering further evidence of the author's deep feeling for pastoral scenes. Here, for example, is the description of the scenery bordering the road between Northchapel and Petworth:

> There were purple vetches in the hedges, meadowsweet, honeysuckle, belated brambles—but the dog-roses had already gone; there were green and red blackberries, stellarias and dandelions, and in another place white dead nettles, traveller's joy, clinging bedstraw, grasses flowering, white campions, and ragged robins. One cornfield was glorious with poppies, bright scarlet and purple white, and the blue corn-flowers were beginning. In the lanes the trees met overhead, and the wisps of hay still hung to the straggling hedges. . . . Here and there were little cottages and picturesque beer-houses with the vivid brewers' boards of blue and scarlet, and once a broad green and a church, and an expanse of some hundred houses or so.

Again and again when reading Wells's novels one is struck by this affection for the unchanging rural scenes he had known and loved as a young man: an emotional attitude in sharp contradiction to the received view that as a writer he was devoid of aesthetic appreciation. We shall have occasion later in this *Companion* to return to this theme: suffice it to note here that from his earliest novels onwards there are indications of a deep tenderness towards the countryside and an awareness of the relationship between man and nature almost Lawrencian in its intensity.

Hoopdriver, the central character of the story, is an embryo version of Arthur Kipps. As imagined by Wells he is rather an absurd figure, vaguely discontented with his lot but lacking the imagination to see how he could escape from a life of drapery. He is, however, possessed of a Walter Mitty-like disposition to day-dream himself into all manner of romantic situations—running an ostrich farm in South Africa, shooting a lion, rescuing young ladies in distress—and it is this quality which lifts him above the commonplace and makes him a characteristically Wellsian hero. At the end of the novel he returns to the drapery emporium a changed man—full of his conversations with Jessica Milton (the 'Young Lady in Grey' with whom he has a romantic encounter) and determined to improve his lot. 'Tomorrow, the early rising, the dusting, and drudgery, begin again—but with a difference, with wonderful memories and still more wonderful desires and ambitions replacing those discrepant dreams.'

The principal interest of the story today from the point of view of Wells's later development as a novelist lies in the character of Jessica, and in the skill with which Wells describes the growing friendship between her and Hoopdriver. Jessie, with her fine features, her bright eyes, 'and a rich swift colour under her warm, tinted skin' is a clear anticipation of Ann Veronica Stanley and possesses the same restlessness and curiosity about life: 'I am resolved to Live my Own Life. . . . I want to Live, and I want to see what life means. I want to learn. Every one is hurrying me; everything is hurrying me; I want time to think. . . . I want to lead a Free Life and Own myself.' Jessica Milton is in fact an embodiment of the New Woman and her attitude and behaviour must have caused some raised eyebrows among the genteel readers of 1896. It is interesting to note that in this, his first novel, there is far more discussion—including discussion of *ideas*—than would have been customary in polite fiction of the period, and for this and other reasons Wells seems to have realised that some of his readers would find the book lacking in taste. (See, for example, his reference to the novel as being 'a little vulgar' in his essay 'Of Conversation', and the numerous apologetic remarks addressed directly by the author to the reader, whom he assumes throughout is female.) Jessica, then, although lacking the vigour and roundness of detail of Ann Veronica, is convincing enough. With her coolness and acumen she is a perfect foil for the impetuous Hoopdriver and retains to the end much of the reader's sympathy.

Writing apropos *The Wheels of Chance* forty years later in his autobiography, Wells observed that 'the bicycle was the swiftest thing upon the roads in those days, there were as yet no automobiles, and the cyclist had a lordliness, a sense of masterful adventure, that has gone from him altogether now'. Because of its theme and humorous descriptions of cycling in its early days the novel now has an important place in the literature of the bicycle. One of the many reasons why reading it today is such a rewarding experience is that it encapsulates so much of the flavour of late Victorian England from the standpoint of an acute and sympathetic observer. But it would be a pity if the novel were to be remembered simply as a rather slight cycling adventure or as an insignificant romance. Slight it undoubtedly is, yet it contains within it sufficient indications of the mature Wells to repay careful study. In its skilful use of dialogue to discuss ideas and conventions, its wealth of social detail, its gentle satire of Victorian society and insight into the lives and aspirations of ordinary people, it foreshadows the central themes of the novels yet to come. Moreover it embodies in the characters of Hoopdriver and Jessie two people who, each in their different ways, are acutely dissatisfied with their station in life and wish to change it. It is this basic attitude of mind and desire to disentangle oneself from a limiting environment which proved to be his most fruitful source of renewal in the years ahead.

LOVE AND MR. LEWISHAM

Apropos *Love and Mr. Lewisham* Wells confided to his friend Elizabeth Healey: 'There is really more work in that book than there is in many a first class F.R.S. research, and stagnant days and desert journeys beyond describing.' It was begun in 1896 in a mood of immense seriousness but not completed until January 1899, when he was living at Beach Cottage, Sandgate. Again and again it was laid aside while Wells pressed on with other projects— *The War of the Worlds*, *When the Sleeper Wakes* and *Tales of Space and Time*. He was determined that *Love and Mr. Lewisham* should not be published until it was as good as he could make it, and he resisted the temptation to let it leave his hands until he was satisfied it was a polished and complete work of art. Of all his books (including *Tono-Bungay*, over which he lavished great pains) it is the most consciously 'written'; it was planned to conform to a carefully worked out scenario and read aloud to his wife Jane to ensure the utmost symmetry and grace of style.

It is one of the most autobiographical of his novels, beginning with a detailed description of 'Whortley Proprietary School, Sussex' (Midhurst Grammar School) where Wells, like Lewisham, was an assistant master. The description of Whortley and the countryside around Immering (Iping) is very skilfully done, as is the account of his adolescent love affair with Ethel Henderson. These opening chapters tell us much about Wells's state of mind at the outset of his literary career. In a revealing passage he admits that:

> In those days much of Lewisham's mind was still an unknown land to him. He believed among other things that he was always the same consistent intelligent human being, whereas under certain stimuli he became no longer reasonable and disciplined but a purely imaginative and emotional person.'[3]

This is one of the earliest indications in his work of a basic conflict in his temperament between classical and romantic elements. Lewisham, with his love of music, his infatuation with Ethel and his appreciative eye for wild flowers and the beauties of nature is very far from being 'always the same consistent intelligent human being', and in recognising this fact his creator was acknowledging a fundamental dichotomy within his own makeup.

The Whortley chapters are followed by an equally careful account of the Normal School of Science, London, where Wells had been a student during the years 1884–7. The account of the School, the students and their interests may be taken to be an accurate picture of student life as he had known it and may instructively be compared with the short story 'A Slip Under the Microscope' (1896) which has a similar setting. He was still a young man in his early thirties when *Love and Mr. Lewisham* was written, and this was only his second novel. He was clearly feeling his way towards his mature style as a man of letters, and there is abundant evidence from letters to his friends that he took immense pains over its writing, and rewrote and revised chapters times without number. Even at this early date there is far more discussion of ideas than was customary in the Victorian novel, and in the dialogues between Lewisham and Chaffery (more especially in Chapter XXIII, 'Mr. Chaffery At Home') there are clear indications of the novelist Wells was to become. The story reveals an acute insight into middle-class marriage problems and both Lewisham and Ethel are drawn with a deeply convincing pen. Yet the book has perhaps the most un-Wellsian conclusion in all his work, for at the end of the novel Lewisham succumbs to domesticity instead of launching out on his programme of educational improvement as might have been expected. The nagging fear of domestic claustrophobia, which almost overwhelmed Wells in his own person, becomes increasingly evident as the novel proceeds. But *Love and Mr. Lewisham* is chiefly of interest because of its insight into the financial and personal problems of a newly married couple. The Lewishams succeed in surmounting their difficulties, but only at the cost of mutual compromise and considerable sacrifice of ambition. It is a carefully thought out parable on the dangers of entering into marriage with inadequate preparation. The author is, in a sense, warning the reader to avoid the mistakes he himself made in his first marriage. Domestic routine can so easily become a trap stifling initiative and personal ambition. Years later he remarked: 'At the time of writing it I did not consciously apply the story of Mr. Lewisham to my own circumstances, but down below the threshold of my consciousness the phobia must have been there'.[4]

It is not difficult to see why *Lewisham* is accepted today as a classic, nor the reasons why it was praised by his friends Arnold Bennett, Henry James and George Gissing. It is a far more ambitious piece of work than *The Wheels of Chance* and approaches much closer to the conventional idea of a full-dress novel. Until its publication in 1900 he had been regarded as a scientific romancer pure and simple, but this 'Story of a Very Young Couple' was plainly the work of a serious and accomplished writer. Contemporary critics, whilst welcoming it as a novel of great promise, appear to have missed one of its most significant aspects: that it encapsulates the conflict between sexual passion and sustained intellectual effort. This motif, which appears again in *The Sea Lady* and in even more elaborate form in *The New Machiavelli*, was destined to be the dominating theme of his life. In his autobiography he termed it his 'Compound Fugue', and to greater or lesser degree it underlies all the novels which follow it.

KIPPS

On 5 October 1898, Wells drew a 'picshua' showing himself sitting on an egg with the caption 'This egg was laid at New Romney in September'. A second sketch shows a tiny top hatted figure emerging from the newly hatched egg. On being asked 'Hullo. What's your name?' he answers 'Kipps, sir.' Wells was convalescing at New Romney after a painful recurrence of his kidney ailment. For a time an operation for the removal of the offending kidney was advised, but the surgeon who was to perform the operation decided on further examination that this was not necessary. It was in the mood of euphoria consequent upon his recovery in health and spirits that *Kipps* was conceived.

With the exception of *The Time Machine* the novel had a longer gestation than any of his works. It was conceived first as a 'great novel on the Dickens plan'[5] under the title *The Wealth of Mr. Waddy*. This was plainly intended to be a work of comic relief, in sharp contrast to *Love and Mr. Lewisham*. From October 1898 to March 1899 he worked steadily on this project, corresponding frequently with J. B. Pinker, his literary agent, in a mood of great enthusiasm. In later years he was under the impression that the manuscript had been lost or destroyed; in fact it survived and is today in the Wells Archive at the University of Illinois. *The Wealth of Mr. Waddy* was published in a critical edition in 1969.

This novel, the first draft of the work we now know as *Kipps*, consists of fifteen chapters (about 35,000 words) of largely finished copy, and twenty chapters of notes and outlines. It has many similarities with *Kipps*, and indeed Wells incorporated some of the *Waddy* material into the later work. The central difference between the two novels is in the character of Mr. Waddy himself: in *Kipps* he occupies merely a minor role, but in *The Wealth of Mr. Waddy* he dominates most of the opening chapters. He is a fully drawn individual, characterised with the wit and observation of the early Dickens, and reminiscent in his irascibility and 'larger than life' quality of Uncle Ponderevo. Yet for all Wells's enthusiasm for it at the time *Mr. Waddy*, in spite of moments of genuine comic vitality, lacks the conviction of his best work. Wells realised that it was commercially impracticable and that, had he developed the idea in accordance with his original plan, would have been far too long.[6] For *Kipps*, lengthy though it is, was to have been merely one part of a much larger design. First was to have been a long section in which Mr. Waddy, Kipps's benefactor, was the central character; then a middle section recounting Kipps's life story; and finally 'the adventures of young Mr. Walshingham as a fugitive in France'. Such a work would have run to two hundred thousand words and would not have found a publisher. By 1900 the three-decker novel of Victorian times was a convention of the past and Wells realised he had no choice but to truncate his original design. At some point between March 1899 and April 1900 he abandoned *Mr. Waddy* and from then on the work is referred to in his correspondence simply as *Kipps*. The book was finally published in October 1905 and was thus, in all, seven years in the making.

Kipps is a totally different kind of novel from the much more carefully wrought *Love and Mr. Lewisham*. Whereas the latter had been written to an elaborately worked out plan, *Kipps* was envisaged from the outset as a work of Dickensian comprehensiveness. Wells wanted freedom to digress and amplify, to philosophise and discuss to an extent which had not been possible in his earlier novels. It is no accident that George Ponderevo in *Tono-Bungay* states: '. . . do what I will I fail to see how I can be other than a lax, undisciplined storyteller. I must sprawl and flounder, comment and theorise, if I am to get the thing out I have in mind.' Wells had a strong admiration for the novels of Dickens and there is no doubt that he felt completely at home in the discursive tradition of Sterne and Fielding. Now at last, he felt, he had the leisure to write a novel on the grand scale.

The opening chapters, 'The Little Shop at New Romney' and

'The Emporium', contain some of Wells's very finest work. These sections brilliantly convey the atmosphere of his early life, first at Morley's Commercial Academy for Young Gentlemen, Bromley, and then the two years (1881–3) he spent as an apprentice at Hyde's Drapery Emporium, Kings Road, Southsea. The whole of the first part, describing Kipps's childhood and adolescence, is written with an assurance he rarely equalled, and justifies the extravagant praise which Henry James, among others, heaped upon the book. The account of the Folkestone Drapery Bazaar and its proprietor Mr. Edwin Shalford is vividly wrought; it is evident that his hatred for the narrow world of retail apprenticeship still rankled in his memory twenty years after his Southsea experiences. This was also the first novel in which his natural gift for characterisation is expressed to the full. Chitterlow, Helen Walsingham, Chester Coote, and, above all, Ann Pornick, are drawn with sensitivity and perception. Arthur Kipps himself, one of his happiest and most verisimilar creations, clearly fascinated Wells as he explored his complex individuality in greater and greater depth as the novel proceeded. Even so fastidious a critic as James had to admit that Kipps 'is a diamond of the first water, from start to finish, exquisite and radiant'. In later years Wells doubted whether, in view of changes in social conditions, the novel would continue to be read and remembered. 'I doubt,' he wrote, 'if any of these persons have that sort of vitality which endures into new social phases. In the course of a few decades they may become incomprehensible; the snobbery of Kipps for example or the bookish illiteracy of Mr. Polly may be altogether inexplicable.'[7] He need not have feared. Today *Kipps* has achieved the status of a classic and seems destined to be one of the handful of books which will earn for him the literary immortality he affected to despise.

The final section, 'Kippses', is only comprehensible in relation to Wells's personal circumstances and attitudes during the period in which the book was written. For the years 1898–1905 were notable, first for his restlessness and protracted search for a congenial and permanent home and, second for his increasing involvement with the socialist movement. During 1898–9 he and his wife Jane were searching actively but with mounting frustration for a house. On health grounds he had been advised by his doctor to seek a house 'on sand or gravel and high and sheltered'. Some indication of his exasperation at this time can be gained from a letter to J. V. Milne:

Sandgate and Hythe and Rye present a certain suitableness of soil and aspect, but the houses! There's no word for it, as the

costermonger said. Servant-murdering basements, sanitary in-
sanities, and not a decent bathroom anywhere. I want a house
with five sane rooms and the proper fitting of kitchen, bathroom
and so forth—I am ready to go to £80 and I can't get it. I'm tied to
this house still—I was in bed to within a few days ago, but my
wife returns from desperate raids, nigh upon tears.'

Tired, overworked and ill, Wells and his wife continued the
house-hunting for a considerable time before deciding to build.
While waiting for Spade House to be built (Spade House, Radnor
Cliff Crescent, Sandgate, built 1899–1900) he rented furnished
houses, first Beach Cottage, Granville Road, Sandgate and then the
neighbouring Arnold House (now 20 Castle Road). Much of the
frustration and worry of these house-hunting experiences is expressed vicariously in *Kipps*. Indeed the whole of the latter part of
the novel is obsessed with architecture, almost as extensively as is
Tono-Bungay. Some readers find this preoccupation with housing overdone, but seen in the context of his private life it is only too
understandable.

He was also at this time becoming increasingly interested in
sociological questions. He had become a member of the Fabian
Society in February 1903, sponsored by Bernard Shaw and Graham
Wallas, and made his debut by presenting a paper entitled 'The
Question of Scientific Administrative Areas in relation to Municipal Undertakings'. (This paper, subsequently published as an
appendix to *Mankind in the Making*, also stems directly from his
housing experiences: apropos of supplying electricity to Spade
House he wrote 'It happens that I have had an object-lesson in this
matter of local government; and indeed it is my object-lesson that
has led to this paper tonight.') The concluding sections of the
novel, written long after the opening chapters, lack the conviction
and ease of the first two-thirds. It is as if Wells, increasingly
fascinated by social issues and beginning to involve himself in
overtly propagandist organisations, was uncertain how to introduce an ideological element into a novel which had begun as a
work of art. The lengthy paragraph at the conclusion of Book 3,
Chapter 2, beginning 'The stupid little tragedies of these clipped
and limited lives!' and ending with the words 'And the claw of this
Beast rests upon them!' is one of a number of passages open to
criticism on the grounds of its clumsiness, although its sincerity
and eloquence are undeniable.

In summary, then, *Kipps* could be described as a flawed masterpiece. Begun when Wells was a rising young author at the begin-

ning of his literary career, it was completed seven years later when he was an established novelist and on the brink of a career as prophet, sociologist and iconoclast which was to carry him to world-wide fame. By the time he came to write the later chapters he was far removed in mood from the boyish young man who had conceived the novel as a picaresque extravaganza in the vein of *Pickwick Papers*. With *Anticipations* and *A Modern Utopia* behind him and *Faults of the Fabian* on the horizon he was now taking himself seriously as a responsible writer on social questions. *Kipps* was his first attempt at a large-scale novel and although it was deservedly successful and has always been counted as among his most enduring works it remains experimental in nature. Wells in 1905 was still learning the craft of the novelist; and his greatest triumphs were yet to come.

TONO-BUNGAY

In his autobiography Wells records that after the building of Spade House 'presently I was finishing *Kipps* and making notes for what I meant to be a real full-length novel at last, *Tono-Bungay*, a novel, as I imagined it, on Dickens–Thackeray lines. . . .'[8] There can be no doubt that he regarded *Tono-Bungay* as a very ambitious novel indeed, and that it is one of the few works by which he would have wished to be judged. In the copy which he presented to Bennett he wrote '*My* novel'. It stands alongside *The Old Wives Tale* as a sustained and coherent work of the imagination, and as an unforgettable picture of the ending of the Victorian age. Indeed 'The End of an Age' was one of the alternative titles he considered for the novel, along with 'A Picture of the World', 'One Man's View of England', and 'Waste'. Each of these titles serves to indicate the scope of his design. On its publication one reviewer perceptively commented: 'And we think that we shall be within the limit of reasonable prophecy if we suggest that *Tono-Bungay* will prove to be H. G. Wells's *David Copperfield*—the full-fledged, four-square epitome of all that modern life and character have to tell him.'[9]

Geoffrey West dates its inception from the suicide of Whitaker Wright in the London Law Courts early in 1904. The novel was not completed until the spring of 1908, so the planning and writing of it occupied in total a span of four years. This is not to say that he was occupied wholly with *Tono-Bungay* during this period. Again and again it had to be laid aside when he was distracted with other projects—the Fabian affray, the writing of *In the Days of the Comet*

1b. 8 South Street, Bromley, which Wells attended as a dame school (1871-2); it was run by Mrs. Knott and her daughter Miss Salmon. Here Wells learned to read and do his tables

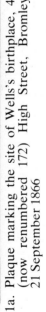

1a. Plaque marking the site of Wells's birthplace, 47 (now renumbered 172) High Street, Bromley, 21 September 1866

2a. Bromley High Street, *circa* 1905. No. 47, Atlas House, is on the left

2b. Morley's Academy, Bromley (now demolished), where Wells was a pupil from 1874 to 1880. Note the classroom extending at the rear of the building

3. H. G. Wells, *circa* 1876. His brother Frank described him as 'a healthy and masterful child from the first'

4a & b.   Two views of 18 Victoria Street, Basford, Stoke on Trent, where Wells stayed for three months during the spring of 1888. Here the short story 'The Cone' was written and parts of 'The Chronic Argonauts' were drafted

5. Etruria Woods, Stoke on Trent. Wells recorded in his autobiography: 'One bright afternoon I went out by myself to a little patch of surviving woodland amidst the industrialised country, called "Trury Woods". There had been a great outbreak of wild hyacinths that year and I lay down among them to think. It was one of those sun-drenched afternoons that are turgid with vitality. Those hyacinths in their upright multitude were braver than an army with banners and more inspiring than trumpets. "I have been dying for nearly two-thirds of a year," I said "and I have died enough."'

6. Up Park, near Petersfield. Wells's mother was housekeeper here from 1880 to 1893. The house figures as 'Bladesover' in his partly autobiographical novel *Tono-Bungay*

7a. Plaque at Spade House, Sandgate, Kent, Wells's home from 1900-09. Here he rose to a position of world-wide fame as novelist and prophet. At Spade House he wrote *Anticipations, Mankind in the Making, The Food of the Gods, A Modern Utopia, Kipps, In the Days of the Comet, New Worlds for Old, The War in the Air, First and Last Things, Tono-Bungay, Ann Veronica* and *The History of Mr Polly*

7b. View of Spade House, Sandgate

8.   17 Church Row, Hampstead, Wells's home from 1909 to 1912

9a & b. Two views of Easton Glebe, Dunmow (formerly Little Easton Rectory), Wells's home from 1912 until his wife's death in 1927. Easton Glebe figures as 'The Dower House' in *Mr Britling Sees it Through*

10. H. G. Wells, *circa* 1930. Wells was now a world figure, and in 1934 held discussions with Stalin and Roosevelt on the prospects for world order. In 1936 he was awarded the honorary degree of D.Litt. by the University of London

11. 13 Hanover Terrace, Regents Park, the elegant Nash Terrace house which was Wells's home from 1937 until his death in 1946. He remained here throughout the war years in spite of air raids, and wrote a serene book, *The Happy Turning*, describing his imaginative world during his final illness

12a & b. Two stills from the film *Things to Come*. (a) The moon rocket about to be fired from the space gun; (b) One of the aeroplanes of the world air force which eventually succeeds in imposing order on a Europe shattered by war and pestilence and *New Worlds for Old*, a visit to the United States in 1906, and much journalism and pamphleteering. The novel was accepted for serialisation in the *English Review* and finally appeared in book form, under the Macmillan imprint, in February 1909. What is so remarkable about it as a work of fiction is that, in this alone of all his works, each aspect of Wells's genius is fused together into a single consistent whole. Previous works had embodied particular facets of his art—the storyteller, the novelist, the scientific romancer, the sociologist, the humorist. Now for the first time all these elements were blended in a social panorama of Dickensian comprehensiveness: the result is a novel of impressive richness and power.

Tono-Bungay can be fully understood only in relation to Wells's own life, for—despite his denials at the time—it is perhaps the most overtly autobiographical of all his novels. Here we find a picture of his childhood impressions at 'Bladesover House' (Up Park, near Petersfield, now the property of the National Trust); his apprenticeship to the chemist's shop at Wimblehurst (Midhurst); his student days in London; and his love affair and marriage with his first wife, Isobel Mary Wells. The novel is not only archetypally Wellsian in this regard but also in its entire mood and philosophy. It is wholly permeated with Wells's temperament and outlook: indeed it would not be too much to say that it is obligatory reading for anyone who seeks to understand the man and his world. It is in a real sense his personal testament. The opening chapter, with its detailed and fascinating description of Bladesover House, should be compared with the references to 'Burnmore Park' in *The Passionate Friends* and to Up Park in his autobiography for a full appreciation of the impact the great house must have made on the young Wells. To a boy brought up in the comparatively restricted world of Victorian Bromley his sojourns at the house must have been a liberating experience:

> About that park there were some elements of a liberal education; there was a great space of greensward not given over to manure and food grubbing; there was mystery, there was matter for the imagination. . . . There were corners that gave a gleam of meaning to the word forest, glimpses of unstudied natural splendour. There was a slope of bluebells in the broken sunlight under the newly green beeches in the west wood that is now precious sapphire in my memory; it was the first time that I knowingly met Beauty.[10]

In reading this chapter, so exquisitely written and beautifully observed—as if Wells is consciously striving to achieve fine prose—one is again struck by that curious ambivalence which lay at the heart of his complex nature. The sensitive, almost romantic response to the scenery of the park can hardly be squared with George Ponderevo's image of himself as a sceptical man of science, or indeed with Wells's image of his own nature. ('Essentially an intellectual with an instinctive dislike for the ... intensities and emotional floors of life ... he was much more the scientific man than the artist, though he dealt in literary forms.'[11]) At numerous points in the novel the narrator reveals a romantic, imaginative approach to life and its problems which is at odds with his outward scepticism. Moreover it is questionable whether George's attitude to the passing of the Bladesover era is one of nostalgia or satisfaction, or whether it is neither—simply an *acceptance* that the old rural order is now no more. It is this co-existence within the novel of apparently opposing emotional responses, corresponding to the author's own unresolved doubts, which provides much of its inner tension and renders it so characteristic of Wells as a man and a thinker.

The characterisation in the novel is assured and convincing. Many critics regard Aunt Susan as Wells's most memorable heroine, and it is difficult to believe that she was not drawn from life. With her irrepressible badinage, her humorous approach to life and her kindly indulgence towards her husband she recalls Rosie Driffield in *Cakes and Ale*. Uncle Ponderevo is a more complex figure. In his ebullience and furious energy he is almost a caricature, oddly reminiscent of some of Dickens's characters in his 'larger than life' quality. Wells does not seem to have had any specific individual in mind when sketching such a distinctive figure: he is in reality a hybrid, with aspects taken from a number of individuals—some from Samuel Cowap (the chemist to whom he was apprenticed for a brief period at Midhurst), others from Northcliffe and Whitaker Wright. Memorable, too, is the picture of George's mother as the housekeeper at Bladesover, a picture drawn in some respects from Wells's mother, Sarah. We find the portrait painted in greater depth in *The New Machiavelli* and *The Dream*.

But the most interesting character in many ways is that of the narrator himself, George Ponderevo. Here is a fully realised portrayal of a man who is intellectually and imaginatively emancipated from the servant class, looking back on his past life and reflecting on his experiences. His idealism, his constant striving towards emotional and personal fulfilment, are at once verisimilar and revealing:

I don't think I'm blind to the fun, the surprises, the jolly little coarsenesses and insufficiency of life, to the 'humour of it', as people say, and to adventure, but that isn't the root of the matter with me. There's no humour in my blood. I'm in earnest in warp and woof. I stumble and flounder, but I know that over all these merry, immediate things, there are other things that are great and serene, very high, beautiful things—the reality. I haven't got it, but it's there nevertheless. I'm a spiritual guttersnipe in love with unimaginable goddesses.'[12]

This continual quest for an ideal which always eludes his grasp gives to the book an exhilarating sense of movement. It is a journey not simply in the sense that George and his Uncle and Aunt are constantly moving onward in their social progression, but also in that George is ever seeking a satisfying personal faith, a rationale which will embody and unify the competing strands in his makeup. He seeks this fulfilment first in Tono-Bungay then, recoiling, in his love for Marion, in his experiments with flying machines, in his love for Beatrice, and finally in the manufacture of destroyers. He is the epitome of Wells in his restlessness, his sceptical attitude towards orthodox religion, his dislike of convention and his almost mystical belief in the veracity of science. At the conclusion of the book he asserts that the 'one enduring thing' he has found in life is scientific truth.

The quap episode, much criticised by some commentators on the grounds that it is too disparate in theme to form a unified part of the novel, is in reality an integral part of the overall design. At numerous points Wells is at pains to emphasise that the dominating theme underlying the book as a whole is 'the broad slow decay of the great social organism of England'.[13] The quap adventure is intrinsic to this theme since, through the skilful use of metaphor, he is able to introduce a range of linguistic devices to emphasise the idea of radioactivity as a creeping harbinger of cancer and decay. By likening the radioactive quap to a cancerous growth in a living organism and then extending the simile to the decay of English culture (as is done explicitly in III, iv, 5) Wells demonstrates that he sees the African adventure as ministering in a fundamental way to this overall motif. The decay of the ship bringing the quap to England is symbolic of the illusory, unstable nature of the world of finance and commerce: it is a satirical reminder that a society based upon profit-seeking and the unscrupulous pursuit of wealth is built on foundations of sand.

The sense of the novel as a journey, as an ongoing experience, is heightened by the final chapter 'Night and the Open Sea'. Here in a series of brilliant images Wells describes a journey by destroyer down the Thames and out to the open sea, in the process 'passing all England in review'. This final section, one of the most carefully written passages in the whole corpus of his fiction, is a further reminder of the malaise at the heart of England, of the crumbling and decay of the social organism. Through the vivid simile of the destroyer cleaving a cross-section through English history, Wells is seeking to convey an awareness of the continual process of decay and change, and of the realities lying behind the outward appearance of mellowness. Reflecting on his experiences, George sees that 'through the confusion something drives, something that is at once human achievement and the most inhuman of all existing things'. The story mounts to both a literal and symbolic coda as he rhapsodises on the one permanent element he has found in life. The one reality George finds is

> . . . something we draw by pain and effort out of the heart of life, that we disentangle and make clear. Other men serve it, I know, in art, in literature, in social invention, and see it in a thousand different figures, under a hundred names. . . . Men and nations, epochs and civilisations pass, each making its contribution. . . . It emerges from life with each year one lives and feels, and generation by generation and age by age, but the how and why of it are all beyond the compass of my mind. . . .[14]

It is with the ambiguous image of the destroyer that the story ends. It is arguable that all Wells's novels have an ambiguous ending, but perhaps none more so than this vivid picture of the ship cleaving through the Thames onwards to an unknown destination. With this enigmatic symbol, so fraught with possibilities for both destruction and human betterment, the novel comes to its close.

Tono-Bungay, then, is a panorama of English society: a panorama seen from the outside though with a richly detailed knowledge. To read it is an invigorating intellectual and emotional experience. Within its pages one finds an extraordinarily detached but loving vision of England: it is as if the events described are seen from the perspective not of 1909 but of the distant future. George narrates the story as if he is an observer, an adventurer passing through the dying phases of the Victorian era—he is in a sense a time traveller commenting upon what he sees and feels but not participating actively in the society he describes. Indeed the detachment of the narrator is the dominant impression which remains in the mind after the last page has been reached: the sense that time and again

George is not expressing an emotional feeling but an intellectual attitude. It is this lack of emotional commitment, this awareness that at certain crucial stages an emotional balance is missing, which constitutes what is arguably the novel's most serious weakness.

But as a picture of a radically unstable society and an indictment of irresponsible capitalism it is unique. Some critics have seen it as an 'exploding' novel, and recognise in the patent medicine 'Tono-Bungay' a symbol of the inherent instability, the radioactive decay, of modern civilisation. Wells himself seems to support this view: 'I have called it *Tono-Bungay*, but I had far better have called it *Waste.* . . . It is all one spectacle of forces running to waste, of people who use and do not replace, the story of a country hectic with a wasting, aimless fever of trade and money making and pleasure seeking.'[15] His prescience not merely in foreseeing modern advertising methods but in his forecast of the economic malaise so characteristic of the twentieth century is remarkable: 'Yet it seems to me indeed at times that all this present commercial civilisation is no more than my poor uncle's career writ large, a swelling, thinning bubble of assurances; that its arithmetic is just as unsound, its dividends as ill-advised, its ultimate aim as vague and forgotten; that it all drifts on perhaps to some tremendous parallel to his individual disaster.'[16] David Lodge has demonstrated convincingly that *Tono-Bungay* is a 'Condition of England' novel, in common with Mrs. Gaskell's *North and South*, Disraeli's *Sybil* and George Eliot's *Middlemarch*. Whilst it is a novel of characterisation in the accepted sense it is also a social panorama, an epic spanning an immense canvas. In relating the life story of his alter ego he is interpreting and analysing the Victorian and Edwardian age in a way which is not matched in any of the later novels. It was not by any means his last attempt to write a conventional novel, but it was the last to be written consciously as a work of art and the only one to be wrought with such consummate vision. *Tono-Bungay* is more than a watershed in his work: it is his finest single achievement.

ANN VERONICA

A Modern Utopia was leading up to *Ann Veronica* (1909) in which the youthful heroine was allowed a frankness of desire and sexual enterprise hitherto unknown in English popular fiction. That book created a scandal at the time, though it seems mild enough reading to the young of today. It is rather badly constructed, there is an excessive use of soliloquy, but Ann Veronica came as near to being a living character as anyone in my earlier love stories. This was so because in some particulars she was drawn from life. And for that and other reasons she made a great fuss in the world.'

Thus wrote Wells in his autobiography of a novel which in its day caused an unparalleled furore.

Ann Veronica, begun while *Tono-Bungay* was still in hand and written during the spring and summer of 1908, has as its central character Ann Veronica Stanley, a vivacious girl who is eager for life and experience. She flees from a respectable, rigidly conventional home to elope with her biology tutor, Capes, a man who is already married. In the story of their flight and defiance of the prevailing moral code there are strong undertones of Wells's own crisis between his first wife Isabel and Amy Catherine Robbins, and of a later affair which occurred during the Fabian imbroglio. It is the fact that Ann Veronica, one of his most memorable heroines, is 'drawn from life' which renders the novel such an intense emotional experience. He was not far wrong when he wrote to Frederick Macmillan 'it is, I think, the best love story I have ever done'.

Ann Veronica Stanley is by common consent one of his most attractive and finely drawn female characters. In her zest for life, her infectious curiosity, her eagerness to sample experience and her radical ideas she symbolised for Wells—and undoubtedly for many of his readers—the spirit of a generation. She *lives* by the sheer vitality of her temperament and personality, whereas by comparison some of his other heroines (V. V. Grammont in *The Secret Places of the Heart*, for example) manifestly lack conviction and vitality. The novel is also rich in a whole range of minor characterisations—her father, 'a lean, trustworthy, worried-looking, neuralgic, clean-shaven man of fifty-three'; Ramage, who attempts to seduce her but is repulsed in a memorable scene; Manning, who for all his ineptitude is sincerely in love with her; Miss Miniver, a well-meaning but completely ineffectual pursuer of Movements; and many others. Structurally there is some evidence that the book was originally planned on a much more ambitious scale but was abruptly brought to a conclusion when it was realised that the original conception could not be satisfactorily carried out. Whatever may be the truth of the matter the indications are that *Ann Veronica*, unlike its predecessors, was written quickly and whilst the events which had inspired it were still fresh and vivid in Wells's mind. The book was rejected by Macmillan (to whom Wells offered it in the first instance) and was finally published by Fisher Unwin in October 1909.

To be fully understood the novel needs to be seen in the context of Wells's personal life and attitudes, and in particular against the background of two events which dominated his intellectual and emotional life during the years 1906–9: first, his abortive attempt to revivify the Fabian Society and second, his affair with Amber Pember Reeves. Each in their different ways shaped his life during these turbulent years, and each is reflected in the pages of *Ann Veronica*.

On 9 February 1906, Wells read a paper to the Fabian Society entitled *Faults of the Fabian*. In it he was highly critical of the Society on the grounds of its smallness and general ineffectiveness, and proposed the setting up of a committee to consider in detail proposals for radical reform. This initiative led directly to the appointment of a Special Committee 'to consider measures for increasing the scope, influence, income and activity of the Society', of which Wells was one of the leading members. Jane Wells was Secretary of the Special Committee, which reported in December 1906 and proposed a fundamental reconstruction of the Society, including the formation of local groups, the creation of a Propaganda and Membership Committee with power to organise a vigorous campaign of literature and publications, a revised statement of aims and objects, and a reshaping of the Society to ensure more effective executive direction of its policy and activities. The Executive Committee—led by Shaw and Sidney Webb—produced in reply a counter report which amounted to a complete rejection of these proposals and an acceptance of the status quo. Wells, who was no match for Shaw's formidable debating powers, was ultimately outmanoeuvred and after two packed meetings at Essex Hall had to concede defeat. This 'storm in a Fabian tea cup' rankled for many years in his memory and in a number of novels written in its aftermath—including *Ann Veronica*, *Tono-Bungay* and *The New Machiavelli*—he took his revenge on what he regarded as the Fabian 'Old Gang'. The Goopses in *Ann Veronica* are characteristically earnest Fabians, and there are a number of passages in the novel in which he is gently poking fun at 'the giant leaders of the Fabian Society who are remaking the world'. Frustrated by his inability to achieve the practical reforms he desired in the world of politics, he relieved his feelings vicariously by satirising the Fabians in his fiction.

Amber Reeves was the daughter of the Hon. William Pember Reeves, Agent-General for New Zealand and later a Director of the

London School of Economics. Mrs. Pember Reeves had been an active member of the Fabian Society for many years and was head of the Women's Section. Amber had had a brilliant academic career at Cambridge, had joined the Society and first met Wells in about 1906. Their affair, which lasted some two years and scandalised some of Wells's friends, has been fully described elsewhere.[17] Suffice it to say here that this was unquestionably a cardinal event in his life, for it dominates not only *Ann Veronica* but also *The New Machiavelli*, where the story is retold in the persons of Richard Remington and Isobel Rivers. In describing the love affair between Ann Veronica and Capes, Wells is apparently recreating the atmosphere of his own encounter with Amy Catherine Robbins (Jane Wells), but in the later chapters describing Ann Veronica's involvement with the suffragette campaign, her imprisonment, and her subsequent flight abroad with Capes, he is clearly writing of Amber as he knew and loved her during these traumatic years.

In a lecture on 'The Scope of the Novel' given to the Times Book Club in 1911[18] Wells declared:

'What is the good of pretending to write about love, and the loyalties and treacheries and quarrels of men and women, if one must not glance at those varieties of physical temperament and organic quality, those deeply passionate needs and distresses from which half the storms of human life are brewed? We mean to deal with all these things, and it will need very much more than the disapproval of provincial librarians, the hostility of a few influential people in London, the scurrility of one paper, and the deep and obstinate silences of another, to stop the incoming tide of aggressive novel-writing.

Ann Veronica, which carries the sub-title 'A Modern Love Story', merits a place in literary history as the first truly modern novel—that is to say, the first in which the heroine openly and cheerfully defies the moral conventions of the day. To the Edwardian reading public it must have come as a revelation.

In the utter frankness regarding emotional discords revealed in both *Tono-Bungay* and *Ann Veronica* Wells was certainly breaking new ground. 'These are the sort of things that are not supposed to happen,' observes Capes apropos incompatibility in married love. 'They leave them out of novels—these incompatibilities. Young people ignore them until they find themselves up against them.' *Ann Veronica* also became a *cause célèbre* because of the spirited determination of the heroine to choose her own partner and to marry only for love. On this score the book would be considered quite unexceptional today, but for readers of her time and class her behaviour was still highly controversial. The book sparked off an immense controversy and was widely read, particularly among the young. Attempts were made to ostracize Wells from social life, but most of his friends, including Bernard Shaw and G. K. Chesterton, spoke vigorously in his defence. The nearest parallel in our own time to the public debate sparked off by the book is that surrounding the publication of *Lady Chatterley's Lover* in 1960. But there are no passages in *Ann Veronica* which could be described as pornographic, or even erotic. What caused so much commotion was the behaviour of the lively and vivacious heroine: she defied the accepted moral code, and did so with the author's obvious approval. It was this which so many critics found unforgivable.

THE HISTORY OF MR. POLLY

Today, seventy years after its original publication, *The History of Mr. Polly* has achieved the status of a classic. It has taken its place alongside *The Pickwick Papers* and *The Diary of a Nobody* as one of those quintessential works which serve to delineate the English character. It is also universally accepted as being among the handful of novels which are destined to carry its author's name forward to posterity, and many critics regard it as Wells's finest single work.

It was begun 'in a mood in which, Wells has remarked, he felt he could go on writing for ever',[19] and indeed it is almost unique among his vast literary output in being written throughout in one consistent form. Time and again in his fiction he was working on several stories simultaneously, or would work for long periods on a novel only to set it aside in favour of some other book or piece of journalism. This inevitably gives some of his novels a disjointed, uneven effect. *Mr. Polly*, however, is written throughout in a sustained mood of happiness which gives the entire work a warm, kindly radiance and which weaves the novel into a coherent, artistic whole. Superficially it is a far less autobiographical work than *Love and Mr. Lewisham* or *Tono-Bungay*—the most overtly autobiographical episodes are the reminiscences of the drapery emporium at Port Burdock (Southsea) in the opening chapter, and of his father (Chapter 4, §1)—yet it remains characteristically Wellsian in concept and plot, and embodies some of his most fundamental themes and preoccupations.

Wells shared with a number of other radical writers, most

notably George Orwell, a nostalgia for England's rural past, a half-concealed affection for the ordered, pastoral, unchanging world he had glimpsed as a child in the Kentish countryside and which was now, with the advent of the motor car and urbanisation, rapidly disappearing. This yearning for a harmonious rural order forms an extremely interesting element in his makeup which becomes evident at numerous points in his work. There is, for example, the unaffected delight in the countryside manifested in such essays as 'Bleak March in Epping Forest' and 'The Amateur Nature Lover'; the careful description of the English village scene in such works as *The Wheels of Chance, Love and Mr. Lewisham* and *The Invisible Man*; and the nostalgia for the rural tranquillity of Up Park in the opening chapters of *Tono-Bungay* and *The Passionate Friends*.

Even in his sociological writings the affection for unspoilt pastoral scenes reveals itself:

> There will be many footpaths in Utopia. There will be pleasant ways over the scented needles of the mountain pinewoods, primrose-strewn tracks amidst the budding thickets of the lower country, paths running beside rushing streams, paths across the wide spaces of the corn land, and, above all, paths through the flowery garden spaces amidst which the houses in the towns will stand.[20]

The truth is that Wells never wholly resolved the conflict within his own temperament between classical and romantic elements, and *The History of Mr. Polly* is, arguably at least, a sustained essay in romanticism. In its pages he permitted his love of nature free rein, and in numerous scenes in the novel—in the wanderings of the 'three P's' through the countryside behind Port Burdock, in Mr. Polly's wanderings as a tramp and, above all, in the finding of the ultimate haven of the Potwell Inn—there are unmistakable indications of his deep feeling for rural England. There are passages which recall Gissing's *The Private Papers of Henry Ryecroft* in their sensitive description of landscape and season. Indeed, there can be no doubt that in creating the character of Alfred Polly he was giving imaginative expression to emotions and attitudes fundamental to his innermost being. Whatever else it is, *Mr. Polly* is a work of utter sincerity.

A second major theme discernible in the novel is that of disentanglement. Again and again in his private life Wells had succeeded in disengaging himself from situations which became unpleasant or intolerable—from the drapers' shops at Windsor and Southsea, from the Holt Academy, and from his unhappy first marriage. All his life he was impressed by the significant part played by chance and hazard, by the way in which one's whole experience could be transformed by a single encounter. As George Ponderevo reflects in *Tono-Bungay*, 'one gets hit by some unusual transverse force. . . '. This again is a continually recurring theme in his fiction, and examples could be multiplied, ranging from the eating of the fungus in 'The Purple Pileous' to the sudden inheritance in 'A Catastrophe', from the unexpected legacy in *Kipps* to the flight from Chatham in *Tono-Bungay*. Mr. Polly's humdrum existence is irrevocably changed by two events: first, the death of his father and second, his decision to set fire to the shop and leave his wife Miriam. Wells draws no moral from either event but the reader is left in no doubt of his conviction that ultimately each individual is responsible for his own actions and has the power to transform his life immeasurably for good or ill.

As a character Polly appears to have been based not so much on Wells in his own person as on his elder brother, Frank, yet it is not difficult to recognise in *The History of Mr. Polly* a fantasia or speculation on what might have happened to himself had he failed to escape from the world of drapery. In this sense the novel is a kind of wish fulfilment. After a series of picaresque adventures Mr. Polly finds his ultimate retreat in the Potwell Inn. Here, at last, after surviving the miseries of 'cribs' and fifteen years as a bankrupt shopkeeper he finds accomplishment and peace. The book can be viewed simply as a comic novel in the vein of *Three Men in a Boat* or as a profoundly serious allegory about human happiness. Either view has much to commend it. However one chooses to interpret the book—whether as a light-hearted extravaganza, a holiday from his main work, or as belonging in the mainstream of his central concerns about man—there is no reason to begrudge its popularity. *Mr. Polly* is regarded as a classic precisely because of those timeless qualities by which literature should be judged. As Geoffrey West rightly observed,[21] '*Mr. Polly* is what it is because it is neither what Wells thought nor what he believed, but what he *knew*.'

THE NEW MACHIAVELLI

The New Machiavelli was written in the years 1908–9 but not published until January 1911. Wells intended it to be 'a sort of companion piece to *Tono-Bungay*, as large and outspoken, but this time it is a picture of political life'.[22] The comparison with *Tono-Bungay* clearly demonstrates that in planning *The New Machia-*

velli Wells envisaged an ambitious novel which would offer a commentary upon political life in Edwardian England.

The novel contains strong elements of autobiography. The second chapter, 'Bromstead and my Father', should be closely studied by any reader who is anxious to learn more of Wells's family background and childhood at Bromley, for in these pages will be found a careful description of his nascent world. The Bromley of the 1870s comes vividly to life in his account of the building bricks which formed the substance of many of his childhood games (and which later bore fruit in *Floor Games* and *Little Wars*); of his early reading; and of the rapid urbanisation which formed the dominant background of his youth. There is a particularly striking passage (Book One, Chapter 2, §5) which summarises the growth of Bromley between 1750 and 1900 and conveys unmistakably the impact of planless despoliation upon the sensitive mind of a child.

Chapters Two and Three contain carefully drawn portraits of Wells's mother and father (which should be compared with similar accounts in *Tono-Bungay* and *The Dream*). These are unforgettable in their compassion and understanding, and contain some of his finest writing. The description of the death of Remington's father whilst pruning a grape-vine is a circumstantial account of an actual event (1877) in which Joseph Wells sustained a broken leg in identical circumstances. These opening chapters, with their sympathetic insight into his parents' mode of life and their regret at the passing of the old rural order, provide further evidence of Wells's ambivalent attitude towards change and his nostalgia for the ordered, harmonious life of the pre-industrial past. The decline of the Ravensbourne must have been one of the cardinal events of his boyhood, for it is referred to not only in *The New Machiavelli* (as 'the Ravensbrook'), but also in *The War in the Air* (as 'the Otterbourne'), in *Experiment in Autobiography* (p. 194), and in a newspaper article, 'The Degeneration of the Ravensbourne' (*Pall Mall Gazette*, 12 July 1894). References to Bromley and the surrounding area are comparatively few in his fiction, but this should not be taken as an indication that these years made little impact on his imagination. 'Bromstead and my Father' contains abundant evidence that the experience made an indelible impression upon him and provided a reference point for his mature reflections on man in society.

Wells had been fascinated by the Potteries ever since visiting Etruria for a three-month stay in 1888. This fascination can be clearly seen in his short story 'The Cone', in the detailed descriptions of the Five Towns landscape in *In the Days of the Comet*, and in the occasional references to the district elsewhere in his fiction.[23] In *The New Machiavelli* he returned to this preoccupation in an elaborate description ('Margaret in Staffordshire') which reveals a penetrating insight into Potteries life and character. The paragraphs immediately following the sentence 'I took myself off for a series of walks, and acquired a considerable knowledge of the scenery and topography of the Potteries' cannot be far from a factual account of his impressions whilst staying with his friend William Burton at the age of twenty-one. Of special interest is the description of Remington's uncle—with his chauvinistic attitude to all foreigners, and his love of 'reet Staffordshire'—and the aptness of Wells's comment 'There are hordes of such men as he throughout all the modern industrial world ... yet it is only in Arnold Bennett's novels that I have ever found a picture of them.'

Much of *The New Machiavelli* is a detailed, if not laboured, account of the London political scene during the opening decade of the twentieth century. Since this has inevitably lost its topicality with the passage of time, the political chapters of the novel have lost much of their vitality and interest. This is compensated in part, however, by the vividness of the writing and the lively descriptions of contemporary personalities under fictitious names—most notably Sydney and Beatrice Webb [Oscar and Altiora Bailey], Charles and George Trevelyan [The Cramptons], Lord Samuel [Lewis], Balfour [Evesham], Graham Wallas [Willersley], and Alfred Harmsworth, later Lord Northcliffe [Cossington]. Nor are Wells's own political ideas as absurd as is commonly supposed. Remington's campaign for the Endowment of Motherhood achieved realisation many years later with the introduction of family allowances.

The novel has been much criticised on the grounds of the alleged priggishness of the central character, Richard Remington. Indeed, it is the first of a series of novels written during the Edwardian years which are known collectively as the Prig Novels. (The phrase appears to have been coined by Wells himself and refers to the group of related works—*The New Machiavelli, Marriage, The Passionate Friends, The Wife of Sir Isaac Harman* and *The Research Magnificent*—in which the quest for 'a purpose in life' is a predominant element.) Certainly the charge of priggishness is not without substance. There is, too, a more insidious aspect of Remington's make-up in that, almost alone of Wells's fictional characters, he bears unmistakable traces of solipsism. Time and time again one has the impression that Remington believes that he and he alone possesses a monopoly of truth. It can be argued that self-righteousness—or, at least, self-pity—is always present to some degree in novels written in the first person, yet this quality is redeemed in Wells's case by a rich and abundant sense of humour. In the Prig Novels, however, humour is markedly deficient, and in the present case it disappears almost completely after the 'Bromstead' chapter.

In seeking to understand *The New Machiavelli* and to form an assessment of it by comparison with its contemporaries it has to be borne in mind that it was written at a time of acute emotional stress. Wells had achieved some notoriety through the outspokenness of *Ann Veronica* and the fact that his private life offended against the prevailing moral codes. He was caught up in a tempestuous love affair which was causing him happiness and distress in equal measure and diverting his energies from the literary and sociological purposes to which he was dedicated. He was also at this time seeking to clarify his approach to the novel (witness his lecture 'The Contemporary Novel', delivered to the Times Book Club in May 1911, and his correspondence with Henry James) and his views on a wide range of political issues.

All these concerns came to a head in *The New Machiavelli*. In telling the story of Remington and his love for Isabel Rivers Wells was presenting an impassioned account of his friendship and love for Amber Reeves, and in analysing his political experiences he was musing over his own encounters with the Fabians and their associates during the previous decade. In its pages Wells is essentially thinking aloud, and for these reasons the book is one of his most revealing. Together with *Boon* it affords an intriguing glimpse into his mental and emotional attitudes during the years 1900–14.

The novel was submitted to the publishers during the spring and summer of 1910, but Frederick Macmillan declined to publish it on the grounds of its strong sexual element (and also, presumably, because he feared legal action from the 'originals' of the characters only too clearly recognisable behind Wells's fictionalisations). Eventually, after a lengthy exchange of correspondence—recorded in detail in Lovat Dickson's admirable *H. G. Wells: His Turbulent Life and Times*—Macmillan agreed to find an alternative publisher, and the book finally appeared under the imprint of John Lane in January of the following year. It is important to bear in mind, therefore, that the book was written before *The History of Mr. Polly*—not *after*, as would appear from the order of publication.

Reflecting on the novel years afterwards Wells realised that it was a compensatory production.... *The New Machiavelli* is quite plainly once more the release of the fugitive urgency, a release completed in imagination if not in fact. I realise now (and the queer thing is that I do realise only now) that the idea of going off somewhere—to Italy in the story—out of the tangle of Fabian disputes, tiresomely half-relevant politics and the routines of literary life, very nearly overwhelmed me in my own proper person, and the story of Remington and Margaret and Isabel is essentially a dramatised wish. I relieved my tension vicariously as Remington.[24]

MARRIAGE

In *Marriage*, written at Pont-de-l'Arche in 1911 and published in 1912, Wells returned to the theme of the successful man who attempts to extricate himself from a marriage which has become unsatisfying. But whereas *Ann Veronica* and *The New Machiavelli* had been severely criticised on the grounds of their overt sexuality and their blatant assault on the prevailing moral code, *Marriage* was warmly welcomed by critics for its apparent innocuousness. It clearly marked a return to the solid, novelistic manner of *Kipps* and book reviewers were almost unanimous in their praise. *T.P.'s Weekly* welcomed it as 'a thrilling and inspiring book, and one that can be placed on a puritan's family bookshelf', while the *Spectator* (which had savaged *Ann Veronica*) proclaimed: 'Mr. Wells has put all his cleverness into this long story of an engagement and marriage between two attractive and, we may add, perfectly moral young people.' Wells himself acknowledged the sharp difference in tone between *Marriage* and its predecessors, for during the protracted correspondence with Sir Frederick Macmillan over the publication of *The New Machiavelli* he had written: 'The next book I'm planning won't cause any of this trouble—I'm passing out of a necessary phase in handling my medium. Sex *must* be handled, and few writers escape the gawky phase.' As if in earnest of his good intentions he dedicated the book to his old friend Arnold Bennett, whose painstakingly written novels he greatly admired.

The heroine, Marjorie Pope, is one of Wells's most attractive characters and the opening chapters, which place her in the setting of the Pope ménage, are written with a care and sobriety he rarely excelled. The book reveals an acute understanding of middle-class marriage problems, and Trafford's gradual realisation of the tem-

peramental differences between Marjorie and himself (see especially Chapter Three, §2) is both perceptive and accomplished.
Whereas in *Tono-Bungay* and *The New Machiavelli* the narrator's
marriage had collapsed through sexual incompatibility, the marriage between Marjorie and Trafford passed through a lengthy
process of disillusionment, during which each becomes increasingly aware of the other's shortcomings. There grew up in Trafford
'a vast hinterland of thoughts and feelings, an accumulation of
unspoken and largely of unformulated things in which his wife
had no share. And it was in that hinterland that his essential self
had its abiding place.' At length, tired and disillusioned with
conventional London society, both agree to leave England for
Labrador, where—untrammelled by distractions and irrele-
vancies—they propose to think out afresh their respective
attitudes to life.

Although told in the third person—Henry James had repeatedly
warned Wells against first person narration, with its consequent
temptations to excessive authorial comment—this did not prevent
him from introducing a considerable degree of sociological comment into the novel. Interspersed with the narrative are strictures
against Movements, reflections on authority and organisation,
social commentary upon the role of women in society, on the
suffragette campaign, on contemporary politics, on sport and
travel as symptoms of restlessness, and so on. James took him to
task for his increasing tendency towards discursiveness, whilst
Edmund Gosse complained of the hardness and rhetorical quality
of the novel. The tendency to *preach* at the reader is uncomfortably
evident, in spite of much good characterisation and skilful
dialogue. In retrospect it is difficult to deny the charge of priggishness which some critics—including Wells himself—have levelled
at *Marriage* and the other novels written at about this time. The
self-righteousness of Trafford becomes embarrassingly obtrusive
as the story proceeds and much of his conversation assumes a
curious wooden quality. The narrative is written with intellectual
conviction but lacks the emotional force necessary to give it life.

Marriage is primarily of interest today for the further evidence it
offers of Wells's preoccupation with the theme of disentanglement.
Trafford is an entirely typical central figure in that, having established for himself a position of some responsibility, he wishes to
escape from what he regards as a constricting and inadequate
environment. Marjorie is also infected with the desire to withdraw
from London with all its irksome routines, and to seek a completely
different life elsewhere. 'A great desire came upon Marjorie to go

away with Trafford for a time, out of their everyday life into strange and cool and spacious surroundings. . . . It was the first invasion of their lives by this conception, a conception that was never afterwards to leave them altogether, of retreat and reconstruction.' There can be no doubt that for Wells this idea of removing oneself from the routines and conventions of life and making a fresh beginning in totally different surroundings had a strong appeal. This mood of restlessness came upon him at frequent intervals, and is evident, for example, in his decision to sell Spade House and move to Hampstead (1909) and in his move to Provence (1924). In this respect Trafford shares with Richard Remington, George Ponderevo and Stephen Stratton a dissatisfaction with his world which was characteristic of Wells's personality. This 'flight impulse' is a continually recurring element throughout his fiction. Critics of his work ascribe it to a basic instability in his makeup, a persistent refusal to face up to the world as it is. Whilst there is unquestionably some substance in this view it is at least arguable that Wells was genuinely obsessed by a vision of an alternative world. In the short stories 'The Door in the Wall' and 'Mr. Skelmersdale in Fairyland', in the flight of Remington and Ponderevo, in Mr. Polly's escape from a bankrupt draper's shop to a life of happiness, and now in the journey of the Traffords to Labrador, there are renewed instances of the idea of escape and renewal. Closely linked to this recurring motif is his insistence that each individual is responsible for his own destiny, that the tenor of one's life is within one's own control, and that if a person is dissatisfied with life as it is then it is within his own power to change it. Wells had lived his private life fully in accordance with these convictions and had no hesitation in commending this philosophy to his readers. But whereas Remington and his mistress Isabel had left England for Italy in the full knowledge that they were facing exile and social disgrace, Marjorie and Trafford know that their journey abroad is temporary in duration and that eventually they will return to play their full part in affairs.

The novel is unlikely to 'live', for despite moments of enduring interest—the birth of Marjorie's daughter (Chapter Two, §7), the description of the Pope household, and the sojourn in Labrador—much of the social comment is inevitably dated. *Marriage* is perhaps the most carefully written of the Prig Novels and yet is possibly the least likely to survive the vagaries of literary fashion. In *The New Machiavelli* Wells succeeded in fusing together the intellectual and emotional elements in his nature in a coherent, though imperfect, work of art. The attempt to repeat this formula from purely cerebral ingredients was less convincing, but a more promising experiment was to follow.

THE PASSIONATE FRIENDS

The Passionate Friends is cast in the form of the autobiography of a middle-aged man, Stephen Stratton, ostensibly written for his son to read in adult life. The device is of considerable interest in the light of Wells's earlier comment to Henry James: 'The only artistic "first person" is the onlooker speculative "first person", and God helping me, this [*The New Machiavelli*] shall be the last of my gushing Hari-Karis.' In April 1911 he gave James the firm impression that he intended to write no more autobiographical novels written in the first person, yet barely a year later we find him doing so on an even broader canvas. Where *The Passionate Friends* differs from its predecessors is precisely in the confessional form Wells chose to adopt, a device which permitted him to lay bare his innermost thoughts to the reader.

This is evident, for example, in the lyrical description of Burnmore Park in the opening pages of the novel, a clear reminiscence of happy childhood days at Up Park (Chapter Two, §1) which it is instructive to compare with similar passages in the 'Bladesover' chapter of *Tono-Bungay*. These passages provide abundant evidence of his nostalgia for the rural peace of his boyhood, and of his romantic yearning for an emotional communion with nature. 'Did I really go into those woods and waving green places as one keeps a tryst, expectant of a fellowship more free and delicate and delightful than any I knew? Did I know in those days of nymphs and dryads and fauns and all those happy soulless beings with which the desire of man's heart has animated the wilderness?' Wells is here committing to paper his most secret imaginative reveries, and the pages describing the Park and its delightful freedoms possess a poetic intensity one associates with the early romances rather than the novels of his middle period.

The substance of the story is concerned with Stratton's love for Lady Mary Christian, later Lady Mary Justin, one of his most attractive and carefully drawn heroines. Her character and temperament are strongly reminiscent of Beatrice Normandy in *Tono-Bungay*, and reveal once again Wells's fictional predilection for aristocratic women. As with Beatrice, the narrator first meets and falls in love with Mary as a child, but as the novel proceeds his feelings towards her intensify into a passionate longing. (There are echoes of *Tono-Bungay* again in the midnight assignation between Stratton and Mary, a scene repeated almost exactly between George Pondervo and Beatrice.[25]) Both she and Rachel More, whom Stratton eventually marries, are drawn with care and tenderness. Both contrive to be more convincing characters than Margaret Reming-ton, for they are described with a frankness and honesty which can only be drawn from real life. Commenting on his emotional at-titude to the mature Lady Mary, Stratton muses: 'Here beside me, veiled from me only by our transient embarrassment and the tarnish of separation and silences, was the one person who had ever broken down the crust of shy insincerity which is so incurably my characteristic and talked intimately of the inmost things of life to me.' Here again we find Wells, through his alter ego, confiding to the reader fundamental truths concerning his own personality. In confessing that his most incurable characteristic was a 'crust of shy insincerity' he was drawing attention to an aspect of his makeup which few observers have commented upon.[26] The phrase 'the one person who had ... talked intimately of the inmost things of life to me' is also significant in the light of his own comment, frequently expressed, that life had meaning only in relation to women, and that he could not adequately convey his appreciation for the intellectual and emotional companionship his friendships with women had brought.

In retrospect it can be seen that *Ann Veronica* was the fore-runner of a series of discussion novels in which the code governing sexual relationships is assailed from a number of differing points of view, in each case using a particular individual or group of indi-viduals as the vehicle of criticism. These are *The New Machiavelli*, *Marriage*, *The Passionate Friends*, *The Wife of Sir Isaac Harman* and *The Research Magnificent*. Together they constitute some of his most serious and painstaking work. The heroes are not especial-ly impressive—most of them are too priggish and dignified to be even lifelike—but the heroines are alive and vital. Re-reading them today, the most memorable sections are the tempestuous love stories which form the kernel. Wells was, in effect, posing a number of individual problems and demonstrating that in each instance the moral code was either unworkable or irrelevant to its solution. He was arguing that there was, in fact, no solution within the framework of accepted morality.

In both *The New Machiavelli* and *The Passionate Friends* he argued that in a world of widening opportunities for friendship and intercourse between the sexes the uneasy compromise which permits intellectual intimacy but forbids physical lovemaking was quite intolerable. 'On the basis of the accepted code the jealous people are right, and the liberal-minded ones are playing with fire. If people are not to love, then they must be kept apart. If they are not to be kept apart, then we must prepare for an unprecedented toleration of lovers.'

Social life was riddled with pretences and secret relationships. It was tacitly assumed that each woman would have one sole man intimate, and vice versa, yet the reality was far more complex than this simple generalisation. Friendship between the sexes was deemed proper provided it did not go beyond a certain unstated point. To transgress this point, if one was already committed in the labyrinth of sex, was to court disaster. The convention encouraged the unscrupulous and clandestine, whilst honest open passion was penalised. Wells was returning to his plea that laws and customs assumed all individuals to be identical in needs and outlook, that the code was far too inflexible and that those persons who chose to live outside its framework should not be ostracized. The novel is an arraignment of jealousy and persecution: a plea for free and intimate friendships between the sexes without incurring the stigma of opprobium.

Much of the latter part of the novel is concerned with Stratton's vision of an 'open conspiracy' (the phrase, which Wells used for the title of a book in 1928, first occurs in *The Passionate Friends*) to bring about the World State. He and an American friend, Gidding, set up an ambitious publishing and printing enterprise which seeks to disseminate knowledge and enlightenment throughout the world. The ideas adumbrated in these chapters were developed and refined in many later works, and may be regarded as the first crude draft of themes which were to become the dominant obsession of Wells's life from 1914 onwards. The First World War, which lay only one year ahead when this novel was published, gave an enormous stimulus to his idea of world unification, but already the main lines of his thought were clear. What is so remarkable is his consistency over a period of thirty years—longer, indeed, for the broad shape was already evident in *Anticipations*, published in 1900—in advocating cosmopolitan ideas long before the need for planetary institutions was widely accepted.

Towards the end of the book occurs one of the most remarkable and self-revelatory passages in the entire corpus of Wells's fiction. This is the sequence of paragraphs in Chapter Eleven beginning with the words 'We idealists are not jolly people, not honest simple people. . . .' and concluding with the words ' . . . a sense of life as of an abyssmal flood, full of cruelty, densely futile, blackly aimless, penetrates my defences'. This passage provides yet further evidence of the pessimism which throughout his life formed an integral part of his most fundamental convictions, and which never deserted him, even when superficially in euphoric mood. The admission that despair was always near to him is a salutary reminder of the complexity of his persona; outwardly ebullient, he could be—like Elgar—intensely withdrawn and, in certain moods, profoundly pessimistic about his fellow men.

What strikes the reader forcibly on re-appraising the novel today is its excessive solemnity. As with all the Prig Novels, Wells's sense of humour seems to have deserted him. The sincerity and earnestness of the narrator are unrelieved by any touches of the humour which infuses so many of his novels with delight. But of his integrity of purpose there can be no doubt. One reviewer—Ward Clark in *Bookman* (January 1914)—went so far as to say: 'Make no mistake, this is real autobiography, not in the mere literal sense, but in the sense that it comes straight at first hand from the man's own experience and thought. The strongest impression that remains of *The Passionate Friends* is of the author's intellectual honesty.' Both Henry James and Arnold Bennett wrote to Wells to say how much they admired the book, and although Wells made it clear in his replies that he was dissatisfied with it,[27] it nevertheless remains an important landmark in his work. It was the first novel in which he sketched out his developing ideas of an educational renaissance and a 'world encyclopaedia' to unify mankind; one of his frankest works of fiction in that it lays bare his innermost soul to the readers' scrutiny; and his last experiment in the autobiographical form before the much more ambitious *World of William Clissold* thirteen years later.

THE WIFE OF SIR ISAAC HARMAN

When Arnold Bennett wrote to Wells praising in fulsome terms *The Passionate Friends*, Wells replied: 'I'm glad you like the book, which I mistrust myself as the end of a phase. The next will be quite different and longer.' In fact *The Wife of Sir Isaac Harman*, published in October 1914, differs from *The Passionate Friends* more in tone than in substance, for both novels take as their predominant theme the problem of sexual jealousy.

Where the new book differs from the other novels of this period is

in the strong element of humorous observation which characterises
the story of Lady Harman. The other Prig Novels had been much
criticised on the grounds of their solemnity and general lack of
vitality: Rebecca West, reviewing *Marriage* in *Freewoman* (September 1912) accused Wells of being 'the Old Maid among novelists' and took him to task for a sex obsession that was 'the reaction
towards the flesh of a mind too long absorbed in airships and
colloids'. There is abundant evidence from the subsequent correspondence between the two writers that Rebecca West took the
liveliest interest in his fiction, and some indications that under the
stimulus of her criticisms he returned to the liveliness and humour
which had earlier typified his writing. Certainly Lady Harman is a
more sympathetically presented heroine than Lady Mary Christian, and one with whom many more readers could identify.
Moreover the novel is peopled with living characters: Mr. Brumley
and Lady Beach-Mandarin are memorable precisely because they
are solid, believable creations with personalities of their own.

The humour which is notably absent from *The Passionate
Friends* now returned in generous measure. With infectious delight Wells describes Sir Isaac hiding in the mushroom shed from
Lady Beach-Mandarin; Mr. Blapton making a brave fight to save his
epaulettes at the party reception; and a host of minor characters and
incidents drawn with manifest relish. But alongside this element
there is an atmosphere of discontent. Underlying the novel is the
mood of claustrophobia and dissatisfaction which affected Wells
increasingly in the years immediately preceding the First World
War. An undercurrent of restlessness is apparent throughout, and
there are again intimations of a theme he returned to many times in
his later novels: the problem of surplus energies and the increasing
'secondariness' of women. As early as 1912 he was fully alive to the
fact that the growing economic independence of women, the trend
towards smaller families and other social factors, would lead to a
situation in which—at least in the independent and wealthier
classes—the responsible part of a woman's life would no longer
engage all her energies and mental powers. A great apparatus of
travel and social routines had arisen in order to consume these
surplus energies and channel them in aimless amusements and
harmless ends.

The Wife of Sir Isaac Harman and *The Research Magnificent*
complete the cycle of discussion novels written in the years
1910–14. Both novels are preoccupied with the problem of sexual
jealousy; both are characterised by a mood of boredom and discontent. Lady Harman, in particular, is the personification of the truth

that wealth and security without emotional happiness leads to frustration and a quest for imaginative release.

Isaac Harman is significant in a wider sense in that it is a picture of a society in a seething state of unrest. Geoffrey West said of Wells that he was in these years 'frankly at odds with his social environment'. Nowhere is the mood more clearly betrayed than in the descriptions of Lady Harman's state of mind, and in her realisation that each individual is responsible for his or her own life and actions:

> All children, I suppose, begin by taking for granted the rightness of things in general, the soundness of accepted standards, and many people are at least so happy that they never really grow out of this assumption. They go to the grave with an unbroken confidence that somewhere behind all the immediate injustices and disorders of life, behind the antics of politics, the rigidities of institutions, the pressure of custom and the vagaries of law, there is wisdom and purpose and adequate provision, they never lose that faith in the human household they acquired amongst the directed securities of home. But for more of us and more there comes a dissolution of these assurances; there comes illumination as the day comes into a candle-lit uncurtained room. The warm lights that once rounded off our world so completely are betrayed for what they are, smoky and guttering candles. Beyond what once seemed a casket of dutiful security is now a limitless and indifferent universe. Ours is a wisdom or there is no wisdom; ours is the decision or there is no decision. That burden is upon each of us in the measure of our capacity. The talent has been given us and we may not bury it.

This attitude of mind, too familiar perhaps in our own existentialist age, was still novel and terrifying in 1914. Wells was perceptive enough to realise that society was in a phase of questioning and flux: that morality, law and conduct would from now onwards be challenged, and that the rigidity of his childhood world could never return.

BEALBY

Bealby: A Holiday was written early in 1914 and published as a book in the following year. The subtitle is significant, for the novel marks a respite from the preoccupation with sexual and social problems which dominated Wells's fiction during these years and a return to the lighthearted manner of *Mr. Polly*.

It is an entirely characteristic piece of writing in that it possesses in abundance that love of the open air, that affection for the English countryside, which was so strong a trait in Wells. His biographer Geoffrey West records: 'Walking and cycling were favourite forms of exercise, and often he would take his work and wander for days about the Kentish countryside on foot or wheel, sleeping at inns and farms.' The same mood pervades *The History of Mr. Polly*. Polly, after escaping from the misery of his life with Miriam, 'came to country inns and sat for unmeasured hours talking of this and that to those sage carters who rest for ever in the taps of country inns, while the big, sleek, brass-jingling horses wait patiently outside with their wagons'. In the description of Bealby's encounter with the caravan party and his adventures *en route* there is ample evidence of Wells's nostalgia for rural England and his intense curiosity about ordinary people and their ways.[28] It reveals a Romanyesque affection for the life of the open road, described by George Ponderevo in these terms:

> . . . nor at the other end of the scale have I had what I should call an inside acquaintance with that dusty but attractive class of people who go about on the high roads drunk but *en famille* (so redeeming the minor lapse), in the summertime, with a perambulator, lavender to sell, sun-brown children, a smell, and ambiguous bundles that fire the imagination.

H. G. Savage, Wells's valet and general handyman at Spade House, told the present writer that Wells was fascinated by gypsies and their ways and never lost an opportunity of mixing and talking with them.

The mood of the novel is, however, quite different from that of its predecessors. In the Preface to the Atlantic Edition Wells acknowledged that *Bealby* 'betrays a writer intensely irritated by his world . . . All the characters are pelted with derision and misfortune.' Whilst this may not be true of the central character, Arthur Bealby, it applies in large measure to some of the minor figures—more especially to William Bridget, the dirty, unscrupulous tramp who forces Bealby to take part in a burglary. Bridget is all the world away from the mood of the earlier novels: one has only to compare him with the kindly Philosophical Tramp in *The Wonderful Visit* to appreciate the vast difference in conception and spirit. Both are aware of the darker aspects of life, but whereas the Philosophical Tramp views his world with humorous detachment Bridget's attitude is one of unmitigated selfishness. The difference cannot be explained simply by the twenty-year gap between the two novels: it is rather a shift of emphasis—some would say a loss of innocence—symptomatic of Wells's mood of irritation. Two years earlier, in *The Passionate Friends*, he had confessed that 'I go valiantly for the most part, I know, but despair is always near to me . . . a sense of life as of an abyssmal flood, full of cruelty, densely futile, blackly aimless, penetrates my defences.' *Bealby*, for all its apparent air of sunny happiness, betrays something of this same mood of discontent.

It is also a novel which, in common with *Mr. Polly*, has disentanglement as its theme. Bealby, rebelling against life below stairs, escapes from Shonts and only returns after a series of picaresque adventures and a long chase through the English country-side—including a memorable pursuit through the village of Crayminster. It is not too fanciful to recognise in this scenario symptoms of that restlessness, that claustrophobia, which very nearly overwhelmed its author during these years and to which he frequently gave fictional expression. *Bealby* is, in fact, as its subtitle suggests, a holiday: an escape from sociological problems and a diversion into the genre of farcical romance. It is also in a real sense a return to characteristic themes: flight from an uncongenial environment, affection for pastoral England, and transitory despair at the folly of his fellow men.

THE RESEARCH MAGNIFICENT

In 1914 Wells wrote in the preface to a new edition of *Anticipations*: 'That conception of an open conspiracy . . . is always with me . . . it forms the substance of the longest novel I have ever written—that is, if ever the war will let me get it written—the novel I am still writing.' This was *The Research Magnificent*, an elaborately planned and written work begun late in 1913 and completed at the beginning of 1915. The novel is principally of interest today for the insight it affords into Wells's philosophical attitudes on the eve of the First World War and, secondly, for its portrait of Rebecca West as Amanda Morris.

To understand the idea of an 'open conspiracy'—the idea which in one form or other dominated his thinking from 1900 onwards—it is essential to grasp that his basic concept of politics was aristocratic rather than democratic. His alter ego William Clissold expressed his basic position in these terms:

> But when I think of revolution I have in mind something quite different from the idea of a Revolutionary that has dominated the human imagination since those violent days in Paris a hundred and thirty odd years ago. . . . I look, indeed, for something antagonistic to that. I look to the growth of a minority of intelligent men and women for the real revolution before mankind. I look for a ripening elite of mature and educated minds, and I do not believe progress can be anything more than casual and insecure until that elite has become self-conscious and effective. I do not look to the mass of people for any help at all. I am thinking of an aristocratic and not a democratic revolution.

This, then, was Wells's personal philosophy, his credo, from which he did not deviate in essence during a career as novelist, journalist and public figure spanning half a century.

In *The Research Magnificent* he sought to explore one man's search for intellectual and spiritual fulfilment through the idea of world government by a natural aristocracy: 'All paths and all enquiries led him back to his conception of aristocracy, conscious, self-disciplined, devoted, self-examining yet secret, making no personal nor class pretences, as the supreme need not only of the individual but the world.' It was this basic conception, expressed in its fullest form as the Samurai of *A Modern Utopia*, which formed his central attitude of mind throughout his adult life. Critics have not been slow to assert that the concept of a voluntary nobility has undertones of priggishness, if not of elitism. Yet there can be no question of his deep sincerity in advancing these views or of the ultimate worth of the philosophy of life elaborated by Benham.

Rebecca West, whom Wells met for the first time in 1912 and with whom he was on terms of intimacy from 1913 to 1923, played an extremely important role in his life during a decade of crucial significance to his literary and intellectual career. Their love affair, alternately idyllic and tempestuous, has been fully documented elsewhere.[29] What is cardinal to the present study is the fact that Wells was deeply in love with Rebecca and that in three of his novels portrayed her in fictional guise: Amanda Morris in *The Research Magnificent*, Martin Leeds in *The Secret Places of the Heart* and Helen in *The World of William Clissold*. Of these, the first is the most sensitive since it records his impressions of her while they were still fresh and glowing in his mind. Indeed, parts of the novel were written at Hunstanton when he and Rebecca were living together under an assumed name.

Amanda, whom Benham meets whilst on a walking holiday near South Harting, is a portrait of Rebecca West as Wells first knew her as a girl of nineteen:

> She had an eyebrow like a quick stroke of a camels-hair brush, she had a glowing face, half childish imp, half woman, she had honest hazel eyes, a voice all music, a manifest decision of character. . . . Everything from her that night that even verges upon the notable has been told, and yet it sufficed, together with something in the clear, long line of her limbs, in her voice, in her general physical quality, to convince Benham that she was the freest, finest, bravest spirit that he had ever encountered.

She is indeed the most living character in the novel, and the passages describing their friendship, marriage and ultimate estrangement are the most vital elements in a work which would otherwise be notably deficient in that *energy* which is so characteristic of Wells's writing.

The Research Magnificent has never been one of the most popular of his novels, and in retrospect it is not difficult to see why. Despite moments of animation—the walking tour in Surrey and Sussex, the encounter with Amanda, the riot scenes in Johannesburg, and much of incidental interest—the work as a whole fails to satisfy. The central character is too consciously aristocratic for most readers to identify with him, and the love scenes are embarrassingly sentimental and contrived.

Most critics regard the book as the last of the Prig Novels. The ambitious scope of its design is undeniable, but its weakness lies in the excessive priggishness, almost other worldliness, of William Benham. By comparison with (say) *Tono-Bungay* or *The New Machiavelli* it lacks vitality; it is dead where they are pulsating with life. Wells is so intent on the discussion of ideas that the novel ultimately fails as a novel and becomes instead a quasi-political treatise. The failure is not in the presentation of the ideas, which are in many ways unexceptional, but in the attempt to introduce discursive sociological comment within a narrative structure appropriate to a novel. Already in *Marriage* there had been signs of an increasing unwieldiness in handling this technique, but in the story of William Benham—'the story of a man who was led into adventure by an idea'—the tendency to prolixity and complicated prose was multiplied.

But let Wells himself have the last word:

Incidentally I may complain that *The Research Magnificent* is a book deserving to be remembered and yet seems to be largely forgotten. I liked it when I re-read it and I find it remarkably up to date with my present opinions. It was blotted out by the war. But Amanda is alive and Benham has his moments of vitality.[30]

BOON

Boon, The Mind of the Race, The Wild Asses of the Devil, and *The Last Trump*—to give it its full title—was first published in 1915 although parts were written considerably earlier. Geoffrey West described it perceptively as 'his most intimate and revealing book, yet comparatively little known', and it remains true that of all his vast output *Boon* is one of the most difficult titles to obtain. It was originally published under the pseudonym Reginald Bliss (in a second edition issued in 1920 its true authorship was acknowledged) and purports to be 'a first selection from the literary remains of George Boon', prepared for publication by Bliss. The book is revealing in the sense that in its pages Wells mocks many of the literary fashions and personalities of his day, and even questions some of his own most fundamental assumptions. It was clearly written in a mood of profound discontent with the world as he saw it, and much of the work is suffused with an atmosphere of self-criticism and self-doubt. Viewed alongside his other writings of this period it provides a most interesting insight into his attitude of mind during the opening months of the First World War.

Boon has achieved some notoriety for its lampooning of Henry James, and the fourth chapter, 'Of Art, Of Literature, Of Mr. Henry James' should be closely studied by all who seek to understand the profound intellectual and temperamental antipathy which separated Wells and James. Of Wells's impressive ability to ape James's elaborate style there can be no doubt, and today—sixty years after its publication—much of *Boon* remains vital and amusing. He subsequently apologised to James for his bad manners, and in a letter dated 8 July 1915, stated 'You may take it that my sparring and punching at you is very much due to the feeling that you were 'coming over'' me, and that if I was not very careful I should find myself giving way altogether to respect. . . . But since it was printed I have regretted a hundred times that I did not express our profound and incurable difference and contrast with a better grace.' Later opinion is divided as to whether this apology was disingenuous or not, but there can be little question that in *Boon* Wells genuinely felt that he was expressing and defining the deep divisions which separated the two writers and that he deliberately chose to do this through the device of a quasi-fictional form rather than through a direct frontal attack which might have antagonised James even more.

It is in many ways regrettable that subsequent literary criticism has concentrated upon those sections of *Boon* which encapsulate the Wells–James debate and virtually ignored the remainder of the work. The book, in fact, embodies some of Wells's most fundamental preoccupations—the idea of a 'Mind of the Race'; the struggle of the 'Mind of the Race' against ignorance and war; and the necessity for constant vigilance in the face of violence and evil. Indeed, much of *Boon* is cast in the form of a debate between the ostensible author and his conscience, Wilkins, who raises objections at various stages of the discussion and thus obliges Wells to continually restate and clarify his propositions. The result is a work of unusual intimacy, as if the author is thinking aloud: the reader has a sense of participating in his innermost reflections on the fundamentals of life and literature.

No part of his philosophy was more characteristic of the man than his conception of the Mind of the Race. This conception of an underlying human memory was slow to form in his mind. It appears in embryonic form in *Anticipations* (1901) and, with much more conviction, in *First and Last Things* (1908). It colours or underlies most of his work written after 1914, most notably *Boon*, *The Undying Fire* (1919), and *The World of William Clissold* (1926). The idea, in essence, was of a racial mind, a collective memory in which all man's achievements were stored and which continued to add wisdom and thought to itself. It was a living being: an undying flow of ideas, an immortal thought process in which ideas were continually being refined and developed. With the invention of speech, writing and printing ideas could be preserved and distributed. Wisdom no longer perished with the individual. An increasing interchange between brain and brain arose and a vast expansion in man's powers of communication. Minds became less and less isolated. They interacted in an endless flow of recorded and published information.

Gradually a race memory emerged, a slow unfolding of consciousness and will, the collective human mind, a synthesis of all man's wisdom and knowledge. This common mental being of the race was greater than the individual life; it would go on into futurity long after the individual had passed away; each separate life was contributory and subordinate to it.

The racial mind, he believed, existed SEPARATELY FROM THE SUM OF INDIVIDUAL MINDS, for it included all literature, all science, all disinterested thought; it was a continuing synthesis, incorporating all recorded knowledge since man's first expression of his ideas. It would gradually become conscious of itself and strain towards knowledge and power. It flowed through all thought, all discussion, all the interplay of ideas and interpretations. The individual was incidental, episodical, a gatherer of experience for the being of mankind.

Much of *Boon* is a lengthy debate in which this concept is discussed and analysed from a number of different points of view, interspersed with critical comments from Wilkins and others who are sceptical of its validity. One of the most revealing passages occurs in Chapter Seven, 'Wilkins makes Certain Objections', in which the following interchange occurs:

> 'You mean really, Boon, that the Mind of the Race isn't a mind that *is*, it is just a mind that becomes.'
> 'That's what it's all about,' said Boon.
> 'And that is where I want to take you up,' said Wilkins. 'I want to suggest that the Mind of the Race may be just a gleam of conscious realisation that passes from darkness to darkness—'
> '*No,*' said Boon.
> 'Why not?'
> 'Because I will not have it so,' said Boon.

It is this ambivalence in Wells's mind and the shifts in mood from optimism to despair which give the book its underlying energy and inner tension. This is equally evident in a second strand of thought underlying the work, the notion of the provisional nature of literature and ideas. In 1912 James had invited Wells to serve as a member of the Academic Committee of the Royal Society of Literature. Wells declined, saying that 'I have an insurmountable objection to Literary or Artistic Academies as such, to any hierarchies, any suggestion of controls or fixed standards in these things. . . . This world of ours, I mean the world of creative and representative work we do, is I am convinced best anarchic.' James pleaded with him to change his mind, but Wells was adamant.[31] In

Boon he returned to this theme (guying the Society as 'the Royal Society for the Discouragement of Literature') and gently mocking many of his contemporaries, including not only James but also Sir William Robertson Nicoll, editor of the *British Weekly* ('Dr. Tomlinson Keyhole'), A. R. Orage, Ford Madox Ford, Hugh Walpole and Bernard Shaw. Amidst all the tomfoolery the idea of pragmatism is restated with unmistakable force: 'With the breakdown of specific boundaries the validity of the logical process beyond finite ends breaks down. We make our truth for our visible purposes as we go along, and if it does not work we make it afresh. We see life once more as gallant experiment.' (*Boon*, 7, §2)

The book concludes with two short stories, 'The Wild Asses of the Devil' and 'The Story of the Last Trump'. Each is complete in itself (the latter is included in *The Complete Short Stories*) and each contains interesting pointers to Wells's fluctuating state of mind. Both are commentaries on human fallibility and on the unending struggle between civilisation and destruction. 'The Wild Asses of the Devil', although virtually unknown, is an entirely characteristic fantasia on the theme of human stupidity, and is akin to other satirical fables including *The Island of Doctor Moreau*, *Mr. Blettsworthy on Rampole Island* and *The Croquet Player*. It is a salutary reminder of man's animal nature and the thinness of the veneer of civilisation.

The interest of these concluding chapters lies not simply in the stories themselves but in the *discussion* of them which follows, in which Wells lays bare his innermost reflections. Speculating on the meaning of the 'Wild Asses of the Devil' and on the dark forces of hatred and extremism unleashed by the world war, 'Bliss' observes:

> Boon's pessimistic outlook on the war had a profoundly depressing effect upon me. I do all in my power to believe that Wilkins is right, and that the hopelessness that darkened Boon's last days was due to the overshadowing of his mind by his illness. (9, §7)

Viewed in the context of Wells's own pessimism during the closing years of the Second World War these are among the most fascinating pages, and serve to underline the central importance of *Boon* in his intellectual pilgrimage.

Some observers have seen *Boon* as marking a watershed in Wells's career: as a symbolic farewell to literature. Others view it as little more than a vitriolic attack upon Henry James and all he stood for. Both interpretations, in my view, are too simplistic. The book should be seen rather as a confessional; as a kind of notebook in which he recorded his impressions of the literary and intellectual scene of his time, sometimes with humour, sometimes with disappointment, but always with shrewd observation. Within its pages he set down his most intimate thoughts on life and literature, frequently—since both Boon and Wilkins are clearly *alter egos* of himself—debating within his own mind on the fundamental issues of the day. It is precisely this interplay between hope and pessimism—between the optimistic, forward-looking aspect of his nature and the scepticism which was so integral to his temperament—which raises *Boon* above journalism and gives it an enduring place in his work.

MR. BRITLING SEES IT THROUGH

It is perhaps difficult for anyone who did not live through it to understand the impact the First World War exercised upon a whole generation of English men and women. The outbreak of war in August 1914 must have come as a cataclysmic shock. Europe had been at peace since 1871; to many thousands of intelligent people war seemed a remote possibility until, in the aftermath of the Sarajevo assassination, the conflagration spread beyond all hope of arresting its advance and the long Edwardian summer was at an end.

In *Mr. Britling Sees It Through*, begun in early 1915 and written almost from day to day throughout the following twelve months, Wells sought to describe the impact of the war upon a representative mind and the reaction of a sensitive intelligence to the carnage in Europe. He deliberately chose to cast the novel in a strongly autobiographical form—indeed *Mr. Britling*, of all his novels, conveys the most accurate picture of his life and mental atmosphere during and immediately preceding the war—although, significantly, it is not written in the first person. The third person narration permits a detachment which *The New Machiavelli*, for example, lacks, whilst allowing a frankness when writing about himself which is wholly salutary. For Hugh Britling is a self-portrait of the mature, successful Wells just as Lewisham is a self portrait of Wells as an impecunious student:

> His was a naturally irritable mind; this gave him point and passion; and moreover he had a certain obstinate originality and a generous disposition. So that he was always lively, sometimes

spacious, and never vile. He loved to write and talk. He talked about everything, he had ideas about everything; he could no more help having ideas about everything than a dog can resist smelling at your heels. . . . He had ideas in the utmost profusion about races and empires and social order and political institutions and gardens and automobiles and the future of India and China and aesthetics and America and the education of mankind in general.

Moreover the *setting* of the novel is totally realistic. In describing Matching's Easy and the Dower House he gives a photographic description of Little Easton and his home at Easton Glebe, while many of his neighbours and friends appear with little attempt at fictional disguise. Lady Warwick, for example, figures as Lady Homartyn, and Karl Bütow, the German tutor the Wellses had engaged for their sons, appears as Herr Heinrich. (*Mr. Britling* should be studied closely for the insight it provides into life at Easton Glebe during the years 1914–16. Further background information on Wells and his milieu at Easton Glebe is contained in *H. G. Wells and his Family* by M. M. Meyer.) This quintessentially reassuring, English background lends verisimilitude to the story and heightens the contrast between the unchanging pastoral order before the coming of the war and the transformation which affects and uproots Matching's Easy with the ending of the long peace.

At the outbreak of war Wells was almost forty-eight, an established writer—already a world figure—with a secure reputation as novelist, scientific romancer, and a writer upon sociological problems. All his life, for as long as he could remember, had been lived against a background of peace and stability in Europe. He had written about war—analysed it, as in *Anticipations*; speculated about the possibility of new weapons, as in 'The Land Ironclads'; fantasised upon the idea of world destruction, as in *The War in the Air*—but had never seriously believed in its imminence. Now at last war had come in earnest and he set out to write a novel which would be at once a personal testament of one man's response and an account of how the disaster affected the whole fabric of life in a sample English community.

That he succeeded is demonstrated by the extraordinary public response to *Mr. Britling*. (The original title bears witness to his conviction that the war would be over by 1916; the words *Sees It Through* were removed for the Atlantic Edition.[32]) The book sold extremely well both in Britain and the United States and went into numerous editions. Never before had Wells touched such a chord of shared experience; never before had he evinced such power to transmute universal suffering into an enduring literary form. There are few more moving moments in the literature of our time than the scene in which Mr. Britling receives the news of the death of his eldest son Hugh:

> This room was unendurable. He must go out. . . . Very softly he went towards the passage door, and still more softly felt his way across the landing and down the staircase. Once or twice he paused to listen. He let himself out with elaborate precautions. Across the dark he went, and suddenly his boy was all about him, playing, climbing the cedars, twisting miraculously about the lawn on a bicycle, discoursing gravely upon his future, lying on the grass, breathing very hard and drawing preposterous caricatures. Once again they walked side by side up and down—it was athwart this very spot—talking gravely but rather shyly. And here they had stood a little awkwardly, before the boy went in to say goodbye to his stepmother and go off with his father to the station. . . .

Wells's own sons Gip and Frank were in fact too young to fight—in 1914 they were aged thirteen and eleven respectively—and his account of his bereavement is wholly imaginary. But death had come to so many of his friends that he was able to write of it with an unaffected simplicity which moved and comforted thousands of his readers. Some, convinced that he had sustained a real loss, wrote him letters of sympathy. It is in this, the ability of the novel to express a generation's trauma and grief, that its real importance lies.[33]

Wells's initial response to the war, as expressed in *Mr. Britling* and numerous articles and pamphlets written at this time, was one of unassuaged patriotism. He felt that England and English values were threatened by German militarism and lent his voice enthusiastically to support for the war effort. Disillusionment quickly set in, however, and as early as March 1915 he was openly criticising the conduct of the allies and advocating the ending of private profit from the armaments industry, a world congress to control the proliferation of armaments and the creation of a world body with supranational powers to enforce peace. From 1917 onwards he devoted an increasing proportion of his energies to propagating the idea of a League of Free Nations. *Mr. Britling* inevitably reflects these changes in attitude; as the novel proceeds there is a shift in emphasis from enthusiasm in the early stages of the conflict to one of increasing disenchantment. Particularly interesting in this connection are the letters Mr. Britling receives from his son at the

Front: these reveal a profound disillusionment with militarism and the war ethos and a growing awareness of the futility of trench warfare.

Mr. Britling has a place in the literature of the First World War as expressive in its own way as Binyon's 'For the Fallen' or Rupert Brooke's 'The Soldier'. It verbalised for many thousands of English-speaking men and women the shattering experience of 1914–18 and the numbing realisation that life could never be the same again. Geoffrey West described it as 'undoubtedly the outstanding example in Wells's work of the journalist turning artist in his own despite'. Critics are agreed that it is one of the best novels of his middle period and some observers count it as among his finest pieces of writing. Much of the novel has the flavour of journalism, inevitably so in the light of the traumatic events which form its substance, yet it is journalism tinged with the quality of greatness. Indeed there could be no more apposite example of Wells's strengths and weaknesses as a creative writer than the final chapter, 'Mr. Britling writes until Sunrise'. This chapter, in which Mr. Britling composes a long letter of condolence to the bereaved father of Herr Heinrich, is by any standards an accomplished piece of writing. Viewed at one level it is simply that—a born journalist seeking to express, in rather laboured fashion, the anguish of a nation to whom death had become all too familiar. Yet viewed at another level it is something more; a hesitant and moving attempt to put into words the real sense of a new beginning which he undoubtedly felt and which he wished his readers to share. The book closes with an exquisite description of sunrise sweeping over the world of Matching's Easy, culminating in 'the sound of some early worker whetting a scythe'. The scythe—instrument of both creation and destruction, of both life and death—is a fittingly ambiguous symbol with which to end this most seminal work.

THE SOUL OF A BISHOP

During the years 1916–19 Wells passed through a phase of religious questioning which found expression in two non-fiction works, *War and the Future* and *God the Invisible King*, and three novels, *Mr. Britling Sees It Through*, *The Soul of a Bishop*, and *The Undying Fire*. During this period he professed a belief in a finite God—in contradiction to the views expressed in almost all his previous writings, and to the confusion of many of his friends and admirers. The phase appears to have been engendered by acute mental and spiritual distress in the wake of the First World War. Grieved by the universal carnage as the war intensified, frustrated in his search for a unifying political and educational creed, he turned for a time to religious and theological speculation. Although he repudiated these religious writings in both *The World of William Clissold* and *Experiment in Autobiography*,[34] admitting that 'God the Invisible King was merely the Humanity of Comte with a crown on', there can be no doubting the sincerity and strength of his convictions during this phase.

The Soul of a Bishop tells the story of Edward Scrope, Bishop of Princhester, a man brought up in a conventional religious background who becomes increasingly disenchanted with orthodox Christianity. He is possessed by a vision of the oneness of mankind:

> For that is the real thing you seek to do today, to give yourselves to God. . . . You profess a great brotherhood when you do that, a brotherhood that goes round the earth, that numbers men of every race and nation and country, that aims to bring God into all the affairs of this world and make him not only the king of your individual lives but the king—in place of all the upstarts, usurpers, accidents and absurdities who bear crowns and sceptres today—of a united mankind.

For Scrope, as for Wells, the building of the 'Kingdom of God on earth', overriding national sovereignty and national loyalties altogether, was the supreme task before man. As the Bishop becomes more and more dissatisfied with the accepted creed and formulas of worship he is increasingly dominated by the idea of a world unified and invigorated by the concept of God:

> God was coming into the life of all mankind in the likeness of a captain and a king; all the governments of men, all the leagues of men, their debts and claims and possessions, must give way to the world republic under God the king. . . . To live and serve God's kingdom on earth, to help to bring it about, to propagate the idea of it, to establish the method of it, to incorporate all that one made and all that one did into its growing reality, was the only possible life that could be lived, once that God was known.

Never a Christian in the accepted sense, nevertheless Wells had a deep respect and admiration for the teachings of Jesus of Nazareth. This is evident from the chapter on Jesus in *The Outline of History*, from his article 'Gethsemane' in *Guide to the New World*, the imaginary conversations with Jesus in *The Happy Turning*, and other writings. With hindsight it is difficult not to be moved by many passages in his work written during the tormented years of the war, as he turned for solace and inspiration to the teachings of the Nazarene. Wells does succeed in *The Soul of a Bishop* in conveying the idea of a man feeling his way towards a nobler concept of religion as a revivifying force working for world unity and an end to intolerance. The novel traces the impact of this idea, first on the Bishop himself and then on his wife Ella, his daughter Eleanor, and on Lady Sunderbund, a wealthy widow who totally misunderstands the spirit of Scrope's new enlightenment.

In retrospect it can be seen that, far from marking a new departure in his work, *The Soul of a Bishop* and its related writings belong with *Boon* as the explorations of a sensitive mind under the influence of a world holocaust. In his illuminating study *H. G. Wells: A Sketch for a Portrait*, Geoffrey West describes the book as 'Wells's least interesting, least vital, and most humourless novel, and the Bishop and Lady Sunderbund are his dreariest characterisations'. Whilst acknowledging that the novel cannot be counted among his finest work, these strictures are not, on a dispassionate assessment, wholly justified. The story is not without moments of vitality and there can be no gainsaying the force and dramatic quality of the three visions which form the substance of the story. But Wells was right to feel discontented with his religious speculations, interesting—even inspiring—though they are. In later years he came to realise that he had fallen into an intellectual cul de sac and confessed that

> In spite of the fact that it yielded Peter's dream of God Among the Cobwebs and *The Undying Fire* I wish, not so much for my own sake as for the sake of my more faithful readers, that I had never fallen into it; it confused and misled many of them and introduced a barren detour into my research for an effective direction for human affairs.[35]

JOAN AND PETER

Joan and Peter is one of the most comprehensive novels Wells ever attempted. The first edition by Cassells occupied more than 700 pages, and indeed it is only rivalled in scope by *Tono-Bungay*, *The New Machiavelli* and *The World of William Clissold*. Its publication coincided with the post-war paper shortage and this fact, together with its high price affected its sales unfavourably. Wells was deeply disappointed that *Joan and Peter* did not receive greater recognition, for it was, in his own view, of far greater merit than the highly praised *Mr. Britling Sees It Through*. The book rapidly faded into oblivion and today is almost totally forgotten.

He recorded in the preface to the Atlantic Edition that it was 'one of the most ambitious of the author's novels. It was designed to review the possibilities of a liberal education in contemporary England—contemporary in 1918 that is—and to reflect upon the types of educated youngster that the period round and about the war years was giving the British world.' Its subtitle is *The Story of an Education*, and the novel traces the educational development of Joan and Peter as samples of their generation, for 'what mankind becomes is nothing but the sum of what we have made of the Joans and Peters'.

The educational ideas which dominate the novel were profoundly influenced by his friendship with F. W. Sanderson, for many years headmaster of Oundle School, whom Wells met for the first time in 1914. In the autumn of that year his two sons went to Oundle as pupils, where they remained until the age of eighteen, and from 1914 until Sanderson's death in 1922 Wells and Sanderson were on terms of warm personal friendship and intellectual communion. Wells's debt to him can be judged from his statement, in *The Story of a Great Schoolmaster*, that 'I think him beyond question the greatest man I have ever known with any degree of intimacy.' Under his stimulating influence Wells produced some of his finest work, *Joan and Peter* (1918), *The Undying Fire* (1919), and *The Story of a Great Schoolmaster* (1924).

The book is saturated with Sanderson's conception that schools should present a vision of life; a vision of all the things that man has done, and all he has yet to do. Schooling should be reorientated in the direction of creative service and co-operation, instead of competition for selfish ends. Wells shared with Sanderson the conviction that service should replace competition as the dominant motive in schools and in the human mind. Instead of 'How can I get on in the world', he wanted the underlying theme to be 'How can I best use my talents to the common good: how can I best serve humanity?' Schoolchildren and students were all players in a limitless team. They should be imbued with the desire to do work and serve mankind, and to do their utmost to work towards world reconstruction.

The novel reflects Wells's growing conviction that the school had a distinctive, indispensable role in the modern world and that the needs of post-war reconstruction were posing unprecedented opportunities for an educational renaissance. A thorough, sound education (asserts his *alter ego*, Oswald Sydenham) should place before the child a general aim in life to which all young people can contribute. It must explain the youngster's place in space and time, setting before him a vision 'of where they are, where they are to come in, what they belong to'. It must link them up to a great human solidarity, to a sense of kinship with all the peoples of mankind, to a realisation of man's common inheritance and common destiny, and an awareness of man's planetary adventure. It should aim, moreover, to provide a spacious introduction to the complex modern world, including a knowledge of non-Western cultures, finance and currency, citizenship, and technical skills such as engineering, in addition to the ability to speak a number of foreign languages. It is axiomatic to Sydenham that 'a world whose schools are unreformed is an unreformed world', and that in education lay whatever hope there was for mankind.

The novel contains some memorable incidents and some brilliant characterisations. There is, for example, the description of Peter's first sunset; the christening of Joan and Peter at the instigation of Lady Charlotte Sydenham ('Lady Charlotte Sydenham was one of those large, ignorant, ruthless, Low-Church, wealthy, and well-born ladies who did so much to make England what it was in the days before the Great War'); the dramatic interview between Oswald Sydenham and Lady Charlotte and her humorous pretence of illness (Chapter 9, §7); and Peter's escape from the High Cross Preparatory School. The opening chapters, with their account of the childhood and adolescence of Joan and Peter, are sensitively written and contain some passages not bettered elsewhere in Wells's fiction.

Such passages as Chapter 11, §5, describing the imaginative awakening of Joan are memorable in their simplicity and beauty and demonstrate an impressive ability to write prose of enduring excellence—albeit in a novel frequently criticised as too overtly ideological.

In his autobiography[36] Wells admitted that *Joan and Peter* 'starts respectably in large novel form and becomes dialogue only towards the end. It is as shamelessly unfinished as a Gothic cathedral.' Perhaps indeed the reason why the novel has never won the recognition Wells felt it deserved is precisely because it is ill-balanced: it fails to live up to the promise of the early chapters. The final sections, recounting in detail the impact of war upon the Stublands and the efforts of Oswald Sydenham to find them an education commensurate with contemporary needs, fail to hold the reader's attention despite their obvious sincerity. Wells seems to have realised that it was not possible to accomplish his original scheme in the manner he had intended[37] and, although he evidently was at pains to write a novel on the grand scale, the intention does not quite succeed.

Joan and Peter has been consistently ignored by literary critics or dismissed as mere propaganda. Its daunting length and occasional slovenliness of structure, however, should not blind the reader to its intrinsic merits nor its importance as a watershed in Wells's intellectual development.

THE UNDYING FIRE

For many years Wells had been attracted by the idea of the 'dialogue novel'. As early as 1901 he confided to his friend Arnold Bennett that he was meditating a book which would have 'an effect of looking into a room in which a number of human beings behave and talk, with someone like Father Shandy giving a lantern entertainment with comments'. Both *A Modern Utopia* and *Boon* were experiments in the dialogue form and towards the end of his life, in *Babes in the Darkling Wood*, he was still trying over variations in the genre.

The Undying Fire is one of his most ambitious dialogue narratives. It is in essence a modernised version of the Book of Job, a prose poem which Wells greatly admired.[38] Job of Uz becomes Mr. Job Huss; Eliphaz the Temanite becomes Sir Eliphaz Burrows, manufacturer of a building substance called Temanite; Bildad becomes Mr. William Dad; and Elihu the son of Barachel is Dr. Elihu Barrack. The pattern of the book follows closely the order of the biblical narrative and the entire work is imbued with a mood of sombre realism reminiscent of *Boon*. Distressed by the horror and carnage of the First World War, uncertain in which direction to move in his search for reconstruction, Wells was clearly in a deeply divided state of mind in 1918–19 when the book was written. In retrospect it seems almost incredible that during this time he not only planned and drafted *The Outline of History* but also wrote both *The Undying Fire* and *Joan and Peter*, in addition to playing an active part in the campaign for a League of Nations. The climacteric experience of the war exercised an impact on his mind which it would be almost impossible to exaggerate. The war affected every aspect of his philosophy, changed his outlook in many significant directions and set him working in new and fruitful fields of enquiry. After 1918 he became quite openly a journalist, educational reformer, historian and apostle of world revolution. This is not to say that he ceased to write novels or works of literary merit, but it is to assert that increasingly his writing was animated by ideas. Had it not been for his experiences during the war it is quite conceivable that *The Outline of History* would not have been written. Certainly his advocacy of a scientifically planned world state would not have received such a decisive impetus. The war underlined in the most dramatic manner possible the need for a new education commensurate with the needs of the new world. In the widespread disillusionment of 1916–18 many formerly sacrosanct notions began to be questioned, and Wells was quick to seize the opportunity presented by this phase of disenchantment. *The Undying Fire* represents a fusion of three distinct elements in his thought: the final phase of his belief in a deified humanism, a conviction that henceforth history must be taught as the adventure of all mankind, and a passionate insistence that there could be no stable world peace without a universally accepted foundation of common ideas and understandings.

It is a sombre work, lit by the burning enthusiasm which flows through its pages as Job Huss, headmaster of Woldingstanton school, explains to his interlocutors the faith which activates his life:

> The reality of a school is not in buildings and numbers but in matters of the mind and soul. Woldingstanton has become a torch at which lives are set aflame. . . . I have given understanding to some thousands of boys. All those routines of teaching that had become dead we made live again there. My boys have learnt the history of mankind so that it had become their own adventure; they have learnt geography so that the world is their possession; I have had languages taught to make the past live again in their minds and to be windows upon the souls of alien peoples. Science has played its proper part; it has taken my boys into the secret places of matter and out among the nebulae. . . . .

The model for Woldingstanton was the public school at Oundle, with whose headmaster, F. W. Sanderson, Wells had been on terms of friendship for some years. Huss plans a new and greater Woldingstanton as a seed-bed of educational revival. It is to include a map corridor, depicting the growth of empires from the beginnings of civilisation and tracing the expansion of human thought and knowledge from the dawn of history. He envisages a picture gallery, a concert hall, displays of ethnological exhibits, a museum building, chapels dedicated to the races of mankind. He dreams of Woldingstanton spreading its ideas across the Atlantic, of a nucleus of outstanding, creative schools developing and reproducing their kind, of one school leading to another, of schools collaborating for the exploitation of the cinematograph and the creation of central libraries.

The book is dedicated 'to all schoolmasters and schoolmistresses and every teacher in the world'. Wells plainly set great store by it and hoped it would be widely read by educationalists, but there is little evidence that it reached a substantial readership. The first edition soon passed out of print, although some years later it was reissued in a cheap edition.

His hopes of an educational renaissance received an unexpected setback with the sudden death of Sanderson in June 1922. Sanderson died of heart failure after delivering a lecture at University College, London, at which Wells was chairman. The suddenness of his friend's passing, cut off in the full vigour of his jovial, buoyant personality, impressed Wells with a sense of irreparable loss. He was convinced that much of Sanderson's finest work was still incomplete; many of his boldest and most inspiring projects were as yet unrealised. He had counted on so much more from this energetic and innovating schoolmaster, at once practical and visionary, who had transformed Oundle from a small country grammar school into one of the most renowned public schools in England. He set to work at once to record all he could of Sanderson's ideas, for it was plain to him that 'there rested upon us an obligation to do all that we could to record and preserve and continue his magnificent beginnings'. Assisted by a small editorial committee he planned and edited an official Life, a symposium to which more than fifty people contributed, which was published anonymously in 1923 under the title *Sanderson of Oundle*. He withdrew from this undertaking before completion owing to editorial dissension—his colleagues insisting that its subject's origins as a pupil-teacher in an elementary school should be omitted—but it is clear from his own statements and from internal evidence that much of the writing is, in fact, his work. The introductory chapter contains some unmistakable Wellsian touches, and the seventh and eighth chapters, 'The Temple of Vision' and 'The Last Lecture', contain many passages identical with those in his own *Story of a Great Schoolmaster*. Characteristically, he then embarked on a personal biographical effort, which may be regarded as a minority report to the official Life. This was published in 1924 as *The Story of a Great Schoolmaster: Being a Plain Account of the Life and Ideas of Sanderson of Oundle*. This is one of the most inspiring and movingly written works he ever wrote, and he confessed later that 'it is so personal and affectionate an impression and it is so expressive of my own educational conceptions as well as his, that if I could I would incorporate it . . . in this already greatly distended autobiography'.

Apart from its dominant educational theme *The Undying Fire* is principally of interest today for the evidence it affords of Wells's pessimism at a time of world holocaust. Job Huss is obsessed by the misery and cruelty of both human and animal life (at one point in his discourse even an image from *The Island of Doctor Moreau* is introduced—that of a rabbit with its head torn off and covered with flies—as an illustration of the wanton destructiveness of nature). Job's mood fluctuates between hope in the undying fire which burns in his own heart and utter despair. There are moments when the idealism which is central to his philosophy flickers and dies: 'I talk. . . . I talk. . . . And then a desolating sense of reality blows like a destroying gust through my mind, and my little lamp of hope goes out. . . .'

Fifteen years later he wrote in his autobiography: 'In many ways I think *The Undying Fire* one of the best pieces of work I ever did. I set great store by it still.' Whilst it fails to match the promise of the introductory 'Prologue in Heaven'—a remarkable piece of writing in which the eternal struggle between God and Satan is brilliantly described—and the later pages are marred by too many passages in which Wells *lectures* the reader, the novel is memorable on many counts. It will continue to be read for the fine dream sequence during Huss's operation (reminiscent of the short story 'Under the Knife'), for the eloquence of God's final rekindling of Job's idealism, for the moving letter from the former pupil, pleading with Huss to continue as headmaster. Wells could rightly be content with such passages. Uneven though it is, the novel stands as a moving testimony to his quest for assurance during the trauma of world war.

THE SECRET PLACES OF THE HEART

The Secret Places of the Heart was written at a time when Wells was obsessed with the teaching of history and it is, in his own words, 'saturated with the historical idea'.[39] It was also written at a time (1920–1) when he was heavily overworked. He had completed the immense task of writing *The Outline of History* and was simultaneously at work on *The Salvaging of Civilisation*, a series of lectures planned for delivery in the United States, and *A Short History of the World. The Secret Places of the Heart* bears all the signs of having been prepared during a phase when Wells was tired and ill, and despite much interesting dialogue it is one of his least successful discussion novels.

In manner it belongs with *The Undying Fire* and *The Soul of a Bishop* as an experiment in the dialogue form. Its central character, Sir Richmond Hardy, is advised by his doctor to embark on a motoring holiday in the west of England and, during the tour, to unburden his worries and 'the secret places of the heart'. During 1917 Wells had been a member of the Civil Air Transport Committee, where his insistence on the imperative need for the organisation of European air transport on an international basis gave him the background for Sir Richmond Hardy's frustrating experiences as a member of the Fuel Commission.

The most successful sequences in the novel—and the most interesting to a student of Wells's personality—are those in which Sir Richmond discusses his emotional life and his craving for sexual fulfilment. 'What stands out in my memory now is this idea of a sort of woman goddess who was very lovely and kind and powerful and wonderful. That ruled my secret imaginations as a boy, but it was very much in my mind as I grew up.' Sir Richmond explains to Dr. Martineau his need for the love and companionship of women, and his lifelong desire for intellectual and emotional communion. He then confesses that, although happily married, he has a mistress, Martin Leeds. In all essentials Martin Leeds is a thinly disguised portrait of Rebecca West, a caricature which Rebecca West seems to have found amusing rather than hurtful.[40] Wells proceeds to describe his mistress and the happiness and frustration the love affair brings in its train. 'When things go well—they usually go well at the start—we are glorious companions. She is happy, she is creative, she will light up a new place with flashes of humour, with a keenness of appreciation....' But there are disappointments, trouble with servants, incompatibilities, which are tending to undermine and mar a once-fulfilling relationship. He cannot bring himself to part from her since they are held together by a web of memories and genuine affection for each other. The portrayal of Rebecca West is revealing in its alternate moods of compassion and bitterness, and should be compared with other fictionalisations in *The Research Magnifi-*

cent (Amanda Morris) and *The World of William Clissold* (Helen) in which Wells seeks to convey something of what he felt for Rebecca during the years 1913–23 and the impact she made on his life.

The final section, in which Sir Richmond meets and fails in love with a young American girl, V. V. Grammont (possibly based on Wells's friend Margaret Sanger), is skilfully handled—the actual moment in which they declare their love for one another being particularly well contrived—yet fails overall to satisfy because of its unreal dialogue and excessive philosophising. The attempt to discuss sociological and historical problems through conversation, which succeeds admirably in *Boon* and in other novels, fails in *The Secret Places* for reasons which Wells, had he been under less mental stress, must have been aware of.

Not the least interesting aspect of the novel is the insight it gives into the topography of the West Country. There are descriptions *inter alia* of Maidenhead, Silbury Hill, Avebury, Tintern and Stonehenge, interwoven with much illuminating comment on local history. The historical and descriptive commentary is fresh and stimulating, and even today cannot fail to hold the attention of the reader.

As a discussion novel *The Secret Places* must be regarded as a failure when measured against, say, *Mr. Britling Sees It Through* or *The Bulpington of Blup*. On closing the book one is left with a sense of dissatisfaction which stems partly from its lack of artistic unity and partly from the manifest irritability of its central figure. Yet the novel occupies an important place between *The Undying Fire* and *The Dream* and still merits re-reading in spite of its defects.

THE DREAM

On its publication in 1924 *The Dream* was well received, selling 15,000 copies within a month, and one reviewer hailed it as 'the richest and most generous thing that Mr. Wells has given us for years and years and years'. Despite this initial reaction the novel is today almost unknown and, along with *Joan and Peter* and other later works, seems destined to fade into total oblivion. This is in many ways regrettable, for *The Dream* is an extremely interesting experiment in literary form and marks a return to the accomplished narrative style of *Tono-Bungay* and *The New Machiavelli*. It is cast in the form of the autobiography of a typical twentieth-century man viewed from the standpoint of two thousand years hence. Sarnac, a citizen of the future, experiences a vivid dream in which he imagines himself to be Harry Mortimer Smith and, on waking, relates the dream to his companions. The substance of the novel is the story told by Sarnac, which describes the life, adventures and death of Harry Mortimer Smith spanning the years 1895–1920.

Wells was clearly in an intensely autobiographical mood at the time of writing, for *The Dream* contains reminiscences of his mother and father, of his childhood home at Bromley, of his apprenticeship at the chemist's shop, and of his Uncle Williams, who is memorably fictionalised as 'Uncle John Julip'. The description of the deaths of his father and mother (Chapter Four, §1 and Chapter Five, §11 respectively) are sensitive pieces of writing and cannot be far from a direct account of his own reactions on the death of Joseph and Sarah Wells. Joseph Wells had died in 1910 and Sarah in 1905; he was deeply moved by both events and had obviously reflected upon them extensively in the intervening years. The impact of these deaths on his mind and emotions can be judged from the fact that one or both play a significant part in *Tono-Bungay, The History of Mr. Polly, The New Machiavelli,* and *In the Days of the Comet.* In *The Dream* there are carefully written portraits of both his parents and of the home background of his early years. Especially memorable is the picture of the underground room at Atlas House in which he had spent so many hours of his childhood:

> . . . the little fire-place with the kettle on a hob, the kettle-holder and the toasting fork beside the fire-place jamb, the steel fender, the ashes, the small blotched looking-glass over the mantel, the little china figures of dogs in front of the glass, the gaslight in a frosted glass globe hanging from the ceiling and lighting the tea-things on the table.[41]

Mingled with his feelings of sorrow for the poverty of his upbringing there is an evident nostalgia for the London of his youth (Chapter Four, §3) with its streets and shops, its river embankment, its ever-changing lights and atmosphere. London never lost its fascination for Wells and for the larger part of his life he regarded it as his home.

For a brief period during January 1881 Wells was apprenticed at the chemist's shop of Samuel Evan Cowap of Church Street, Midhurst. His indentures were cancelled on his own initiative when he realised that his mother could not possibly afford the fees involved, but it is clear that although the experiment was brief in duration, lasting only one month, it made a strong impression upon him (see *Experiment in Autobiography*, 138–9), and figures prominently in *Tono-Bungay* as 'The Wimblehurst Apprenticeship'. Harry Mortimer Smith becomes a 'boy in general' at a chemist's shop in Pimlico, and here again Wells draws on his Midhurst memories—not only in describing the shop with its coloured bottles in the window and its jars with abbreviated Latin inscriptions, but also in recounting his efforts to learn Latin and the genuine appetite for learning which was stimulated by this endeavour.

All his life he had been fascinated by the meteoric career of Alfred Harmsworth, Lord Northcliffe, and had even suggested to Geoffrey Harmsworth that the latter should write the story of the family under the title *The Harmsworth Adventure*. In sketching the life and career of Edward Ponderevo in *Tono-Bungay* he appears to have been inspired, at least in part, by Northcliffe's example and to have embodied some of his 'Napoleonic' mannerisms in the novel. He returned to this theme once again in *The Dream*, and in the description of Thunderstone House, the headquarters of the publishing enterprise of Crane & Newberry, conveys vividly a picture of such organisations as Newnes, Pearson and Harmsworth as they were in the opening years of the twentieth century. Northcliffe himself, whom Wells had known for many years, is caricatured as one of the central characters, Richard Newberry. Northcliffe had died in 1922, and it may well be that with his passing Wells felt able to write about him and his enterprises in a way that would not have been possible during his lifetime.

Judged simply as a piece of storytelling *The Dream* must be regarded as a conspicuous success, certainly Wells's finest for more than a decade. The narrative is convincing, the writing is assured, the characterisation is skilful and remains in the memory long after the story has been read. The novel is rich in characters drawn with a skilful pen, including not only the narrator's parents, Martha and Mortimer Smith, but also Martha's friend Matilda Good, Harry's sister Fanny, his wife Hetty Marcus, and his uncle John Julip. These are notable creations and the fact that some, at least, were drawn from life serves to give the story a verisimilitude it might otherwise have lacked. The novel has to carry a large—some would say excessive—amount of authorial comment. But, save at the beginning of the dream, this is not obtrusive, and is more than compensated for by the pace and vigour of the narrative. Seen in retrospect it is not difficult to understand the enthusiastic

welcome *The Dream* was accorded on publication. It represents not
so much a fresh departure as a return to the strong narrative line
and vivid characterisation of his earlier novels and romances, and
as such deserves a high place within the conspectus of his work.

CHRISTINA ALBERTA'S FATHER

Originally serialised under the title 'Sargon, King of Kings', *Christina Alberta's Father* was published (by the then recently established firm of Jonathan Cape) in 1925. Wells was nearly sixty. For
ten years and more he had been preoccupied with the immense
issues arising from the war and reconstruction; he had devoted
enormous energy to the writing of *The Outline of History* and *A
Short History of the World*; he was busily engaged on all manner of
literary, political and educational projects. Now in the mid-1920s
he was affected by a phase of restlessness and discontent.

> The huge issues of the War and the Peace held my mind steady
> and kept it busy for some years,' he recorded later. 'But in 1924
> the same mood returned, [the mood of disentanglement] so
> recognisably the same, that I am surprised to realise how little I
> apprehended the connection at the time. If I did not get to writing
> in Italy in the pose of the New Machiavelli, I got to the south of
> France. It was much the same thing. It was the partial realisation
> of my own fantasy after twelve years.[42]

The novels written during these post-war years—*The Secret
Places of the Heart*, *Men Like Gods*, *The Dream* and *Christina
Alberta's Father*—each reflect in varying degrees this profound
discontent with the thing that is and a longing amounting to
nostalgia for the saner world of his dreams.

Christina Alberta's Father, the last of the group, is in essence a
fantasia on the idea of the 'dramatised self'. A continually recurring
theme in Wells's fiction was the idea of the man who imagines
himself to be something other than he is—the man who projects
himself into a different and more grandiose personality. As early as
The Wheels of Chance, Hoopdriver betrays a Walter Mitty-like
propensity to wish himself into romantic situations; Mr. Polly
betrays the same tendency on a more ambitious scale. Later he was
to write a much more elaborate novel, *The Bulpington of Blup*, in

which the psychology of the reverie personality is explored in even greater depth, but already in the character of Mr. Preemby there are clear intimations of his leading idea. Albert Edward Preemby, a humble widower who imagines himself to be a reincarnation of Sargon, King of Sumeria, is one of his most fully realised creations. In a sense he is akin to George McWhirter Fotheringay in *The Man Who Could Work Miracles*: the little man who believes he has a divine mission in life and is released from all earthly constraints in the execution of his task. Edward Ponderevo in *Tono-Bungay* is by no means free of the same delusion. This was unquestionably a theme which both repelled and fascinated Wells and it reappears in various guises in the novels and short stories.

Christina Alberta, the central character of the novel and nominally Preemby's daughter, is by common consent one of his most convincing and lifelike heroines. A criticism frequently levelled against his fiction—and one in which there is some substance—is that his female characters as a whole lack inner conviction; the aristocratic heroines such as Beatrice Normandy and Lady Mary Christian are too remote from everyday experience to engage the reader's sympathy, whilst such personalities as Margaret Siddon and Ethel Henderson, carefully drawn as they are, fail in some indefinable way to match the lifelike quality of their protagonists. The exceptions to this general criticism are those instances in which the heroine is clearly drawn from life; such vital personalities as Ann Veronica, Susan Ponderevo and Dolores immediately come to mind. Christina Alberta plainly belongs to this category and is moreover one of the most attractive and vivacious of Wells's creations precisely because she embodies all that curiosity about life and experience which he found such an appealing quality in the opposite sex. With her intellectual and emotional vivacity, her freedom from social inhibitions and infectious gaiety she is a child of the 1920s, just as Ann Veronica Stanley is a product of the Edwardian era. In each of these respects she is a solid and believable character, one which any assessment of Wells as a novelist must reckon with. In the vitality and realism of the female characters in the novels written during the following decade there are indications of the influence of Odette Keun, his close friend and adviser during these years. Certainly of all the novels of the immediate post-war decade this was one of the most successful and it remains one of the most original and fertile.

Wells observed in his autobiography that Christina Alberta 'is a much more living figure than Ann Veronica and her morals are far easier; but times had changed and not a voice was raised against her. That *Spectator* reviewer, and much else, had died since 1909. That particular liberation had been achieved.' Certainly the moral climate in 1925 was vastly different from that of Edwardian society—a transformation of attitudes to which Wells had in no small measure contributed. Yet the novel has a wider significance than this factor alone. It can be read as an entertaining story and nothing more, but on a deeper level it is an allegory about human behaviour—as Arnold Bennett was quick to recognise.[43] Preemby on his deathbed admits that he is not the only Sargon, and that 'the real thing was to be just a kingly person and work with all the other kingly persons in the world. . . . I have to find out what particular gifts I have and how I may best give them to our kingdom. Each king must glorify his particular reign with his particular gift.' Through the fantasia of Mr. Preemby and his delusions of world domination Wells is expressing in parable form the notion that each individual must use his or her own talents to the full in the building of a finer civilisation. To an admirer who once wrote to him professing to be a Wellsite he replied: 'The true Wellsite ceases to be a Wellsite and becomes instead a Smithite, a Jonesite, a Brownite and a Robinsonite.' This is the same concept expressed in a rather different form. Although his views fluctuated widely over the fifty years of his public career, he never deviated in substance from a basic humanist position—the view that if there is to be any improvement in human society it must be achieved through man's own efforts, that we cannot rely on any supernatural agency, and that it behoves every intelligent individual to use his skills to the utmost in the service of mankind. Kingly qualities—wisdom, vision, altruism—were dispersed throughout humanity and needed to be canalised in the great project of creating a harmonious world community. It is this central idea, that all men are the inheritors of the past, that we are all in some measure descendants of Sargon and that the future is our common heritage, that underlies the surface narrative. As always with Wells's fiction a didactic element lies behind the firm outlines of his vision.

THE WORLD OF WILLIAM CLISSOLD

At the end of his life Wells described *The World of William Clissold* as 'a vast three decker, issued in three successive volumes of rigmarole, which broke down the endurance of readers and booksellers alike'.[44] Never a best seller, the book today is one of the

least-regarded of his works. Yet it remains true that of all his novels
William Clissold is possibly the most criticised and at the same
time the least read by those who disparage it. It was written during
the years 1924-6 at his winter home, Lou Bastidon near Grasse, and
was clearly intended to be an extremely ambitious novel. Just as
Tono-Bungay set out to describe 'nothing more nor less than
Life—as one man has found it', so *William Clissold* aimed to be 'a
description of my world . . . my world and my will. I want it to be a
picture of everything as it is reflected in my brain.' The book is
planned on a spacious canvas and its daunting length and frequent
philosophical digressions have probably deterred many readers.
At first sight it has the form of a collection of disparate essays rather
than a novel, yet in a 'Note Before the Title Page' Wells insisted that
'it is claimed to be a complete full-dress novel, that and nothing
more'.

By the mid-1920s he had reached a turning point in his life.
Throughout the preceding decade the immense issues of the war
and reconstruction had occupied his mind and consumed all his
energies, but in 1924 he felt the urgent need of a change of climate
and mental rest. In Provence he found the respite he desired and
here, accompanied by his close friend Odette Keun (to whom the
book is dedicated) he set out to describe the world and outlook of
his alter ego William Clissold, an industrialist possessed by a
vision of planetary order.

The opening section, 'The Frame of the Picture', which describes
Clissold's mental attitudes, contains some of Wells's most engaging writing. In an early chapter, for example, 'The Treacherous
Forget-Me-Nots', there is a clear reminiscence of his childhood
days at Up Park, totally disarming in its fluency and charm. The
adjacent chapters, 'The World in the Crystal' and 'Infantile', are
almost equally memorable for their insight into his childhood
world. It is perhaps the chapter entitled 'View From A Window in
Provence' which merits the closest study of this first part, for here
Wells gives a minutely detailed description of the house in which
the book was written and its surrounding countryside. Here he
reflects upon the dominating theme of the book, flux universal, 'all
things flow'. 'There is no enduring pain, there is no eternal tragedy.
Toil passes like the straining of a rootlet or the opening of a bud.
Supreme above wars and disasters, surpassing and at last redeem-
ing all the present torments of man, is the growth of a being of
thought.'

In the following sections, 'My Father and the Flow of Things' and
'Essence of Dickon', the story of the Clissold family is continued,

interspersed with reflections upon economics and political theory. These reflections are either fascinating asides or irritating digressions, depending on one's point of view. It can be argued with some justification that the philosophising would be more appropriate in a volume of essays than in a novel, but this is not to deny their intrinsic qualities. Two in particular, 'Psycho-Analysis of Karl Marx' and 'Reincarnation of Socialism' are brilliant pieces of polemical journalism which deserve to survive. Wells was perenially fascinated by the career of financial adventurers such as Northcliffe and Whitaker Wright, and in *Clissold* he again returned to this theme, sketching brilliant pen pictures of Northcliffe and reflecting on the rise of patent medicine and drug empires.

The story is continued in a lengthy middle section, 'Tangle of Desires', in which Wells *qua* Clissold writes honestly and movingly of his emotional life. The chapters of reminiscence on Sirrie Evans and on Helen are among the finest in the entire novel, none the less interesting for being based in part on real persons (Jane Wells and Rebecca West respectively). In these pages Wells sets before the reader his innermost thoughts on human love and friendship. 'Always through my fuller years there was a feeling, a confidence I never had the power or will to analyse, that somewhere among womankind there was help and completion for me. . . . I have never found that completion. For me, at any rate, it has been no more than a sustaining illusion. But I do not repent of my love experiences.' Here, too, he describes his friendship with Clementina (Odette Keun) and the search for a house in Provence in which he could write and think without distractions.

In his autobiography (page 742) Wells stated that *The World of William Clissold* 'has a rambling manner but it seems to ramble more than it actually does from my main preoccupation. Its gist . . . is the possibility of bringing the diffused creative forces of the world into efficient co-operation as an Open Conspiracy.' The whole of Book Five of the novel is devoted to an elaboration of the idea of world revolution through an open conspiracy of intelligent men and women, an ideal which he had toyed with, revised, and speculated about since *Anticipations* in 1900. Briefly summarised, he forecast the emergence of a new functional class, a new social stratum of managers, engineers and educationists who would share certain common ideals and interests. This scientifically trained middle class would gradually detach itself from the community and recognise its distinctive character; it would become aware of a growing common consciousness of itself and a dawning sense of common purpose. This new element of technical and functionary workers would comprise capable administrators and operatives: men of skill and enterprise who would be experienced in the techniques of organisation and leadership. Its members would tend inevitably to be drawn together by a basic similarity of attitude and a belief in a common theory of social order.

In course of time this open conspiracy would be linked together in a definite movement, which would at first be informal and only loosely organised but would slowly gather strength and confidence as its influence increased. It would infiltrate into governments and the machinery of administration until by the close of the twentieth century it would be influencing and controlling the whole apparatus of power; the ostensible governments would probably remain in operation but it would become apparent, perhaps quite suddenly, that executive power was now in the hands of a world revolutionary movement dedicated to the final abolition of war and national animosity. This confrontation between the new order and the old would occur in the shadow of war, as the outcome either of its imminence or the resultant disorder: the crucible of war would be the flux in which the revolution would be accomplished. The strategy of revolution would have been worked out by the open conspirators over a period of generations; ultimately the details would be tried and tested and generally accepted and the new order would be ready to begin. Simultaneously with the development of the conspiracy, and as a concomitant of it, the influence and vitality of existing states and institutions would be on the wane, until at last a stage would be reached when the old order would have insufficient strength to resist. The real task of achieving world order would then commence.

This theory was elaborated, refined and polished in numerous works and reappeared in many different guises, but always its basic outline remained constant: (a) an insistance that the world revolution would be set in motion not by the mass but by an intelligent minority of mature and sentient minds, 'the salt of the earth'; (b) the leadership would be provided by the new managerial class of technocrats and artisans; (c) the ultimate seizure of power would be accomplished during or in the immediate shadow of world war. Wells spent many years speculating about this idea, restating, revising, and trying out new ways of expression. Remington in *The New Machiavelli,* Trafford in *Marriage,* Stratton in *The Passionate Friends* and Benham in *The Research Magnificent* were all open conspirators; the Samurai of *A Modern Utopia*, the Modern State movements of *The World Set Free* and *The Shape of Things to Come*, these and many others were trial forms of the same basic idea.[45]

The concluding section, 'Venus as Evening Star', is a long,

discursive summary of his moral beliefs in which his personal
attitudes are made transparently clear:

> For most of us sexual life is a necessity . . . as a real source of
> energy, self-confidence and creative power. It is an essential and
> perhaps the fundamental substance of our existence. For me and
> my kind the house of ill-fame is of no more use than the
> monastery. My need is for the respect, friendship, sympathy and
> willing help of a woman or women just as much as for her sexual
> intimacies.

He insists that in a saner world men and women will love and
mate on terms of equality, and returns to the idea of the 'compan-
ion-mate', the 'sister-lover' (first discussed in *First and Last Things*
and *The Passionate Friends*)—the concept of lovers mating and
associating freely without rigid bonds or legal contracts binding
them together. The institution of marriage, he argues, is continually evolving—it is not an unchanging formula—and shifts of emphasis are periodically being made by law and social usage. It
would ultimately be narrowed down to 'a child-protecting
bond. . . . The community only becomes concerned with sexual
affairs when the public health is affected or a child is begotten and
born.' At these points public responsibilities were incurred and
obligations to the community needed to be acknowledged and
fulfilled. Throughout the book there is an insistence—as indeed
there is in almost all his writings on this subject—on the need for
diversity in emotional relationships and for many variations in
association. He advocates an end to the stereotyped uniformity of
the formal marriage bond, and predicts that the wider, more
generous civilisation to which we are moving will be much freer in
its attitude to these questions. The entire section is essentially a
recapitulation of views he had held and maintained consistently
since *Anticipations* and *A Modern Utopia*.

   William Clissold, for all Wells's high hopes for it as a novel, does
not fulfil the expectations he had for it. In spite of many passages of
fine prose and brilliant journalism it lacks the life and energy
which are so abundantly present in *Tono-Bungay* and *Ann Veronica*. D. H. Lawrence described the work as 'a mouse's nest', and
certainly on first reading it gives the impression of a plethora of
ideas, chewed and mulled over at inordinate length. The novel will
in fact repay reading more than once for the flashes of genius
present in all his books—even the dullest—and for the impressive
symmetry of its construction. But ultimately, as with *Joan and*

Peter, it is unlikely to find a permanent place in English literature since it lacks that vitalising *force* which makes so much of his work memorable and alive.

The most living moments in the novel are the scenes written from his own direct experience—the childhood sequences at Mowbray, the description of Clementina and his house at Grasse, the account of his marriage and love affairs. There is also a curious 'Epilogue', supposedly written by Clissold's brother Richard, in which Wells views Clissold dispassionately *from the outside* and in doing so comments most illuminatingly on his own temperament and personality. It is these sequences which irradiate the book with vitality and lift it above the commonplace.

The book remains an uneasy hybrid. The attempt to fuse together a fictional story with sociological discussion succeeds admirably in *Tono-Bungay* precisely because the ideas do not overwhelm the characters. The experiment is less successful in *The New Machiavelli* and less still in *William Clissold*, for here the ideas become all important. Although Wells never overtly admitted his error, it is perhaps significant that after 1926 he abandoned the spacious treatment and concentrated instead on more compact forms in which to develop his leading ideas.

MEANWHILE

Meanwhile, commenced in 1926 immediately after the General Strike and published in 1927, is at first sight a novel describing a disparate group of people who assemble at an Italian villa and discuss, in a witty and characteristically Wellsian manner, social and economic problems of the day. It has the appearance and something of the flavour of a novel of manners. That Wells intended more than this is evident from the 'Preface Dedicatory' which describes the book as 'this fantasia of ideas, this picture of a mind and of a world in a phase of expectation'.

Both the introduction and the novel itself are dominated by the image of his wife Jane (Amy Catherine Robbins) who died of cancer in 1927. After her death he paid tribute to her qualities of gentleness and devotion in *The Book of Catherine Wells*, a collection of her short stories prefaced by a long and moving account of their life together. Whilst none of the characters in *Meanwhile* is intended as a portrait of Jane, he drew a composite picture embodying many of her characteristics in the personality of Cynthia Rylands, one of his most sympathetic heroines:

How clear and lucid was her mind, like a pool of crystalline water. He thought about the life he had led with her so far and the life they were going to lead together. He thought of the way in which all his interests and purposes had been turned about through her unpremeditated reaction upon his mind. He thought of the way in which fragility and courage interwove to make her at the same time delicate and powerful. So that for all that she was to him the frailest, most fastidious and inaggressive of women, she was plainly and surely his salvation. A wave of gratitude swept over his mind, gratitude for certain exquisite traits, for the marvellous softness of her hair, for her smile, for her fine hands and her characteristic movements, for moments of tenderness, for moments when he had seen her happy unawares and had rejoiced that she existed.

It is difficult not to recognise in this passage Wells lost in speculation about his wife, overcome with affection for her as he realised afresh all that she meant to him. They had been partners and companions for more than thirty years and her passing was a crucial watershed in his life. In describing Cynthia Rylands and her search for intellectual and emotional fulfilment Wells was giving fictional expression to many of his thoughts concerning Jane and womankind in general.

The second main strand in the novel is the discussion of the General Strike and of the political and social unrest of which it was a symptom. The Strike is discussed in a series of letters from Philip Rylands to his wife (enlivened by a number of delightfully droll 'picshuas') which criticise the government's handling of the dispute and indict both Baldwin and Churchill for their part in the affair. This was a device he had previously employed in *Mr. Britling Sees It Through*—in which Hugh Britling writes a number of letters to his father criticising the conduct of the war—and whilst it is handled here with less subtlety the overall effect is to compel admiration at the candour and penetration of Wells's indictment. His description of *Meanwhile* as a 'picture of a mind and of a world in a phase of expectation' is suggestive. His thesis was in essence that the whole world is 'meanwhiling', simply dissipating time and energy in the pursuit of meaningless distractions whilst the real issues before mankind remain unresolved. From this standpoint the General Strike was an irrelevance, neither side being wholly right or wholly wrong. It was a side issue, an evasion of the fundamental problem—that of achieving a cosmopolitan world order, a planetary civilisation in which economic stability would be assured.

Meanwhile has never been one of his most popular works (it was not until 1962 that a second edition appeared) and, in common with *The Soul of a Bishop* and *The Wife of Sir Isaac Harman*, it seems destined to fade into oblivion. Despite passages—whole chapters even—of witty and incisive dialogue, the total effect of the book is one of *talking at* the reader rather than engaging the imagination. Yet the danger with Wells is always to underestimate him. It would be easy to dismiss *Meanwhile* as a potboiler, a mediocre work on a par, let us say, with Bennett's *Teresa of Watling Street* or Gissing's *Eve's Ransom*. But the quality of the work shines through its unevenness. The dialogue on beauty between Cynthia Rylands and Mr. Plantagenet-Buchan in Book Two, Chapter Seven ('The Epicurean') is a perfect example of his artistry and illustrates his gift for writing in a natural, apparently effortless style. Moreover it has that poetic quality which lifts his work above the commonplace and imbues it with gravity and life. It is precisely these qualities which will ensure for his fiction an audience and critical acclaim in the years which are yet to come.

MR. BLETTSWORTHY ON RAMPOLE ISLAND

Wells described *Mr. Blettsworthy on Rampole Island* as 'a caricature-portrait of the whole human world'.[46] The book is dedicated 'to the Immortal Memory of *Candide*', which surely gives the clue. In common with Voltaire's *Candide*, Swift's *The Tale of a Tub* and Orwell's *Animal Farm*, *Mr. Blettsworthy* is a satire written in the form of an allegory. The book has frankly puzzled many readers who have failed to understand the hidden meaning underlying the events depicted; and it is certainly true that, if read as a straightforward novel, much of the story remains inexplicable. The whole of Chapter Three, containing the account of Rampole Island, is allegorical; and much of the remainder contains parabolic undertones. The entire work is written with vitriolic sarcasm and wit.

Arnold Blettsworthy, a shy young man who has led a sheltered, conventional life shielded from all intimations of evil, embarks on a long sea voyage for his health's sake. After many adventures he is shipwrecked and taken prisoner by the Rampole Islanders, cruel and uncouth savages who decide to adopt him as their Sacred Lunatic. The laws and customs of the Island (caricatures of civilisation) are described in detail and its religion, tribal system and military organisation commented upon.

The most biting satire is reserved for the description of the

Megatheria, the Giant Sloths, which still abound on Rampole
Island. These ungainly creatures symbolise such institutions as the
state, the church, the army and the law—the clumsy Megatheria
are symbolic of those traditional organisations and institutions
which refuse either to adapt or to die. The Giant Sloths are depicted
as powerful and cunning adversaries, possessing formidable reserves of strength and skill.

Eventually Rampole Island goes to war. An obscure tribal dispute is inflamed into a *cassus belli* and the whole island is plunged
into war hysteria. Blettsworthy draws an unfavourable comparison
between the bloodstained stupidity of the savages and the enlightened sanity of Europe, bound together by liberal treaties and
civilised procedures of arbitration. He succeeds in escaping from
this squalid conflict and at last returns to civilisation.

He finds himself in New York, where it is explained to him that
the Island has existed in his imagination only, that for some years
he has lived in a state of reverie preoccupied with a mental world of
his own creation. Blettsworthy concedes that this must be so, and
that in spite of his intensely vivid memories of Rampole Island and
its barbarity he is after all living in the real world. Yet he perceives
that the Island was 'only the real world looming through the mists
of my illusions ... no better than a mild caricature of the harsh
veracities of existence'.[47]

A sensitive, thoughtful man, he is conscripted into the army (for
it is now 1916) and sent to the battlefields of France. Then follows a
passionately moving account of the horrors of trench warfare. At
the time of writing the book, Wells had recently read Gristwood's
The Somme (for which he wrote the Preface) and in *Mr. Blettsworthy* he poured forth in unforgettable terms his detestation of
military stupidity.

Blettsworthy perceives that he is still upon Rampole Island, that
it has indeed enlarged and swallowed all the world. He returns to
England, wounded and disillusioned, to take up the threads of
civilian life once more. For him, as for Edward Prendick, there is no
enduring peace of mind. He is haunted by his recollections of
cruelty and insanity. The world of reality becomes increasingly
translucent; it gives way at times to visions of the Megatheria and
the tribal sages, to glimpses of the Island's military chiefs—now
exercising greatly enhanced power. He is distressed by the enormous fund of evil manifested by the Great War and such harrowing
events as the trial and execution of Sacco and Vanzetti in the
United States.

The book ends, in a section entitled 'Sanguine Interlude', with a long conversation between Blettsworthy and his old friend Graves. The dialogue gives a revealing insight into the author's state of mind at the time and is indicative of his fluctuating moods.

Wells strongly reinforces the theme that there is no hope for man unless war can be restrained and abolished; that there can be no advancement of mankind without a revolution in educational methods and political institutions throughout the earth. Cruelty and evil are acknowledged but, the author insists, these are due to fear and ignorance rather than ineradicable defects. They are *curable* in whole or in part.

There was still room for hope in human life—an optimism tempered with caution, perhaps—but still hope. Meanwhile, the only satisfying faith for the individual life was Stoicism.

The individual life had been overvalued in the past and insufficient attention paid to mankind as a species. To insist on the betterment of humanity was not an evasion of the individual problem. It was an enlargement of horizons from limited and petty ends to a larger vision; it was an escape from mean impulses to generous and disinterested service.

In his autobiography Wells observed that *Mr. Blettsworthy* was 'another breach of established literary standards with which, in spite of its very tepid reception, I am mainly content',[48] and lamented the fact that it was so little known. It is in my view one of his very finest stories and the time is long overdue for its rescue from neglect. It contains some of his most telling irony, one of his best descriptions of adolescent love (the whole of the section entitled 'Love and Olive Slaughter' is especially memorable) and is moreover a first-rate piece of storytelling in the vein of the early romances. In itself it is a refutation of the commonly held view that Wells departed from literature after 1914.

THE BULPINGTON OF BLUP

Wells gave *The Bulpington of Blup* the sub-title 'Adventures, Poses, Stresses, Conflicts, and Disaster in a Contemporary Brain'. This phrase aptly describes what the novel is: a sustained and remarkably consistent study of an acutely divided individuality. Robert Bloom, in his perceptive study *Anatomies of Egotism*,[49] has pointed out that the novel is in reality an anti-Bildungsroman, and it is fascinating to compare the literary technique employed here with that adopted in the earlier novels such as *Kipps*. In this long and elaborately conceived character study he produced one of his finest novels. for many years and a work of considerable artistic merit.

The Bulpington succeeds most effectively in describing the leisurely, effete, cultured circles in which the wealthy intelligentsia moved during the closing years of the Victorian era and the opening decade of the twentieth century. Theodore Bulpington grows up in a comfortable, kindly, limited world shielded from all the coarser aspects of life and far removed from any contact with poverty or deprivation. In much the same manner Arnold Blettsworthy spent his adolescent years. The account of Theodore's upbringing, his speculations about religion and science and his first experience of sexual love, is excellently done. Rarely did Wells achieve a more polished effect than in these chapters, notable for their consummate ease of storytelling. It is the First World War with its implicit challenge to English manhood which provides the necessary shock to jolt Theodore from his daydreamings and present him for the first time with a direct assault on his secure private world. The description of the oncoming of war (see especially Chapter 6, 1, 'The Great Framework Cracks') conveys brilliantly the sense of foreboding as the façade of European stability crumbled and broke asunder. After much prevarication Theodore reluctantly decides to enlist, but is only able to make his subsequent experiences tolerable by fabricating a web of falsehoods about his military career.

The novel is dominated by the image of the Delphic Sybil (Michaelangelo's painting is reproduced as the endpapers in the first edition) which becomes for the hero a symbol of all that he desires in feminine companionship. He is haunted by 'that lovely being, with her sweet wide eyes, her awakening youth' and adopts her as his idealised picture of womankind. Stephen Stratton in *The Passionate Friends* was also obsessed by the same image—clearly a powerful motif in Wells's imagination. The two central female characters, Rachel Bernstein and Margaret Broxted, are both finely realised—the latter recalling Joan Debenham in her manifest sincerity and integrity of purpose. Gradually Theodore identifies Margaret with the Delphic Sybil but becomes disenchanted with her when he realises ultimately that she embodies ideas and attitudes which he cannot share—scientific enlightenment, feminism and a concern for human betterment. At the end of the novel he deliberately defaces his painting of Sybil because she has come to stand for all those forces he refuses to face up to. The story ends, as it began, with Bulpington living wholly in a world of the imagination, protected from reality by layer upon layer of illusions and pretences.

Some critics have seen *The Bulpington of Blup* as a thinly disguised satire on Ford Madox Ford (Ford Madox Hueffer, 1873–1939), with whom Wells had had an uneasy friendship for some years. Ford had unkindly satirised him in *The New Humpty-Dumpty* and it may well be that Wells wished to pay off an old score. In his autobiography he described the novel as 'a very direct caricature study of the irresponsible disconnected aesthetic mentality'.[50] What is so remarkable about the work, particularly in the light of his earlier fiction, is the unusual degree to which he succeeds in describing the mental world and attitudes of a character so totally alien to his own views. The fact that Theodore Bulpington engages the reader's sympathy and understanding even while deluding himself in a series of increasingly extravagant poses is testimony to Wells's skill in building up a portrait of a completely convincing personality. By the end of the book it is clear that he detests Bulpington as a type, yet page by page and chapter by chapter he has woven an elaborate tapestry of emotional and introspective experiences which have helped to mould Theodore and make him what he is.

As a study of aestheticism *The Bulpington of Blup* is unique, not only in his own work but in the entire span of twentieth-century literature. Wells, unlike Henry James and Arnold Bennett, is not normally regarded as a novelist of character, but in this study of a deeply confused personality he succeeded in a way he had not done before in presenting a complete picture of a complex human being.

BRYNHILD

Brynhild, published in 1937, represents an interesting departure in Wells's work. In style and manner it is quite unlike any of his other novels—not least in its almost complete absence of either implied or overt didactic content. In its restrained language, carefully modulated structure and precise shaping of incident and conversation it resembles much more a novel by L. P. Hartley or Somerset Maugham than himself. It is, moreover, the most Jamesian of all his novels in the sense that he appears for once to be subscribing to Jamesian standards of form and refinement and to abandon the picaresque, discursive manner he had previously embraced as the mainstream of the English literary tradition.

George Ponderevo, the narrator in *Tono-Bungay*, defines his approach to the novel in these terms:

> I've reached the criticising, novel-writing age, and here I am writing mine—my one novel—without having any of the discipline to refrain and omit that I suppose the regular novel-writer acquires ... do what I will I fail to see how I can be other than a lax, undisciplined storyteller. I must sprawl and flounder, comment and theorise, if I am to get the thing out I have in mind.... My ideas of a novel all through are comprehensive rather than austere.

This was the stance which Wells in his own person adopted throughout his career and which he elaborated in detail in his lecture of 1911, 'The Contemporary Novel'.[51] It formed the substance of his famous quarrel with Henry James, a quarrel which led to the termination of their friendship in 1915. When James wrote to Wells remonstrating against *Boon* he replied:

> I have set before myself a gamin-esque ideal, I have a natural horror of dignity, finish and perfection, a horror a little enhanced by theory.... There is of course a real and very fundamental difference in our innate and developed attitudes towards life and literature. To you literature like painting is an end, to me literature like architecture is a means, it has a use.... I had rather be called a journalist than an artist, that is the essence of it, and there was no other antagonist possible than yourself.'

In the light of this posture—which Wells maintained with passionate conviction and deep sincerity, and which he elaborated yet again in his autobiography—it is all the more surprising to find in *Brynhild* a novel that in its chasteness and overall symmetry can only be described as a work of art.

That he intended it to be regarded as a major work is made clear in the introductory note: 'If you like this story you will like *The Bulpington of Blup*, *Christina Alberta's Father*, *Kipps*, *Tono-Bungay* and *The History of Mr. Polly* by the same author.' This selection is significant in that each is a novel which takes as its principal or leading theme the exploration of an individuality. In the case of *Brynhild* there are two personalities whose character and psychology form the substance of the book: Rowland Palace, aesthete and writer, and his sensitive, beautiful wife Brynhild. The novel is concerned throughout with an examination of the manner in which each impinges on the other and the impact of both upon a third personality, Alfred Bunter—the latter being apparently modelled on D. H. Lawrence. This is, for Wells, an alien world— the world of refined, aesthetic, art-conscious creative artists— and he now proceeded to explore it with penetrating relish and insight.

The book carries the subtitle 'The Show of Things', a phrase which reinforces the novel's concern with the theme of appearances and with the exploration of outward images. Rowland Palace is obsessed with the image of himself as a successful writer, and his search for an effective means of publicising his reputation provides Wells with ample scope for gentle mockery of the public relations industry. He himself cared deeply about his public image as a writer despite his protestations to the contrary, yet Palace is in no sense an alter ego. Wells does not seek to identify himself in any way with his central character but rather to demonstrate, through his use of a certain ironical detachment, the intrinsic shallowness of the aesthetic mentality. But the novel, significantly, takes its title not from Palace but from his beautiful, enigmatic wife; its thematic substance is concerned equally with her quest for fulfilment. Whereas he achieves his end in an increasingly diffuse mask of self-deception, Brynhild finds her completion in total honesty and integrity. In the completest contrast to her husband (Brynhild appears to have been modelled on Moura Budberg, a close friend and intimate of Wells's during the final decade of his life) she remains steadfast throughout to her own ideals of candour and tenderness. Much of the novel's fascination lies in the way in which these differing personalities impinge upon each other and affect the lives and attitudes of their acquaintances. Moreover, underlying the surface narrative is a web of symbolic reference —seen at its height in the lengthy description of the charade at Valliant Chevrell—which reinforces the central preoccupation with the themes of image and reality, appearance and truth.

Brynhild looks back to earlier literary models—*The Portrait of a Lady* is an obvious and peculiarly apposite precursor—and at the same time anticipates in its extensive use of mythological symbols and precise employment of language such a novel as John Fowles's *The Magus*. It is above all else a novel of characterisation—a work concerned through and through with the delineation of individual character—in marked contrast to the bulk of his fiction which is concerned more typically with an examination of ideas and social forces. In exploring the mental and emotional world of Brynhild and Rowland Palace Wells seems to have deliberately opted for a dignified, graceful style as if he is consciously seeking to make amends for his previous lapses and to demonstrate his ability to produce a polished and cohesive whole. (At one point in the narrative he even interjects a comment apropos of himself: 'Wells was pinned down by his always being linked with 'The Future of—this or that.' But Wells at the best was a discursive intractable writer with no real sense of dignity. A man is not called "H. G." by all his friends for nothing.') Behind the central theme—that of the shallowness of appearances and façades, and the contrasting reality of the true self—lies a wealth of observation and incident woven together in a tapestry of Jamesian complexity.[52] The result is a wholly satisfying piece of writing which deserves to be more widely known and which merits considerably more critical attention than it has thus far received.

THE BROTHERS

In *The Brothers*, a novella published in 1938, Wells returned to a literary genre in which he had always excelled: the satire written in the form of an allegory. That the story is satirical in intent is indicated by the introductory note: 'If you like this story you will probably also like *The Croquet Player*, *Star Begotten*, *Mr. Blettsworthy on Rampole Island*, *The Time Machine*, *Men Like Gods* and such short stories as "The Pearl of Love", "The Country of the Blind" and "The Beautiful Suit" by the same author.' This selection of stories, each of which contains allegorical or parabolic elements, suggests at once that here again Wells is embarking upon a satirical fable.

The story is set against the background of a civil war and was clearly influenced by the traumatic events in Spain: Orwell's *Homage to Catalonia* had been published in the same year and something of its atmosphere of internecine strife permeates the book. Orwell had concluded his account with a moving reaffirmation of his faith in human decency, and Wells's story is also suffused with a message of human brotherhood. But what distinguishes *The Brothers* from so much of his fiction is the complex interplay of narrative and parable.

In essence the story concerns two brothers, Bolaris and Ratzel, who are leaders of opposing factions in a bitterly divisive civil war. Their very names contain symbolic undertones: Bolaris is apparently a pun on the word 'polarise', and Ratzel is immediately suggestive of Rasselas, the hero of Johnson's satirical romance which Wells first read as a boy at Up Park and which helped to sow the seeds of a youthful scepticism. (It will be recalled that Rasselas is confined to a paradise, 'the Happy Valley', just as Ratzel is a prisoner in the world of communist ideas and does not wish to escape.) Ratzel is captured by Bolaris's troops; the brothers confront one another and, in the course of a lengthy dialogue, realise that, whilst differing in their language and preconceptions, each has far more in common with the other than either had appreciated: that although their experiences of life have been different their basic aims are remarkably akin.

In their conversation there is a growing awareness of how much they share a common view of life:

> Until this remarkable fact that we two people, who may be almost identically alike inside, find ourselves here in the most direct antagonism. That sets us thinking again in spite of ourselves. . . . This imbecile civil warfare of sham loyalties, stale dogmas, perverted traditions and fragmentary ideas has got to end. . . . The left and right in any age are just the two faces of the Common Fool, and nothing more, and you have been on one face and I the other.

Bolaris and Ratzel are in fact symbolic of Right and Left: what Wells is saying in fictional terms is that the struggle between capital and labour, between 'right wing' and 'left wing', is outmoded and unnecessary—a tragic waste of human resources.

All his life he had rejected the Marxist interpretation of society, arguing that this was a dangerous oversimplification which concealed a much more complex reality. William Clissold expressed his basic attitude in these terms:

> But I do not think I was quick enough to realise in those days that the Proletariat and Bourgeoisie about which these new Socialists gabbled endlessly were absolutely indefinable classes, and still less to apprehend that this Capitalist System of theirs was a phantasmagorical delusion, a sort of Pepper's Ghost, thrown upon the face of reality. Nowadays I do not succumb so easily to our human disposition to believe that where there is a name there is a thing, and I have learnt to look behind the logical surface of every argument and conviction.

Again in *The Way the World is Going*, he summed up his fundamental antipathy to Marxism:

> I believe this conflict between Capital and Labour is like that great struggle between Arianism and Trinitarianism, which tore

the Roman world to pieces thirteen or fourteen centuries ago; that is to say, I regard it as a struggle about theoretical definitions having only the remotest relationship to any fundamental realities in life.

Seen in these terms it is evident that *The Brothers* is a parable worthy of Voltaire or Swift. It is an attempt to discuss a fundamental human problem in the guise of realistic narrative. The satire rises to its height in a lengthy chapter, 'Coup D'État', in which Bolaris and his five advisers discuss what is to be done with the prisoner. His assistant Handon (another pun is evident here: possibly Handy Andy, the incompetent hero of Samuel Lover's novel) expresses grovelling subservience, whilst the remaining four, described with ironic humour, indicate varying degrees of disapproval of Bolaris's plans. In the final chapter Bolaris, after an eloquent plea for human brotherhood, is accidentally killed by the bungling Handon who has also shot Ratzel whilst trying to escape. The story ends on a note of ambivalence, entirely characteristic of Wells's work, with the two protagonists dead and the outcome of the civil war uncertain. Bolaris's lover stoops over the dead body. 'No,' she whispered to the still face close to hers. 'It cannot end like this. We were the first. We were just the beginning. It was a beginning. . . .'

Viewed in the context of his lifelong advocacy of reconstruction, *The Brothers* is an uneven yet oddly moving work; it combines the tautness of the novella form with the dialogue effect he had sought to achieve in more ambitious works such as *The Undying Fire*. On the whole he succeeds admirably in his intention. Within its terms it is as fine a piece of writing as almost any of the later fiction; it has flashes of impatience but is composed on the whole with restraint and humour; there is as yet no sign of any diminution in his powers as a storyteller. Just as *Boon* reflected his distress and uncertainty in the wake of the carnage of world war, so in 1938 he gave vent to his frustration at the needless slaughter in Spain. That he chose to do so in the form of a morality play rather than an orthodox polemical essay is fully consistent with all that had gone before. From his earliest writings onwards his favourite literary weapons were irony and satire.

APROPOS OF DOLORES

In a series of articles in *Time and Tide* (October 1934) which appeared under the title 'H. G. Wells—The Player', Odette

Keun—who had been Wells's close friend and companion for the previous decade—strongly criticised him for his alleged inconsistency and disingenuousness and asserted that *Experiment in Autobiography*, which was then being published, was 'an enormous reel of self-justification'. For ten years Wells and Madame Keun had enjoyed a friendship from which both no doubt gained much—his warm appreciation of her may be seen in the dedications of both *The World of William Clissold* and *The Bulpington of Blup*—but by 1934 the relationship had considerably deteriorated. Instead of replying to the *Time and Tide* articles Wells bided his time and, four years later, expressed his mature reflections on the Madame Keun affair in a bitingly amusing novel in which she is caricatured as Dolores Wilbeck.[53] This is not to say that Dolores is simply a fictional portrait of Odette Keun—the reality is more subtle than that—but rather that Wells drew on many of her distinctive characteristics and mannerisms in sketching this wryly malicious vignette. He was careful to state in the Preface 'If a character in a book should have the luck to seem like a real human being that is no excuse for imagining an "original" or suspecting a caricature. . . . Nothing in this book has happened to anyone; much in this book has happened to many people.' Several publishers declined to accept the book, presumably because they felt the fictionalisation was too recognisable and they feared a libel action. The book was finally published in 1938 by Jonathan Cape. In looking back on his years of friendship with Odette, Wells recalled their association not with rancour or bitterness, as might have been expected, but a resigned whimsicality—in much the same manner as George Ponderevo in *Tono-Bungay* looked back on his marriage to Marion. The result is that *Apropos of Dolores* is one of Wells's happiest creations. The story is told throughout with a delicious sense of humour and with an ease of manner he was never to recapture.

The novel is cast in the form of a journal kept by the narrator, Stephen Wilbeck, who reflects on his past life and in particular on Dolores and the impact of her unique personality on his philosophy and outlook. The journal is saturated with sociological comment on a wide range of issues on which Wells in his own person had frequently written—racial intolerance, the teaching of universal history, the insidious effect of nationalism and so on—but in *Dolores* his touch is so light and accomplished as to render the book an exhilarating intellectual and emotional experience.

It is rich in episodes of enduring humour. The opening chapter,

'Happy Interlude', is written with a benign goodwill and a delight in his fellow men which recalls the happy mood of *The History of Mr. Polly* thirty years earlier. Wilbeck confides to the reader that he has a 'Boswell self': moods in which he is contented with life and looks charitably on all around him. The mood comes upon him all too rarely but under its influence he begins to describe himself and his world and the manner in which he first met Dolores, who comes at last to exercise a dominating influence in his life.

Some of the finest incidents occur in the chapter entitled 'Dolores at Torquestol'. There is, for example, the unforgettable scene in which she and Wilbeck arrive at the hotel and demand lunch; the hilarious sequence at the dinner table when Dolores' dog, Bayard, becomes involved in an amorous encounter with the pet of the Baroness Schenitzy; the conversation with the English fisherman, culminating in the profound observation that one never sees a woman fishing. After the death of Dolores—which comes as a total surprise to the reader—there is an extremely amusing description of the funeral, with Wilbeck wearing ill-fitting formal clothes so that he looks like 'an unmitigated scoundrel ... the villain in a Victorian melodrama'. He imagines Dolores remonstrating with him for his lack of chic. Each of these episodes is written with a felicity and an infectious good humour which is wholly delightful.

The entire novel is in reality a sustained analysis of egotism, using Dolores as a case study in obstructiveness and resistance to ideas. It is a characteristically Wellsian novel in that the narrator is not content to describe his personal experiences but speculates whether his story might not have a wider relevance to mankind. Could it be, he asks, that humanity is not one species but a mixture: that some people are 'Homo Doloresiform, a widespread, familiar type, emphatic, impulsive and implacable', and that others are 'Homo Wilbeckius, probably a recent mutation, observant, inhibited and disingenuous'? The question, once posed, leads on to much intriguing psychological and biological comment, but this is not obtrusive. In this respect, as in others, Wells's literary technique is skilful and self assured: more so than in some of the earlier novels. Moreover, much of the artistry of *Dolores* lies in the fact that Stephen Wilbeck is truly an invented personality, and Wells does succeed to a considerable degree in reaching inside the mind of a completely imaginary human being.

Although *Apropos of Dolores* was written at a time when the clouds of world war were clearly visible on the horizon, it is on the whole a refreshingly cheerful work. Wilbeck speculates on the probable shape of the future but, for all his caution, concludes that 'there were no biological precedents to guide us to a prophecy of

the outcome, because man's limited but incessant intelligence
makes his case unique. . . . Stoical agnosticism is the only possible
religion for sane adults. Accept and endure what happens to you,
from within just as much as from without. . . . Go on without either
absolutes of believing or disbelieving, without extremities either of
hope or despair.'[54] So it is that at the conclusion of one of his most
humorous stories, undeservedly neglected today, Wells returns to
the stoicism of Edward Prendick and Arnold Blettsworthy. The
novel ends, as it began, with a visit to Rennes—where Wilbeck had
found much happiness—and, in forgiving Dolores for all her
implacabilities and exasperating behaviour, he concludes on a
note of 'complacency and benediction'.

THE HOLY TERROR

At intervals since the publication of *The Open Conspiracy* in 1928
Wells sought opportunities to clothe his political ideas, in one
guise or another, in fictional form. His most ambitious effort in this
direction was *The Shape of Things to Come* (1933) but in *The Holy
Terror*, published in 1939, he produced a long novel constructed
from much the same materials as his history of the future but in
which the Open Conspiracy takes the form not of a dedicated
minority of enlightened revolutionaries but a political party.

Throughout the 1930s he was active in furthering his ideas. His
address 'Liberalism and the Revolutionary Spirit', delivered at the
Liberal Summer School at Oxford in 1932 (reprinted in *After
Democracy*) reached many young people who would not otherwise
have encountered his sociological writings. In the following year
he prepared a memorandum entitled 'There should be a common
creed for Left parties throughout the world' which was subsequently adapted as the basis of the Federation of Progressive Societies
and Individuals—a body with which he briefly flirted and which
was satirised in *The Holy Terror* as 'The New World Society'. The
truth is that he was too anarchic in temperament for any sustained
involvement in a political organisation, but in *The Holy Terror* he
produced a rambling, splenetic novel in which Sir Oswald Mosley
is caricatured as 'Lord Horatio Bohun' and in which the leadership
of Bohun's party is wrested from him by a young man consumed by
an ambition for world domination. The most interesting section of
the novel from the standpoint of literary history is the opening
three chapters describing the childhood and adolescence of the
central character, Rud Whitlow. These provide clear indications

that Wells in his seventies still possessed vivid memories of his years at 47 High Street, Bromley, and was able to render these memories in novelistic form. In the account of Rud Whitlow's childhood battles with his brothers and his imaginary military skirmishes there are numerous echoes of the young Bertie Wells:

> Since he was a day-boy and not very fond of games, and since he could do his school work very quickly, he was free to take long, solitary walks in which he could let his imagination run riot in anticipatory reverie. To the passing observer he seemed to be a small, rather slovenly boy ... but in imagination he rode a magnificent charger, or occupied a powerful car, and his staff and orderlies and messengers buzzed about him, and his embattled hosts stormed the farmhouses and villages of the landscape and swept over the hills, while his pitiless guns searched their recesses. The advance was always victorious, and with the homecoming came the triumph.[55]

There is no doubt that a penchant for imaginary warfare and scenes of destruction was a powerful element in Wells's imagination, as may be seen from the gusto of the descriptions of violence in such stories as *The War of the Worlds* and *The War in the Air*. In later years he was inclined to be rather shamefaced in admitting this trait, but in *The Holy Terror* it is clearly in evidence in Whitlow's youthful visions and dreams of conquest.

Where the book differs from the scenario adumbrated in previous political fantasies is in its exploration of the pathology of the world leader. Once Whitlow becomes master of the world he is consumed by megalomania and seems bent on destroying the unified order he has sought to create. It is not too fanciful to see in this inversion of the familiar scenario Wells's deep mistrust of political parties and their apparatus of power. His insistence that Whitlow was a divided personality—driven partly by disinterested motives and partly by animal greed, like the Beast Folk on Dr. Moreau's island—is a recognition of the duality in man and of his potential altruism:

> That peculiar intelligence that he showed at times! ... It seemed to be something almost entirely independent of his personal self ... I suppose it's something of the sort you get in real poets—or in cardinal men of science. Like something hidden in the dark suddenly lit by a searchlight. As though a higher mind is imprisoned somewhere behind the human brain. Getting free now and then—partially.'[56]

The Holy Terror is in essence a fantasy rather than a novel, as Wells himself conceded in his introduction:

> Every person, place and thing in this story—even the countries in which it happens—are fictitious, and any resemblance, though it runs to the pitch of identical names and circumstances, is at most a realistic device and free of any libellous intention whatever. It is an imagination about everyone and nobody, about everyland and nowhere, justified by the *Lives* of Seutonius and our present discontents.

As a vehicle for the presentation of his ideas it is one of the least successful of the later novels, since it is so plainly divorced from reality. Whereas *The Shape of Things to Come* aroused considerable critical interest because of its underlying fertility and prescience, this Mosleyesque fantasia failed to bring the idea of an Open Conspiracy to a wider audience. Its significance is, however, twofold: first, it bears witness to Wells's consistency in advocating constructive world revolution even at a time when the clouds of war were gathering. It is in this sense a Utopia, an apocalyptic novel in direct line of descent from *Anticipations* and the long list of blueprints and fantasias which had issued from his pen since the turn of the century. Second, it provides extremely interesting evidence of the importance to his imaginative development of the first fourteen years of his life. Just as Lawrence in his later years looked back with affection and nostalgia to his early days at Eastwood, so Wells returned in his reveries to his years at Bromley—years in which the forces which moulded him as novelist and prophet made their deepest impact.

It was as if in old age he sought renewal and imaginative release in returning to the world of his boyhood. As late as *The Happy Turning* (1945) he was recalling with vividness and charm his experiences as a child. And even when writing an ambitious political extravaganza, a fable on the theme of the rise and fall of a world dictator, he was unable to resist the temptation to infect his leading character with his own childhood fancies.

BABES IN THE DARKLING WOOD

Wells described *Babes in the Darkling Wood*, written in 1939–40, as 'the most comprehensive and ambitious dialogue novel I have ever attempted'.[57] It was clearly designed on a large scale and conceived as an attempt to discuss a range of issues and ideas which were topical on the eve of the Second World War and to stimulate his readers by an imaginative presentation of these ideas in fictional form. In short, it was to do for the Second World War what *Mr. Britling* and, to a lesser extent, *Joan and Peter* had achieved for the First: to verbalise the experiences and attitudes of a generation at a time of trauma.

In form it belongs to a genre to which he had always been much attracted, the 'dialogue novel', and which is discussed in depth in the introductory essay, 'The Novel of Ideas'. This introduction may well prove to be the most permanent part of the book. It should be closely studied by anyone who seeks a fuller understanding of Wells's approach to the novel and of his intellectual position in relation to the 'stream of consciousness' school of writers. In it he makes his final defence of the dialogue novel and places *Babes in the Darkling Wood* in its context within the conspectus of his fiction. It belongs, he claims, to a 'great literary tradition', that of 'discussing fundamental human problems in dialogue form'. He acknowledges that he has made a number of experiments in the genre (beginning with *Ann Veronica*) and proceeds to outline his attempt in the present novel to render 'in terms of living human beings' the profound changes in human thought now taking place. Taken together with his essay 'The Contemporary Novel' and the preface to *Stories of Men and Women in Love* this introduction provides a comprehensive statement of his theory of literature and a summary of his aims as a novelist.

'Tried by Henry James's standards I doubt if any of my novels . . . satisfy his requirements fully. . . . The main indictment is sound, that I sketch out scenes and individuals, often quite crudely, and resort even to conventional types and symbols, in order to get on to a discussion of relationships.' Thus wrote Wells, with salutary candour, in 'Digression About Novels'.[58] *Babes in the Darkling Wood* is perhaps the supreme example of the novel of ideas overtaken by the march of events. The ideas discussed at such inordinate length by Gemini Twain and Robert Kentlake must have seemed topical and alive in 1940 yet—so rapid has been the transformation in our social and intellectual climate—today sound remote, almost alien. The result is to infuse the novel with a transitory flavour which militates against its power to endure. There is no reason to suppose that Wells was not aware of this transitory quality: indeed he claimed to welcome it. 'What I write *goes now*—and will presently die.' He would have fully accepted the thesis that once the issues presented in a novel have ceased to have relevance to the times then the novel ceases to have life and may be permitted to fade away.

Yet the argument clearly goes deeper than this, for otherwise *Ann Veronica* (for example) would have long since disappeared from public regard and met the fate of much other forgotten Edwardian fiction. *Babes* is the weakest of the later novels in the sense that Wells forsakes the attempt to weave his didactic materials into a cohesive imaginative whole and is content instead to *talk at* the reader. The resultant dialogue has a hectoring, impatient quality which eventually jars and inevitably dilutes the effectiveness of the book as a whole. Moreover his protagonists Gemini and Stella are in reality creatures of a much earlier generation: in their conversation and attitudes they are more characteristic of 1910 than of thirty years later. The endeavour to transpose the values of Edwardian England into the mental atmosphere of 1940 is ultimately unsatisfactory and leads to a blurring of vision, a distortion of critical focus, which weakens the novel as a polemical work. From this point of view *You Can't Be Too Careful*, which immediately followed it, is a much more assured piece of writing and one which is satisfying in precisely the areas where *Babes* is not.

The real significance of *Babes in the Darkling Wood* lies in its defiant optimism, almost utopianism, at a time when the clouds were darkening throughout the world. Throughout the novel, and especially in the conversations of Gemini and Uncle Robert, there is an aura of hope, a conviction that a nobler order of civilisation is not only possible but practicable—given only the will to achieve it. Yet the book was written in a mood of growing pessimism. In *The Fate of Homo Sapiens*, published in August 1939, he had reaffirmed in the starkest possible terms his assessment of the alternatives facing man:

> Either the human imagination and the human will to live rises to the plain necessity of our case and a renascent Homo Sapiens struggles on to a new, a harder and a happier world dominion, or he blunders down the slopes of failure through a series of unhappy phases, in the wake of all the monster reptiles and beasts that have flourished and lorded it on the earth before him, to his ultimate extinction. Either life is just beginning for him or it is drawing very rapidly to its close.

Anthony West has remarked apropos of Wells's optimistic writing: 'Wells's "progressive" writing represents an attempt to straddle irreconcilable positions, and it involved a perpetual conflict of a wasteful character. In all too much of his work he is engaged in shouting down his own better judgment.'[59] There are many indications in this, the last and most comprehensive of the dialogue novels, that he is giving vent to an ironic expression of his deepening despair for mankind; that it is in fact a profoundly pessimistic work masquerading as a testament on progress. There could be no more apposite instance of Wells 'shouting down his own better judgment' than Gemini's final speech, 'Hope and Plan for Living', a naïve yearning for a better world which his creator in his innermost heart must have known was incapable of realisation. The death of Uncle Robert, so reminiscent of the deathbed scene of Edward Ponderevo, can be interpreted as a symbolic as well as an actual ending. It marks the onset of a deepening scepticism over the prospects for mankind. Henceforward, dogged by illness and old age, increasingly depressed by the cruelty and destruction wrought by war, Wells's work was to be coloured more and more by his hardening doubts for the future of man.

YOU CAN'T BE TOO CAREFUL

With the publication of *You Can't Be Too Careful* in 1941 Wells's career as a novelist, which had begun nearly fifty years earlier with *The Wheels of Chance*, came to an end. His final novel, despite the fact that it has never found favour with literary critics,[60] is in many ways one of the most remarkable of all and embodies his characteristic approach to the art of fiction in all its strength and weakness.

The novel, which is subtitled 'A Sample of Life 1901–1951', tells the life story of Edward Albert Tewler, a Pollyesque figure who blunders from one misadventure to another, and relates his gradual awakening into sexual and political consciousness. The story is told with a frankness which would have been unthinkable in Wells's early fiction, and which is strongly reminiscent of the Orwell of *Coming Up for Air* and *Keep the Aspidistra Flying*. The second and third parts, 'The Adolescence of Edward Albert Tewler' and 'The Marrying, Divorce and Early Middle Age', are brilliantly executed and are convincing evidence that his ability to entertain and amuse the reader was undiminished even at the age of seventy-five. There are, for example, the cricket match (Book Two, 2) in which it is not difficult to imagine reminiscences of his father on the cricket pitch at Bromley; the boarding house at Doober's (Book

Two, 11), an institution almost worthy of Dickens; and the description of his courtship and marriage to Evangeline Birkenhead. The latter is told with pitiless clarity and yet with a freshness and insight which compel admiration.

Tewler himself is a pitiful figure who never at any stage accepts responsibility for his own actions, but in spite of his manifest shallowness and posturing he succeeds, like Theodore Bulpington, in holding the reader's sympathy. That Wells deliberately intended this effect is plain from his comment at the end:

> I have told his poor sordid story and that of the people whose lives he helped to spoil; I have mocked at his absurdities and misfortunes and invincible conceit; but all the way along as I wrote it something has protested, 'This is not fair. Given a broader education, given air, light and opportunity, would he have been anything like this?' He is what our civilisation made of him, and this is all it made of him. I have told the complete truth about a contemporary specimen man. . . . My case is that Edward Albert is not so much detestable as pitiful. . . .

It is instructive to compare this passage with a similar admission at the conclusion of *The History of Mr. Polly*:

> I have failed in presenting Mr. Polly altogether if I have not made you see that he was in many respects an artless child of Nature, far more untrained, undisciplined, and spontaneous than an ordinary savage.

Tewler is, however, a more complex (if less sympathetic) figure than Polly, because he sees life with fewer illusions. But whereas Mr. Polly succeeded in transforming his life by escaping from an environment which had become intolerable, Tewler simply accepts life as it is. He reacts to external pressures but seems incapable of initiating change. The atmosphere of the two stories is similar in a number of respects but the later novel is told with a candour and bitterness altogether lacking in the former.

The essential theme of *You Can't Be Too Careful* is that man has not yet attained the status of Homo Sapiens, that all mankind is still Homo Tewler, and that no advancement beyond his present stage is possible without a world wide moral and intellectual revolution. Wells had been arguing much the same case for many years—most recently in a series of polemical works, *The Fate of Homo Sapiens*, *The New World Order*, and *The Commonsense of War and*

Peace—but now he chose to illustrate and illuminate his thesis by telling the story of a 'contemporary specimen man' who grew to painful maturity during the years between the two world wars.

It is fashionable to dismiss *You Can't Be Too Careful* as a malicious, almost hopeless, work of despair written by an elderly man who was tired and ill. Such a reading is too simplistic. Anthony West has argued cogently[61] that the pessimism which overtook Wells at the end of his life was not a final cry of despair but a reversion to deeply felt convictions he had felt from the outset of his intellectual career. Indeed, the final impression of the novel is not one of hopelessness—as is the case with such early works as *The Time Machine* and *The Island of Doctor Moreau*—but a resigned stoicism.

> Yet a vista of innumerable happy generations, an abundance of life at present inconceivable, and at the end, not extinction necessarily, not immortality, but complete uncertainty, is surely sufficient prospect for the present. They [future generations] may be good by our current orientation of things; they may be evil. Why should they not be in the nature of our good and much more than our good—'beyond good and evil'?

Thus it is that at the end of his literary pilgrimage we find not the unrelieved pessimism of *Mind at the End of its Tether* but a serene impassivity: a refusal to be committed to any ultimate certainty regarding the human future. B. Ifor Evans in his *A Short History of English Literature* has pointed out that the danger with Wells is always to underestimate him. His final novel, flawed as it is by unevenness and a too overt didacticism, is nevertheless a remarkable piece of writing which will live through the force of its invective and the abundant vitality of its ideas.

Part VI

KEY TO THE CHARACTERS AND LOCATIONS

Key to the Characters and Locations

This section consists of an alphabetically arranged dictionary of the characters and places having a significant role in the novels and stories. These are, in many cases, described in Wells's own words. Where the 'original' of a character or location can be identified with reasonable certainty this information is given in square brackets.

The following abbreviations are used throughout:

Air	*The War in the Air*
Ararat	*All Aboard for Ararat*
Argonauts	*'The Chronic Argonauts'*
Babes	*Babes in the Darkling Wood*
Begotten	*Star Begotten*
Bishop	*The Soul of a Bishop*
Blettsworthy	*Mr. Blettsworthy on Rampole Island*
Britling	*Mr. Britling Sees It Through*
Brothers	*The Brothers*
Bulpington	*The Bulpington of Blup*
Camford	*The Camford Visitation*
Careful	*You Can't Be Too Careful*
Christina	*Christina Alberta's Father*
Clissold	*The World of William Clissold*
Comet	*In the Days of the Comet*
Croquet	*The Croquet Player*
Days to Come	*'A Story of the Days to Come'*
Dolores	*Apropos of Dolores*
Dream	*The Dream*
Experiment	*Experiment in Autobiography*

First Men	The First Men in the Moon
Food	The Food of the Gods
Friends	The Passionate Friends
Gods	Men Like Gods
Harman	The Wife of Sir Isaac Harman
Holy Terror	The Holy Terror
Invisible	The Invisible Man
Joan	Joan and Peter
King	The King who was a King
Lewisham	Love and Mr. Lewisham
Machiavelli	The New Machiavelli
Miracles	Man Who Could Work Miracles
Moreau	The Island of Doctor Moreau
Parham	The Autocracy of Mr. Parham
Polly	The History of Mr. Polly
Research	The Research Magnificent
Secret Places	The Secret Places of the Heart
Sea Lady	The Sea Lady
Set Free	The World Set Free
Sleeper	When the Sleeper Wakes
Time Machine	The Time Machine
Undying Fire	The Undying Fire
Veronica	Ann Veronica
Visit	The Wonderful Visit
Waddy	The Wealth of Mr. Waddy
Wheels	The Wheels of Chance
Worlds	The War of the Worlds

A.J. The dedicatee of *Veronica*. Presumably 'Amber' (Amber Pember Reeves, the 'original' of Ann Veronica, and a close friend of Wells's during the years 1906–1910) and 'Jane' (Jane Wells, his wife from 1895–1927).

ALLBUT, CLARA. Wife of William Clissold, 'a dark-haired, slender, restless, talkative girl, with aquiline features and hazel eyes'. After a short, unhappy marriage she becomes the lover of Philip Weston, an artist, and has a daughter by him. Clissold is unable to obtain a divorce as the child is ostensibly his; they separate, and when her liaison with Weston breaks down Clissold assists her financially. Clara dies of influenza many years later. *Clissold*.

ANGEL, THE. His adventures in the village of Siddermorton are recounted in *Visit*. He was a 'youth with an extremely beautiful face, clad in a robe of saffron and with iridescent wings, across whose pinions great waves of colour, flushes of purple and crimson, golden green and intense blue, pursued one another'. After being shot down by the vicar, a keen ornithologist, he · remains in the village for some time observing earthly institutions and learning the rudiments of social behaviour. Following his death in a fire at the vicarage the name 'Thomas Angel' is inscribed over his grave. *Visit.*

BAILEY, ALTIORA [Beatrice Webb]. The wife of Oscar Bailey. She is 'a tall commanding figure, splendid but a little untidy in black silk and red beads, with dark eyes that had no depths, with a clear hard voice that had an almost visible prominence, aquiline features and straight black hair that was apt to get astray'. After her marriage she makes her home in Chamber Street a centre of political and social activity; she encourages Remington and Margaret to marry and helps to further his political career. *Machiavelli*, Book Two, 2.

BAILEY, OSCAR [Sidney Webb]. Husband of Altiora Bailey. He is a 'short, sturdy figure with a rounded protruding abdomen and a curious broad, flattened, clean shaven face that seemed nearly all forehead'.He and his wife comment upon Remington's book *The New Ruler* (*Anticipations*) and encourage him at the outset of his political career. (Wells, in *The Way the World is Going*, commented apropos the Baileys: 'They are not the Webbs, but only Webby people. I succumbed to the temptation of making it rather a lark. But every one recognised the "originals", so what was the good of the sham concealment?') *Machiavelli*, Book Two, 2.

BARNET, FREDERICK. Upon the outbreak of war in 1956 he is sent to France as an infantry officer and has a year's experience of soldiering. With the coming of peace he returns to England and is employed at the Winchester wireless station. His autobiographical novel *Wanderjahre*, published in 1970, records his impressions of life during the war years and is quoted extensively in Wells's account of the holocaust. *Set Free.*

BARNSTAPLE, ALFRED. 'Sub editor and general factotum of the *Liberal*, that well known organ of the more depressing aspects of advanced thought.' Advised by his doctor to take a complete rest, he embarks on a motoring holiday; during an experiment with space-time dimensions initiated from a different planet he is accidentally transported to another world with a highly advanced civilisation. After studying Utopian institutions and customs he is returned to earth, filled with nostalgia for the ideal world he will see no more. *Gods.*

BARRACK, DR. ELIHU.The doctor at Sundering on Sea consulted by

Job Huss. He is an 'agnostic by habit and profession. A Doubting Thomas, born and bred.' He disagrees with Job's religious views and has a lengthy argument with him on matters of belief. In Job's dream he appears as Elihu the son of Barachel the Buzite. *Undying Fire.*

BEALBY, ARTHUR. Stepson of the gardener at Shonts. Rebelling against a life of servitude, he runs away from Shonts and joins a caravan party. After becoming involved in a series of escapades, including an encounter with a tramp and taking part in a burglary, he eventually returns to the servants' quarters resolved to work harder in the future. *Bealby.*

BECHAMEL, GEORGE. An art critic who attempts to compromise and seduce Jessica Milton. He was 'a man of thirty or more, with a whitish face, an aquiline nose, a lank, flaxen moustache, and very fair hair'. He is outmanoeuvred by Hoopdriver who helps Jessica to escape from him while staying at a hotel at Bognor. *Wheels.*

BEDFORD. Narrator of *First Men.* An undischarged bankrupt, he rents a bungalow at Lympne while writing a play. Here he encounters Cavor, inventor of an anti-gravity substance. Together they travel to the moon in a sphere constructed of Cavorite. Bedford eventually returns to the earth alone, abandoning Cavor to his fate as a prisoner of the Selenites. While writing an account of his adventures he receives a number of wireless communications from the moon. *First Men.*

BELLOWS. Narrator of several of the early short stories including 'Le Mari Terrible', 'The Poet and the Emporium', 'The Remarkable Case of Davidson's Eyes', and 'The Triumphs of a Taxidermist'.

BENHAM, WILLIAM PORPHYRY. Son of a clergyman and schoolmaster, he is obsessed with the idea of aristocracy and decides to devote his life to the study of nobility, to 'studying and experimenting in the noble possibilities of man'. He falls in love with and marries Amanda Morris. Throughout his life he struggles against what he terms the four limitations: fear, indulgence, jealousy and prejudice. *Research.*

BENSINGTON. One of the discoverers of Herakleophorbia, the Food of the Gods. He was 'short and very very bald, and he stooped slightly; he wore gold rimmed spectacles and cloth boots that were abundantly cut open because of his numerous corns'. Following the public outcry at the effects of the discovery he retires to Tunbridge Wells with his housekeeper. *Food.*

BERNSTEIN, RACHEL. Sister of Melchior Bernstein and friend of Margaret Broxted and Theodore Bulpington. She and her brother are convinced Marxists and involve Theodore in a series of political discussions. Rachel seduces Theodore in her London flat and for a time the two are lovers. *Bulpington*.

BIRKENHEAD, EVANGELINE. Wife of Edward Albert Tewler. She was 'a remarkable dark young woman who had been in France for some months, and he had become temporarily Frenchified by that experience'. Repelled at first by Tewler's clumsiness as a lover, she relents and then marries him. They have a son, also named Edward Albert, but soon after become estranged. *Careful*.

BLADESOVER. *See* UP PARK.

BLAYPORT. A sea port situated on the River Blay, the childhood home of Theodore Bulpington and his parents, Raymond and Clorinda. In his imaginative daydreams Theodore christens himself 'The Bulpington of Blup', partly because he imagines 'Blup' to be the ancient name of Blayport. *Bulpington*, 1–3.

BLETTSWORTHY, ARNOLD. An effeminate young man, descendant of an ancient English family, who is advised to embark on a sea voyage for the sake of his health. After a series of harrowing adventures he has a mental breakdown, during which he imagines he sees the Megatherium still living. On his return to normal health he serves as a soldier in the First World War and finally becomes a director of the wine and brandy firm of Blettsworthy and Christopher. *Blettsworthy*.

BLISS, REGINALD. Author of 'The Cousins of Charlotte Bronte', 'A Child's History of the Crystal Palace', 'Firelight Rambles', 'Edible Fungi', 'Whales in Captivity', and other works. He is a friend of George Boon, and his literary executor; he prepares for publication Boon's 'literary remains'. *Boon*.

BOLARIS, RICHARD. Leader of one of the rival factions in a civil war and opponent of Ratzel. When Ratzel is taken prisoner he and Bolaris realise that they have far more in common than either had appreciated and that, in fact, they are brothers. *Brothers*.

BONOVER, GEORGE. Headmaster of Whortley Proprietary School. He dismisses Lewisham for evading school duties in order to go for a long walk with Ethel Henderson. *Lewisham*.

BOON, GEORGE A popular writer whose 'literary remains' are edited by Reginald Bliss. Bliss recalls his 'round, enigmatical face, an affair of rosy rotundities, his very bright, active eyes, his queer, wiry, black hair that went out to every point in the heavens, his ankles and neck and wrists all protruding from his garments in their own peculiar way, protruding a little more in the stress of flight'. The ephemera reproduced by his literary executor includes 'The Mind of the Race', 'The Spoils of Mr. Blandish', 'The

Wild Asses of the Devil' and 'The Story of the Last Trump'. *Boon*.

BRAMBLEHURST. *See* MIDHURST

BRITLING, HUGH. A successful English writer, the central character in *Britling*. The novel records his reaction to the First World War and the gradual involvement of himself, his household and family in the war effort. His eldest son, also named Hugh Britling, is killed in 1915. The description of Britling, his ménage at Matching's Easy and his circle of friends, is modelled closely on that of Wells himself when living at Easton Glebe, near Dunmow. *Britling*.

BRITTEN. Remington's chief friend at the City Merchants School; 'as boys, we walked together, read and discussed the same books, pursued the same enquires. We got a reputation as inseparables and the nickname of the Rose and the Lily, for Britten was short and thick-set with dark close curling hair and a ruddy Irish type of face; I was lean and fair-haired and some inches taller than he.' They meet again as adults and Britten becomes sub-editor of the *Blue Weekly*. He attempts to dissuade Remington from eloping with Isobel Rivers and thus destroying his political career. *Machiavelli*.

BROMLEY. Wells was born at 47 High Street, Bromley (now number 172) on 21 September 1866 and spent his childhood there. The town figures as 'Bromstead' in *Machiavelli* (Book 1, 2) and as 'Bun Hill' in *Air* (1). (Cf, *Experiment*, 38–112, 192–8).

The underground kitchen in which Wells spent a considerable part of his boyhood is described in *Comet*, Chapter 3 (see also the essay, 'This Misery of Boots', 1907); the opening chapter of *Dream* also gives much of the flavour of his home background as a child.

BROMSTEAD. *See* BROMLEY.

BROXTED, MARGARET. Daughter of Professor Broxted of Kingsway College and a close friend of Theodore Bulpington. Theodore meets her first as a schoolgirl and is immediately attracted; for him she is the personification of the Delphic Sybil, a 'lovely being, with her sweet wide eyes, her awakening youth'. For a time Theodore and Margaret are lovers but she rejects him when she realises his fundamental shallowness. *Bulpington*.

BRUMLEY, GEORGE. A well-known author who falls in love with Lady Harman, wife of Sir Isaac Harman. He has 'a round, ruddy, rather handsome, amiable face, a sort of bang of brown hair coming over one temple and a large silk bow under his chin and a little towards one ear'. Sir Isaac becomes jealous and warns his wife that she must forsake Brumley; following Sir Isaac's death she declines to marry him, preferring to retain her freedom. *Harman.*

BULPINGTON, THEODORE. Son of Raymond and Clorinda Bulpington of Blayport. Aesthetic and effeminate, he grows up in a mental world of his own making, obsessed by increasingly elaborate daydreams in which he is 'The Bulpington of Blup', a conquering hero. His whole life ministers to his daydreams until at last he romanticises his period of military service, becoming in his imagination 'Captain Blup-Bulpington,' the man who took the Kaiser prisoner. Wells observed that the character was intended to be 'a very direct caricature study of the irresponsible disconnected aesthetic mentality'. *Bulpington.*

BUN HILL [Bromley]. The home of the Smallways family. In the opening chapter of *Air* there is a vivid description of the urbanisation of Bun Hill, once 'an idyllic Kentish village'. (Cf. the 'Bromstead' chapter of *Machiavelli.*) *Air,* 1, 2.

BUNTING, RANDOLPH [Arthur Popham]. Randolph Bunting and his wife 'rescue' the mermaid when she comes ashore at Sandgate because they believe she is drowning, and invite her to remain with them as a paying guest. While staying with them the mermaid adopts the name Doris Thalassia Waters. (The character is based on Wells's neighbour at Arnold House, of whom he wrote: 'It was in '97 or '98 in a little house we occupied at Sandgate that we found congenial next door neighbours, a Mr. Arthur Popham and his wife, with two jolly children, and a coming and going of pleasant cousins and other friends'.) *Sea Lady.*

BURLEIGH, CECIL [Arthur Balfour]. 'The great Conservative leader. He was not only distinguished as a politican; he was eminent as a private gentleman, a philospher and a man of universal intelligence.' When Mr. Barnstaple is accidentally transported to Utopia, Burleigh is one of the party of seven who are transferred with him. *Gods.*

BURNMORE PARK. *See* UP PARK.

BURROWS, SIR ELIPHAZ. A governor of Woldingstanton school who plans to remove Job Huss from the headmastership. During a long discussion with Huss he expresses his belief in personal immortality and his disagreement with Job's ideas. In Job's dream he becomes Eliphaz the Temanite. *Undying Fire.*

CADDLES, ALBERT EDWARD. One of the Giant Children. He is the grandson of Mrs. Skinner, who feeds him with Herakleophorbia. He grows up in isolation, working in a chalk quarry; after several years he decides to visit London, consumed with curiosity about the meaning of life. After spending the night in Regent's Park he is killed by the rat police, the first of the giants to lose his life. *Food*.

CAMBRIDGE. Richard Remington was a student at Cambridge (Trinity College), and comments in detail upon life at the university. Here he meets his friend Willersley. Peter Stubland also spends his student years at Cambridge. 'Camford' (in *Camford*) is apparently an amalgam of Oxford and Cambridge. *Machiavelli*, Book 1, 4; *Joan*, 11; *Camford*, *passim*.

CAMPBELL, CLEMENTINA [Odette Keun]. Companion and mistress of William Clissold. Clissold first meets her in Paris and is immediately attracted by her 'abstracted countenance, elfin and pensive, infantile and sage'. She lives with him at the Villa Jasmin, near Grasse, but has little interest in or understanding of his social and political ideas. *Clissold*.

CAPES, GODWIN. Demonstrator in the biological laboratory of the Central Imperial College at Westminster, and a Fellow of the Royal Society. He was 'an exceptionally fair man of two or three and thirty, so ruddily blond that it was a mercy he had escaped light eyelashes, and with a minor but by no means contemptible reputation of his own'. Unhappily married, he and Ann Veronica Stanley fall in love and decide to live together. Some years later Capes obtains a divorce from his wife and he and Ann Veronica marry. He becomes a successful playwright, writing under the pseudonym Thomas More. *Veronica*.

CARNABY, THE EARL OF. Lover of Beatrice Normandy who, despite her love for George Ponderevo, becomes Carnaby's mistress. He is described as 'that remarkable vestige of his own brilliant youth. . . . a man of sixty five who had sinned all the sins, so they said, and laid waste the most magnificent political debut of any man of his generation. He was a lean little man with grey-blue eyes in his brown face, and his cracked voice was the worse thing in his effect.' *Tono-Bungay*.

CATSKILL, RUPERT [Winston Churchill]. Secretary of State for War, a 'slow moving, intent, sandy complexioned figure in a grey top hat with a black band'. When Mr. Barnstaple is accidentally transported to Utopia, Catskill is one of the party of seven who are transferred with him. He is critical of Utopian institutions and devises an abortive plan for the conquest of the planet. *Gods*.

CAVOR. Scientist and inventor of Cavorite, a substance opaque to all forms of radiant energy. 'He was a short, round-bodied, thin-legged little man, with a jerky quality in his motions; he had seen fit to clothe his extraordinary mind in a cricket cap, an overcoat, and cycling knickerbockers and stockings.' He and Bedford travel to the moon together in a sphere constructed of Cavorite; Bedford eventually returns to earth, leaving Cavor behind as a prisoner of the Selenites. *First Men.*

CHAFFERY, JAMES. Ethel Henderson's step-father, a charlatan who poses as a spiritualist medium. He is 'a benevolent looking, faintly shabby gentleman, with bushy iron-grey side whiskers, a wide thin lipped mouth tucked in at the corners, and a chin like the toe of a boot'. After defrauding Lagune of his savings he absconds with his female assistant. His wife, Ethel's mother, then appeals to Lewisham for support. *Lewisham.*

CHATHAM. The home of George Ponderevo's cousin Nicodemus Frapp and his family. George escaped from Chatham by walking to Bladesover House, a distance of 17 miles. *Tono-Bungay,* Book One, 2.

CHATTERIS, HARRY. 'The nephew of an earl and the hero of a scandal, and a quite possible candidate for the Hythe division of Kent.' He is more and more attracted to the mermaid and, under her spell, neglects his political career and breaks off his engagement to Adeline Glendower. Ultimately the mermaid lures Chatteris to his death. (Wells remarked of him: 'Chatteris is a promising young politician, a sort of mixture of Harry Cust and any hero in any novel by Mrs. Humphry Ward'.) *Sea Lady.*

CHEAPING [Woking]. One of the neighbouring villages of Lady Grove (*q.v.*) During George Ponderevo's aeronautical experiments gas is brought up from Cheaping. *Tono-Bungay,* Book 3, 3.

CHECKSHILL. *See* UP PARK.

CHERRY GARDENS [Cheriton]. The suburb in which Harry Mortimer Smith spent his childhood. 'The name of the place was Cherry Gardens; it was about two miles from the sea at Sandbourne [Sandgate], one way lay the town of Cliffstone [Folkestone] from which steamboats crossed the sea to France, and the other way lay Lowcliff [Shorncliffe] and its rows and rows of ugly red brick barracks. . . .' *Dream,* 2, 3.

CHESSING HANGER PARK [Penshurst Place]. 'Uncle John Julip, my mother's brother, who was gardener to Lord Bramble of Chessing Hanger Park.' In describing the gardener's cottage at Chessing Hanger, and the walk from Cherry Gardens to the Park, Wells gives a fictionalised account of the Penshurst estate, where his father, Joseph Wells, was born in 1827 (Cf. *Experiment,* pp. 53–4, 195). *Dream,* 2, 3.

CHISELSTEAD [Chislehurst]. The scene of many of the boyhood escapades of George Ponderevo. *Tono-Bungay,* Book 1, 1.

CHITTERLOW, HARRY. A playwright who accidentally knocks Kipps down while cycling, takes him home to make amends, and becomes his lasting friend. He tells Kipps of the advertisement which brings him his fortune. Subsequently Kipps buys a share in Chitterlow's play 'The Pestered Butterfly' which enjoys a huge success. The character also figures prominently in *Waddy*, but is developed on rather different lines. *Kipps*.

CHRISTIAN, LADY MARY. Sister of Philip and Guy Christian of Burnmore House. She and Stephen Stratton are childhood companions and he falls deeply in love with her. Unwilling to face a life of poverty with Stratton she marries Justin, a wealthy financier. Years afterwards Stratton and Mary meet again and become lovers; they are discovered by Justin and forced to part. They correspond and, after meeting accidentally, Justin threatens divorce. Mary commits suicide rather than risk the destruction of Stratton's career. *Friends*.

CLAVERINGS [Easton Lodge]. The home of Lady Homartyn, Mr. Britling's neighbour in Essex. *Britling, passim. See* MATCHING'S EASY.

CLAYTON. Clayton, Swathinglea and Overcastle were 'contiguous towns in the great industrial area of the Midlands' (*Comet*), apparently corresponding to Etruria, Hanley and Newcastle under Lyme. 'Clayton Crest' is Basford Bank, Etruria. Wells stayed at Basford for three months in the spring of 1888 whilst convalescing after an illness. *Comet, passim. See* STOKE ON TRENT.

CLEWER. *See* WINDSOR.

CLISSOLD, WILLIAM. An industrialist who retires to the Villa Jasmin near Grasse, to write his memoirs. His character and mental attitudes are closely akin to those of Wells himself, and the description of Clissold's villa in Provence resembles Wells's villa, Lou Bastidon, his winter home from 1924 to 1926. Clissold advocates an 'open conspiracy' of intelligent men and women throughout the world. *Clissold*.

COOTE, CHESTER. A local house-agent, 'a refined and amiable figure ... a most active and gentlemanly person, a conscious gentleman, equally aware of society and the serious side of life'. After Kipps has inherited a fortune Coote acts as his mentor in introducing him into polite society. Coote's sister takes it upon herself to foster Kipps's appreciation of the arts. The character also figures briefly in *Waddy*. *Kipps*.

COSSAR. A civil engineer, 'a large-bodied man with gaunt inelegant limbs casually placed at convenient corners of his body, and a face like a carving abandoned at an early stage as altogether too unpromising for completion'. A friend of Redwood and Bensington, he plays a leading role in the destruction of the Experimental Farm. His three sons are fed on the Food. *Food*.

CREST HILL [Witley Park Manor, Godalming]. The vast house built by Edward Ponderevo at the zenith of his fame and power. It was the building of Crest Hill which led directly to the collapse of the Tono-Bungay empire. Wells records perceptively: 'It is curious how many of these modern financiers of chance and bluff have ended their careers by building. It was not merely my uncle. Sooner or later they all seem to bring their luck to the test of realisation. . . . Then the whole fabric of confidence and imagination totters—and down they come. . .'. The account of Crest Hill given in 'Our Progress from Camden Town to Crest Hill' is a photographic description of Witley Park Manor, near Godalming, the never-completed mansion of the financier Whitaker Wright. Indeed the idea of writing *Tono-Bungay*, a vast panorama of 'this strange advertising commercialised civilisation', seems to date from the suicide of Whitaker Wright in the London Law Courts in 1904. (Cf. Geoffrey West, *H. G. Wells: A Sketch for a Portrait*, p. 180.) *Tono-Bungay*, Book 3, 2.

DAD, WILLIAM. A governor of the Woldingstanton school, manufacturer of the Dad and Showite car. He advocates a 'simple, straightforward, commercial and technical education' and disapproves strongly of the educational ideas of Job Huss. During a long discussion with Huss he expresses his belief in a simple religious faith; in Job's dream he becomes Bildad the Shuhite. *Undying Fire*.

DAVIS, JOSEPH. A successful writer, author of a series of historical romances, 'a sensitive, intelligent and cultivated man'. He becomes obsessed with the idea that cosmic rays are in reality thought rays emanating from a superior civilisation on the planet Mars. Eventually he realises that both he and his gracious, enigmatical wife Mary have been infected by the thought rays. *Begotten*.

DEBENHAM, JOAN. The daughter of Will Sydenham; after her mother's death she is adopted by Arthur and Dolly Stubland and brought up under their name. She falls in love with Peter Stubland, whom she had believed to be her half-brother, and eventually marries him. In the Preface to the Atlantic Edition Wells remarked: 'Joan, the author fell in love with himself as she grew; and she is still his favourite and, he thinks, in many ways his best done heroine.' *Joan*.

DENTON. A young attendant on a London flying-stage, in love with

Elizabeth Mwres. Elizabeth and Denton run away together and live for a time in exile, but return to London when they realise the impracticality of living in the countryside. They eventually find happiness when Elizabeth inherits a legacy from her admirer Bindon. *Days to Come.*

DEVIZES, WILFRED. Mental specialist and father of Christina Alberta. A 'lank, dark, shock-headed man', he realises that he is Christina's true father when she consults him regarding the reincarnation fantasies of Albert Edward Preemby. *Christina.*

DOLORES. *See* WILBECK.

DREW, LADY. The owner of Bladesover House. 'Head and centre of our system was Lady Drew, her "leddyship", shrivelled, garrulous, with a wonderful memory for genealogies and very, very old.' George Ponderevo, son of her housekeeper, has a fight with Archie Garvell and is banished from Bladesover by Lady Drew. *Tono-Bungay.*

DIRECK, MR. Secretary of a Massachusetts cultural society, on behalf of which he visits Mr. Britling in the summer of 1914. He stays with Mr. Britling at the Dower House, Matching's Easy, for several weeks, falling in love with Cicely Corner. In the second year of the war he becomes a soldier in the Canadian army. *Britling.*

DUFFIELD [Sendgrove]. The dependent village of Lady Grove (*q.v.*). Searching for epitaphs in the churchyard, George and Edward Ponderevo find 'a marble crusader with a broken nose, under a battered canopy of fretted stone'. *Tono-Bungay*, Book 3, 2.

ELOI, THE. The frail and child-like race which inhabits the world above ground in the year 802701. Physically weak, the Eloi are preyed upon by the Morlocks and live in fear of them. One of the Eloi, Weena, is rescued from drowning by the Time Traveller and follows him on his journeyings. *Time Machine.*

EWART, SIDNEY. A schoolfellow of George Ponderevo who meets him again in London after an interval of six years. The two become firm friends and Ewart, now a monumental mason, advises George on his emotional life. 'His was essentially the nature of an artistic appreciator; he could find interest and beauty in endless aspects of things that I marked as evil ... commonness vanished before Ewart, at his expository touch all things became memorable and rare.' (Cf. *Experiment*, 611). *Tono-Bungay.*

FARR, JOSEPH. Head of the technical staff of Woldingstanton school and candidate for the post of Headmaster. He disapproves strongly of the educational theories of Job Huss and argues with

Job over his religious and philosophical ideas. In Job's dream he becomes Zophar the Naamathite. *Undying Fire*.

FINCHATTON, DR. A doctor in a country practice near Ely who, while recuperating at Les Noupets from a breakdown, encounters a young croquet player, George Frobisher. He relates to Frobisher the story of 'the haunting fear in Cainsmarsh'. The croquet player is deeply impressed with Finchatton's story but, despite the unsettling effect on his mind, insists on returning to the normal routines of his life. *Croquet*.

FISHBOURNE. A village (near Chichester) in which Mr. Polly is a shopkeeper for fifteen years. It is several times referred to as 'Foxbourne', but this appears to be simply carelessness on Wells's part: the error was corrected in the Atlantic edition. *Polly*, 1, 7–8.

FOLKESTONE. Wells lived at Sandgate (Spade House, Radnor Cliff Crescent) from 1900–9. Prior to this he had lived at Beach Cottage, Granville Road, Sandgate (1898–9) and Arnold House, Sandgate. Folkestone and the surrounding area figure in much of his fiction. See especially *Kipps*, passim; *Sea Lady*, passim; *Dream*, 2; and the short story 'The New Accelerator'. Spade House figures in *Christina* as 'Udimore'. *See also* CHERRY GARDENS; HYTHE; NEW ROMNEY.

FOTHERINGAY, GEORGE McWHIRTER. An assistant at the drapery emporium of Grigsby and Blott, who discovers that he possesses the ability to work miracles. A 'commonplace, pale-faced young man', he embarks on a series of increasingly elaborate miracles, culminating in the cessation of the rotation of the earth. Alarmed by the disastrous consequences of his gift, he chooses to forego his miraculous powers. *Miracles*.

FOXFIELD. A 'hairy untidy biologist', friend of the publisher Stephen Wilbeck. He has a 'big red talkative mouth with a vast fuzz of brindled black and grey hair, he looks at you through his spectacles like the lamps of a big car coming at you fast and rather out of control, and his voice is a rich continuum'. Foxfield does not share Wilbeck's innate hopefulness. Dolores, although taken aback by his untidiness, is impressed with his biological knowledge. (Also mentioned in *Camford* and *Begotten*.) *Dolores*.

FRAPP, NICODEMUS. Cousin of George Ponderevo, a baker at Chatham. He was 'a bent, slow-moving, unwilling dark man, with flour in his hair and eye-lashes, in the lines of his face and the seams of his coat'. George is sent by his mother to stay with Frapp and learn the bakery trade; he wearies of the atmosphere of dinginess and religious intolerance and eventually runs away, walking the 17 miles back to Bladesover House. *Tono-Bungay.*

FROBISHER, GEORGE. An effeminate young man, brought up in a sheltered and comfortable way by his paternal aunt. While holidaying at Les Noupets he encounters Dr. Finchatton, who unfolds to him the story of 'the haunting fear in Cainsmarsh'. Despite the unsettling implications of the story he insists on returning to the normal routines of his life and keeps his appointment to play croquet with his aunt. *Croquet.*

GARVELL, ARCHIE. Half brother of Beatrice Normandy and childhood acquaintance of George Ponderevo. As a consequence of George's fight with Garvell, George is banished from Bladesover House. Years later, by which time Ponderevo has become wealthy in his own right, the two meet again; Garvell was now 'a smart, impecunious soldier of no particular distinction, who would, I think, have been quite prepared to develop any sporting instincts I possessed, and who was beautifully unaware of our former contact'. *Tono-Bungay.*

GIDDING. A wealthy American, friend of Stephen Stratton. Together he and Stratton establish the firm of Alphabet and Mollentrave, a giant publishing enterprise which aims to make available cheap editions of all the world's finest books. *Friends.*

GOOD, MATILDA. A kindly boarding-house keeper who invites Martha Smith and her family to come and live with her at Pimlico. 'She was much larger than any lady I had hitherto been accustomed to; she had a breadth and variety of contour like scenery rather than a human being; the thought of her veins being varicose, indeed of all her anatomy being varicose and fantastic, seemed a right and proper one.' She is admired and respected by Harry Mortimer Smith, who continues to live with her after the death of his mother. *Dream.*

GRAHAM. A young politician who falls into a trance in 1897 and awakes in the year 2100. Because of his accumulated wealth he finds himself Master of the World. He is killed while pursuing Ostrog, a political rival who attempts to seize his power. *Sleeper.*

GRAMMONT, MISS V. V. 'An extremely pretty young woman of five or six and twenty.... She had a clear sun-browned complexion, with dark hair and smiling lips. her features were finely modelled, with just that added touch of breadth in the brow and softness in the cheek bones, that faint flavour of the Amerindian, one sees at times in American women.' Sir Richmond Hardy meets her while visiting Stonehenge and is immediately attracted by her beauty and vivid historical imagination; the two fall in love. *Secret Places.*

GRAVES, LYULPH. Friend of Arnold Blettsworthy and a partner in Blettsworthy & Graves' bookshop at Oxford. After a disagreement Blettsworthy loses touch with him for many years, but the two meet again when both are convalescing after being wounded in the First World War. Graves is eventually employed as marketing adviser in the family business. *Blettsworthy*.

GRIFFIN. A demonstrator of physics in a provincial college who, while conducting experiments in optical density, discovers a method of making himself invisible. After various adventures in London he travels to the village of Iping, determined to find some way of making himself visible again. At length, after renting a room at the Coach and Horses for two months, his supply of money runs out; he flees to Port Stowe, where he goes into hiding and embarks upon a campaign of murder. He is killed in a fight with a gang of navvies. *Invisible*.

HALLIFORD. The narrator in *Worlds* and the curate shelter from the Martians in an empty house at Halliford. (Halliford is situated between Walton on Thames and Chertsey.) *Worlds*, Book Two, 1–5.

HAMMERGALLOW, LADY. Owner of Siddermorton house [Up Park], 'a dear old lady with a ropy neck, a ruddled countenance and spasmodic gusts of odd temper, whose three remedies for all human trouble among her dependents are a bottle of gin, a pair of charity blankets, or a new crown piece'. She rules the village of Siddermorton with an autocratic rule, and believes that the angel is an illegitimate son of the vicar. *Visit*.

HARBURY, *See* WINDSOR.

HARDY, SIR RICHMOND. A member of the Fuel Commission who is advised by his doctor to embark on a motoring holiday in south west England to recuperate from a nervous breakdown. During the holiday he unburdens his soul to the specialist, Dr. Martineau, talking freely and frankly of his sexual history and of the ideas which dominate his life. Whilst at Stonehenge he meets Miss Grammont and falls in love with her. Several months later Sir Richmond becomes seriously ill with pneumonia and dies, after hearing that his proposals to the Fuel Commission have been rejected. *Secret Places*.

HARMAN, LADY (*née* ELLEN SAWBRIDGE). A sensitive, thoughtful woman who, at the age of eighteen, marries Sir Isaac Harman. When Lady Harman wishes to widen her circle of friends and become involved in suffragette politics Sir Isaac is consumed with jealousy and attempts to keep his wife a prisoner. She becomes infatuated with a writer, George Brumley, and Sir Isaac tells her she must forsake him. After the sudden death of her husband she resolves to retain her freedom and never to marry again. *Harman*.

HARMAN, SIR ISAAC. Husband of Lady Ellen Harman. He is a 'lean, grey-headed, obstinate-looking man with a diabetic complexion'. He is extremely wealthy, having made a considerable fortune in the catering trade; his knighthood is granted for his financial support of the Liberal press. His conception of marriage is strict and conventional, and he is totally opposed to his wife's liberal attitudes. *Harman*.

HARROWDEAN, MRS. [Elizabeth von Arnim]. A young widow with whom Mr. Britling is emotionally involved in the early part of 1914. 'She had an intermittent vein of high spirits that was almost better than humour and made her quickly popular with most of the people she met, and she was only twenty miles away in her pretty house and her absurd little jolly park.' Mr. Britling seeks to disentangle himself from the liaison, and following the outbreak of war resolves to see her no more. *Britling*.

HELEN. [Rebecca West]. Friend and lover of William Clissold. 'For me she was wonderful and mystical; she was beautiful and lovely for me as no human being has ever been; she had in my perception of her a distinctive personal splendour that was as entirely and inseparably her own as the line of her neck or the timbre of her voice'. Clissold meets Helen during the First World War, when she is a comparatively unknown young actress. For a while they are extremely happy and travel much together, but eventually they quarrel and agree to part, since in the ultimate neither is willing to permit their relationship to interfere in any way with their respective work. (Cf. Gordon N. Ray, *H. G. Wells and Rebecca West*, 161–6.) *Clissold*.

HENDERSON, ETHEL. Chaffery's step-daughter, with whom Lewisham falls in love while a schoolmaster at Whortley (Midhurst). Two years later, when a science student in London, he encounters her again, neglects his studies on her account and marries her. Although physically attractive she is intellectually shallow and becomes jealous of Lewisham's friendship with his fellow student Alice Heydinger. After a bitter quarrel he and Ethel are eventually reconciled. *Lewisham*.

HENLEY, WILLIAM ERNEST. The dedicatee of *Time Machine*. W. E. Henley, a notable editor and poet, was editor of *The New Review* and encouraged Wells to write *The Time Machine* for serialisation in that journal (January–June 1895).

HEYDINGER, ALICE. A biology student at the Normal School of

Science who admires Lewisham and is secretly in love with him. She lends him books and encourages his socialist activities. She is greatly distressed by the news of his marriage to Ethel Henderson but continues to write to him. *Lewisham*.

HICK, MARJORIE. The dedicatee of *The Adventures of Tommy*. This story was written in 1898 when Wells was convalescing after an illness. It was written for the amusement of Marjorie Hick, his doctor's daughter. In 1929 Wells gave the copyright to Hick to help him establish a younger daughter—Wells's godchild—in medical practice.

HICKLEYBROW. It is at Hickleybrow that Redwood and Bensington set up their experimental farm in order to study growth in plants and animals. *Food*, 2, 3.

HILYER, REV. K. Vicar of Siddermorton and an enthusiastic amateur ornithologist. He shoots the angel under the impression that it is a rare bird; discovering his error he invites the angel to the vicarage to have his wounds tended. He chaperones the angel into local society and permits him to explore the village under his guidance. After the angel's death in the fire the vicar declines into a state of apathy and dies within a year. *Visit*.

HOLT. A village near Wrexham where Wells spent a brief period as a schoolmaster during the summer of 1887. He appears to have recalled some of the details of the village and its surrounding countryside in describing the Welsh setting of *Argonauts*, which is set in and around the village of Llyddwdd. Wells also draws on his Holt experiences in describing the Calvinistic religion of Nicodemus Frapp in *Tono-Bungay*. (Cf. *Experiment* pp. 292–298). *Argonauts, passim*; *Tono-Bungay*, Book One, 2.

HOOPDRIVER, J. E. An assistant at the drapery emporium of Antrobus and Company of Putney. In August 1895 he sets off on a cycling holiday through Surrey and Sussex, having recently learned to ride the bicycle. Whilst on tour he encounters Jessica Milton and becomes romantically involved with her; he helps her to escape from her pursuer, Bechamel. *Wheels*.

HORRABIN, J. F. The dedicatee of *Brothers*. Frank Horrabin was a friend of the Wells family for many years and collaborated closely with Wells in the production of *The Outline of History*, preparing many of the maps, charts and illustrations for the first and subsequent editions.

HORSELL COMMON. The site of the landing of the first Martian cylinder. The Common is situated between Woking and Chobham. Wells lived at Woking (Lynton, Station Road) during the year 1895 and knew the district well. 'Our withdrawal to

Woking was a fairly cheerful adventure. . . . There I planned and wrote *The War of the Worlds*, *The Wheels of Chance* and *The Invisible Man*. . . . I wheeled about the district marking down suitable places and people for destruction by my Martians.' (*Experiment*, pp. 542–3.) *Worlds*, 2–11.

HUSS, JOB. Headmaster of Woldingstanton School. Like Job in the Biblical narrative, disasters fall upon him: his son is reported dead, he discovers he is suffering from cancer, there are deaths at the school, and there are moves afoot to deprive him of the headmastership. Despite this adversity he remains steadfast in his religious beliefs. While under the anaesthetic for his operation he has a vision in which he is Job of Uz; God speaks to him and pleas for courage and endurance. *Undying Fire*.

HYTHE. It was at Hythe that Kipps chose to locate his bookshop. 'The bookshop of Kipps is on the left-hand side of the Hythe High Street coming from Folkestone, between the yard of the livery stable and the shop window full of old silver and such-like things—it is quite easy to find. . . .' *Kipps*, Book Three, 3.

IMMERING. *See* IPING.

IMMERING COMMON [Iping Common]. The scene of the 'scandalous ramble' between Lewisham and Ethel Henderson. The Common also figures as 'Iping Hanger' in *Visit. Lewisham*, 6; *Visit*, 2.

IPING. A village in West Sussex, the focal point of many of the incidents in *Invisible*. The Invisible Man arrives at the Coach and Horses at Iping and creates havoc among the local population. Iping also figures as 'Immering' in *Lewisham* and as 'Iping Hanger' in *Visit. Invisible*, 1–12; *Lewisham*, 6; *Visit*, 2.

JIM, UNCLE. The villainous nephew of the plump woman of the Potwell Inn. On his release from prison he returns to the Inn to terrorise her. He tells Mr. Polly to 'scoot' and threatens violence when he refuses to leave. He and Mr. Polly then attempt to outmanoeuvre each other in the possession of the Inn; Uncle Jim is finally defeated and is drowned in the River Medway. *Polly*.

JOHNSON, HAROLD. The married cousin of Alfred Polly, and ticket-clerk at Easewood Junction. He is a sober, practical man who gives Mr. Polly much well-intentioned advice and urges him to set up a draper's shop of his own. Johnson's home is the setting for the funeral feast following the death of Mr. Polly's father. Polly lives with him and his wife, Grace, until his own marriage. *Polly*.

JULIP, UNCLE JOHN [Wells's Uncle Williams]. Brother of Martha Smith and gardener to Lord Bramble. 'He was very short and fatter than was usual among gardeners. He had a smooth white face and a wise self-satisfied smile.' After being dismissed for stealing produce he degenerates into a life of drinking and gambling. Finally, after an argument, he is forcibly ejected from the house by Martha Smith's eldest son. *Dream*.

JUSTIN. A wealthy financier who marries Lady Mary Christian. He was 'an undersized, brown-clad middle-aged man with a big head, a dark face and expressive brown eyes. . . . This then was Justin, the incredibly rich and powerful, whose comprehensive operations could make and break a thousand fortunes in a day.' After discovering his wife's infidelity with Stephen Stratton, Justin insists that Stratton must leave the country for three years. *Friends*.

KEMP, DR. Formerly a student at University College, London, then becomes engaged on scientific research at his home near Port Burdock. Griffin enters his house by chance, recognises him, and relates the story of the discovery of invisibility and his subsequent adventures. Kemp promises to shield Griffin but, realising that his friend has become a danger to society, alerts the police of his whereabouts. *Invisible*.

KENTLAKE, STELLA. Wife of Gemini Twain. Attractive and intelligent, she lives with Gemini in a Suffolk cottage before marrying him. After Gemini's breakdown she wins him back to health. *Babes*.

KENTLAKE, UNCLE ROBERT. Uncle of Stella Kentlake. Stella appeals to him for help when her mother intervenes in her emotional life; Uncle Robert takes Stella to live with him at Cambridge. A talkative man 'with that invariable confidence of his that he was quite all right and knew it, when all the rest of the world was wrong', he embodies in his general philosophy many of Wells's own attitudes. *Babes*.

KEUN, ODETTE. The dedicatee of *Clissold* and *Bulpington* and a close friend of Wells's during the years 1923–33.

KIPPS, ARTHUR. The illegitimate son of James Waddy and Margaret Euphemia Kipps, brought up by an uncle and aunt at New Romney. He is apprenticed to Mr. Edwin Shalford at the Folkestone Drapery Bazaar, but unexpectedly inherits a fortune from his paternal grandfather. After trying unsuccessfully to become a member of polite society he marries his childhood sweetheart, Ann Pornick. He eventually opens a bookshop at Hythe. (Kipps is also one of the central characters in *Waddy*.) *Kipps*.

LADY GROVE [Sutton Place, near Guildford]. 'Lady Grove, you know, is a very beautiful house indeed, a still and gracious place, whose age-long seclusion was only effectively broken with the toot of

the coming of the motor-car.' This ancient house was purchased
by Edward Ponderevo who lived the life of a lord of the manor for
some years before eventually tiring of its outmodedness. (Cf.
Geoffrey   Harmsworth,   *Northcliffe*,   261.)   *Tono-Bungay*,
Book 3, 2.

LAGUNE. A fellow student of Lewisham's at the Normal School of
Science, 'a grizzled little old man with a very small face and very
big grey eyes . . . he wore a brown velvet jacket and was reputed
to be enormously rich'. An ardent spiritualist, he invites
Lewisham to a seance where the latter encounters once again
Ethel Henderson, now Lagune's typist. Lagune continues to have
faith in Chaffery's integrity as a medium, but is eventually
defrauded by Chaffery of his savings. *Lewisham*.

LAMMAM [Wallingford]. The neighbouring village to Potwell, a
short distance away by boat. *Polly*, 9, 10.

LAMMOCK, NOAH. A writer, the modern personification of Noah the
son of Lamech. He has a series of conversations with God, who
tells him that he wants Noah to construct a new Ark to save
civilisation: 'We will save all the living seeds of civilisation for a
new sowing. Off we will go. And when this inundation of foul
warfare is over and the stench has subsided, the Ark will rest
again on another Ararat and out you will come, all of you, to a
cleansed, renascent world.' *Ararat*.

LAMONT, FLORENCE. The dedicatee of *Gods*. Florence Lamont and
her husband Thomas were friends of Wells's during the 1920s.

LARKINS SISTERS. Annie, Miriam and Minnie, the daughters of Mr.
Polly's maternal aunt. Mr. Polly first meets them at the funeral of
his father; he finds them attractive company and spends an
increasing amount of time in their company. He eventually
proposes to Miriam, the most serious of the three, and is unhappily married to her for fifteen years in a little drapery shop at
Fishbourne. Weary of his marriage and desperately unhappy, he
abandons Miriam and ultimately finds happiness in the life of a
general handyman at a country inn. Five years after his desertion
he returns to Fishbourne and finds Miriam and Annie have
converted the shop into tea rooms. *Polly*.

LEADFORD, WILLIAM. Narrator of *Comet*, a clerk in the office of
Rawdon's pot-bank at Clayton, in the Four Towns. He lives with
his mother and is a close friend of Parload [R. A. Gregory]. The
entire district is in a state of industrial unrest and Leadford
becomes an enthusiastic convert to socialism. He falls in love
with his cousin, Nettie Stuart, and pursues her when she elopes
with her lover, Verral. *Comet*.

LEEDS, MARTIN [Rebecca West]. Mistress of Sir Richmond Hardy, a young artist who does 'a peculiar sort of humorous illustrations usually with a considerable amount of bite in them'. While on a motoring holiday recuperating from a nervous breakdown, Sir Richmond confides to his doctor that he and Martin Leeds are lovers and that she is the mother of his young daughter. After his death she visits him and weeps over his body. *Secret Places*.

LEWISHAM, GEORGE EDGAR. An assistant master at the Whortley Proprietary School, Sussex, who, at the age of eighteen, becomes romantically involved with Ethel Henderson. After being dismissed from his post at the school, he gains a scholarship to the Normal School of Science, London, where he studies biology under Huxley. Later he meets Ethel Henderson again and marries her, neglecting his studies on her behalf; finally he abandons his academic career altogether in the interests of domesticity. The character of Lewisham and the description of his surrroundings at Whortley [Midhurst] and London are based closely on that of Wells as a student. *Lewisham*.

LIMPSFIELD. The Ingle-Nook near Limpsfield (Surrey) is the childhood home of Joan and Peter Stubland. The description of the house (Chapter One), corresponds to Spade House, Sandgate, Wells's home from 1900–9. *Joan, passim*.

LLYDDWDD. A village in Carnarvonshire (fictitious), the setting for the events recounted in *Argonauts*, an early draft of *Time Machine*. Some of the details of the setting were apparently recalled from Wells's brief period as a schoolmaster at Holt, near Wrexham, during the summer of 1887. *Argonauts, passim. See also* HOLT.

LONDON. Wells knew London and its surrounding area extremely well, and felt a strong affection for it. '. . . London, for all my outrageous radicalism, is a very friendly and pleasant city for me. If I have no garden of my own, Regent's Park just outside my door grows prettier every year; there are no gardens like Kew Gardens and no more agreeable people in the world than the people in the London streets.' (*Experiment*, 742.)

He lived at various addresses in London for much of his working life: 12 Fitzroy Road, Primrose Hill, July 1888–May 1889; 46 Fitzroy Road, May 1889–October 1891; 28 Haldon Road, Wandsworth, October 1891–August 1893; 4 Cumnor Place, Sutton, August 1893–December 1893; 7 Mornington Place, January–March 1894; 12 Mornington Road, March 1894–October 1895; 6 Clements Inn, 1902–3; 17 Church Row, Hampstead, 1909–12; 52 St James's Court, 1913–23; 4 Whitehall

Court (Flat 120), 1923–8; 614 St Ermins, 1928–9; 47 Chiltern Court Mansions, 1930–7; 13 Hanover Terrace, Regents Park, 1937–46.

References to London in Wells's fiction are too numerous to itemise in any detail, but the following is a summary of the more important scenes:

Hoopdriver was a draper's assistant at Putney, and the opening chapters of *Wheels* describe the emporium and Hoopdriver setting off from Putney on his cycling holiday. *Wheels*, 1, 2.

Griffin was engaged on research in London, and his early adventures in invisibility take place in and around the city. *Invisible*, 20–23.

The Martians attack London and attempt to establish a permanent base at Primrose Hill. Much of the action of *Worlds* takes place in and around the city. *Worlds*, Book One, 14, 16; Book Two, 6–10.

Sleeper and *Days to Come* are essentially Wells's vision of London in the 21st century. *Sleeper* and *Days to Come*, *passim*.

Lewisham was a student at the Normal School of Science (now the Imperial College of Science and Technology) South Kensington. After his marriage to Ethel Henderson he lived in lodgings at Brompton. Following the disappearance of his father in law, Chaffery, Lewisham and his wife moved into a house at Clapham. *Lewisham*, 8–32.

George Ponderevo was also a science student at South Kensington. During his courtship with Marion, he meets her parents at their home in Walham Green. The patent medicine Tono-Bungay is launched from a building in Raggett Street, E.C. After his marriage to Marion, George lives at Ealing. Later, following the immense financial success of the Tono-Bungay enterprise, George's uncle occupies a suite of rooms at the Hardingham Hotel. *Tono-Bungay*, *passim*.

Ann Veronica fled from her unhappy home at Morningside Park to a hotel 'in a little side street opening on the Embankment'. She studied biology at the Central Imperial College. Her encounter with Ramage takes place at the Hotel Rococo. Later she participates in a suffragette raid upon the House of Commons. *Veronica*, 5, 8, 9, 10.

Richard Remington was a schoolboy at City Merchants School. Later, as a married man, he lives at Westminster and becomes an M.P. He encounters Oscar and Altiora Bailey [Sidney and Beatrice Webb] at their house in Chambers Street, Westminster. *Machiavelli*, Book One, 3: Book Two, 2, 4: Book Three, 1–4.

Harry Mortimer Smith lived with his widowed mother at Lupus Street, Pimlico. He obtains employment in the editorial department at Thunderstone House, a popular publishing enterprise. *Dream*, 4–7.

LOW, WALTER. The dedicatee of *Visit*. Low was editor of the *Educational Times* at the time (*circa* 1891) when Wells was a frequent contributor.

LYMPNE. It is at Lympne (Kent) that Bedford first encounters Cavor and becomes involved in his plans to construct an anti-gravity substance. *First Men*, 1–3.

MAGNET, WILL. A writer of humorous books, 'one of those quiet, deliberately unassuming people who do not even attempt to be beautiful'. He is engaged to Marjorie Pope, but Marjorie breaks off the engagement in favour of Richard Trafford. Magnet then marries Daphne, the eldest of the five Pope children. *Marriage*.

MANNING, HUBERT. A civil servant, 'a tall young man of thirty seven with a handsome, thoughtful, impassive face, a full black moustache, and a certain heavy luxuriousness of gesture'. He asks Ann Veronica to marry him, and although she rejects his offer at the time they are engaged for a period after her return from London. She realises the depth and sincerity of Manning's feelings towards her but ultimately breaks off the engagement in order to elope with Capes. *Veronica*.

MARCUS, HETTY. An attractive school teacher, 'dark eyed, warm skinned, wayward and fragile'; she meets and falls in love with Harry Mortimer Smith before he embarks for the front in 1914. Smith divorces her because of her infidelity with Sumner; later he takes pity on her and assists her to emigrate to Canada. *Dream*.

MARTINEAU, DR. A distinguished Harley Street physician, author of *The Psychology of the New Age*. He advises Sir Richmond Hardy to embark on a motoring holiday for the sake of his health and accompanies him for most of the journey. During the holiday he encourages Sir Richmond to discuss his emotional problems and state of mind. *Secret Places*.

MARVEL, THOMAS. A tramp with a 'copious, flexible visage, a nose of cylindrical protusion, a liquorish, ample, fluctuating mouth, and a beard of bristling eccentricity'. Griffin enlists his help to retrieve his clothes and notebooks from the Coach and Horses; Marvel gives Griffin the slip and eventually becomes the landlord of an inn, The Invisible Man, still with the notebooks in his possession. (Cf. the Philosophical Tramp in *Visit* and William Bridget in *Bealby*.) *Invisible*.

MATCHING'S EASY [Little Easton]. The home of Hugh Britling. Many observers have commented that the account of the Dower House in *Britling* is in fact a photographic description of Easton Glebe (near Dunmow, Essex), Wells's home from 1912 to 1930. However, it is interesting to note that in the preface to *Clissold* Wells appears to deny this. For an account of daily life at Easton Glebe see Meyer, M. M., *H. G. Wells and his Family* (Edinburgh, 1956). *Britling*, passim.

MIDHURST. Wells was apprenticed for a brief period (January 1881) to the chemist's shop of Samuel Evan Cowap of Church Street, Midhurst. Subsequently he had lessons in Latin from the headmaster of Midhurst Grammar School, Mr. Horace Byatt (February–April 1881), and was later a pupil-teacher at the school (1883–4). Wells was greatly attracted to Midhurst and the town figures in many of his novels. It is the 'Wimblehurst' of *Tono-Bungay*, the 'Bramblehurst' of *Invisible* and the 'Whortley' of *Lewisham*. There is also a careful description of Midhurst in *Wheels* in which his landlady, Mrs. Walton, appears as 'Mrs. Wardor'.

Wells records in his autobiography '. . . I had taken to Midhurst from the outset. It had been the home of my grandparents and that gave me a sense of belonging there. It was a real place in my mind and not a morbid sprawl of population like Bromley'. (*Experiment*, p. 139). *Tono-Bungay*, Book 1, 3; *Invisible*, 1; *Lewisham*, 1–7; *Wheels*, XIV, XVII–XIX.

MILTON, JESSICA. 'A girl of eighteen, dark, fine-featured, with bright eyes, and a rich swift colour under her warm, tinted skin.' Frustrated by the conventional environment of her home at Surbiton she runs away with her suitor Bechamel. Whilst on a cycling tour she encounters Hoopdriver, a draper's assistant on holiday, and becomes attracted towards him. She encourages him in his ambition to better himself. *Wheels*.

MINTER, UNCLE. Husband of Richard Remington's maternal aunt, a Five Towns pottery manufacturer and father of two daughters, Gertrude and Sybil. A big man with strong bodily appetites, he sneers at Remington's political ambitions and urges him to become a business man. He 'hated all foreigners because he was English, and all foreign ways because they were not his ways. Also he hated particularly, and in this order, Londoners, Yorkshiremen, Scotch, Welsh and Irish, because they were not "reet Staffordshire", and he hated all other Staffordshire men as insufficiently "reet".' *Machiavelli*.

MONTGOMERY. Moreau's assistant, formerly a London medical student. He was 'a youngish man with flaxen hair, a bristly straw-coloured moustache and a drooping nether lip. He had watery grey eyes, oddly void of expression.' He is instrumental in rescuing Prendick when the latter is shipwrecked and in persuading Moreau to allow Prendick to sojourn on his island. After the death of Moreau, Montgomery becomes drunk and is killed by one of the Beast Folk. *Moreau.*

MORE, RACHEL. Wife of Stephen Stratton, whom she first meets at the age of seventeen. She admires and loves Stratton deeply but they do not marry until some years later; they have three children, Stephen, Rachel and Margaret. Rachel has 'the supreme gifts of belief and devotion', and sustains Stratton with her love and steadfastness despite his emotional involvement with Lady Mary Justin. *Friends.*

MOREAU, DR. A prominent vivisectionist who is compelled to leave England because of the cruelty of his experiments. For eleven years he lives upon a remote Pacific island studying the limits of plasticity in living forms and seeking to transform animals by surgery into a semblance of humanity. He is killed by a puma which breaks loose from the operating table. *Moreau.*

MORLOCKS, THE. The underground inhabitants of the year 802701, descendants of the manual workers. By day the Morlocks live below the earth's surface, emerging at night to capture and kill the Eloi for food. Ape-like and cunning, much of their energy is consumed in the maintenance of vast underground machinery. *Time Machine.*

MORRIS, AMANDA [Rebecca West]. Wife of William Benham, whom she first meets while he is on a walking tour in Sussex. She is attractive and vivacious but has little understanding of Benham's ideas. Benham finds her 'the freest, finest, bravest spirit that he had ever encountered'. (Cf. *Experiment*, 498.) *Research.*

MOURA. Baroness Moura Budberg (Marie von Benckendorff), the dedicatee of *Croquet*, and a close friend of Wells's for many years.

MOWBRAY. *See* UP PARK.

MWRES, ELIZABETH. Daughter of Mwres (Morris), an official of the Wind Vane and Waterfall Trust. She runs away with Denton and lives with him in exile rather than marry the wealthy Bindon. *Days to Come.*

NEBOGIPFEL, DR. MOSES. A mysterious stranger who arrives at the Carnarvonshire village of Llyddwdd and takes up residence in a derelict building, the Manse. His weird appearance and solitary habits soon arouse fear and suspicion in the villagers, who determine to storm the Manse and investigate his strange experiments. It transpires that Nebogipfel has constructed a time machine, the Chronic Argo, upon which he intends to journey to a future age. 'Thirty years of unremitting toil and deepest thought among the hidden things of matter and form and life, and then that, the Chronic Argo, the ship that sails through time, and now I go to join my generation, to journey through the ages till my time has come.' *Argonauts.*

NEWBERRY, RICHARD [Alfred Harmsworth]. Director of Crane and Newberry, publishers, of Thunderstone House, 'a good looking youngish man with rather handsome regular features and a sort of bang of brown hair over his forehead'. He is the lover of Fanny, Harry Smith's sister, and marries her when he is free to do so. He employs Smith in an editorial capacity at Thunderstone House and encourages him in his literary ambitions. *Dream.*

NEWCASTLE UNDER LYME The home of Richard Remington's Uncle Minter, a wealthy Five Towns pottery manufacturer. The town also figures in *Comet* as 'Overcastle'. *Machiavelli*, Book Two, Chapter One; *Comet, passim. See* STOKE ON TRENT.

NEW ROMNEY. The childhood home of Arthur Kipps. 'He knew all the stones in the yard individually, the creeper in the corner, the dustbin and the mossy wall, better than many men know the faces of their wives.' *Kipps*, 1.

NORMANDY, BEATRICE. Stepdaughter of Lady Osprey and a cousin of Lady Drew. George Ponderevo meets her first at Bladesover House as a child; he notes 'the infinite delicacy of her childish skin and the fine eyebrow, finer than the finest feather that ever one felt on the breast of a bird'. The two are immediately attracted to one another but do not meet again until many years later, by which time Ponderevo has become a wealthy man. After the collapse of the 'Tono-Bungay' empire he and Beatrice become lovers but she refuses to marry him, having decided to marry Lord Carnaby instead. *Tono-Bungay.*

OSTROG. Head of the Wind Vanes Control and a rival of the White Council. He wakens Graham by injected stimulants and uses him as an unwitting pawn in a bid to seize power for himself. *Sleeper.*

OVERCASTLE. *See* NEWCASTLE UNDER LYME. *See also* CLAYTON *and* STOKE ON TRENT.

OXFORD. Arnold Blettsworthy was a student at Oxford, and here he opened his first bookshop. After his graduation he took 'modestly comfortable lodgings in the hamlet of Carew Fossetts, towards Boars Hill, on the outskirts of Oxford. . . .'. 'Camford' (in *Camford*) is apparently an amalgam of Oxford and Cambridge. *Blettsworthy* 3–7; *Camford, passim.*

PALACE, BRYNHILD. Wife of Rowland Palace, 'the daughter of a country rector who had been a great classic and had not so much educated her as made up his old classical clothing for her mind to wear'. Sensitive, refined and beautiful, she possesses qualities of integrity and compassion, in the completest contrast to her husband. Dissatisfied with her life, she finds fulfilment in motherhood; she permits a young writer, Alfred Bunter, to make love to her and passes the child off as her husband's. *Brynhild*.

PALACE, ROWLAND. A successful writer, author of *Bent Oars* and *The Supple Willow Wand*. A poseur by nature, he seeks professional advice on how he may improve his public image. He is aesthetic and disingenuous in his approach to life, in contrast to his wife Brynhild. *Brynhild*.

PARHAM, MR. An Oxford don, 'tolerant, broad minded, and deliberately quite modern', he imagines himself to be the embodiment of a Martian war lord, the Lord Paramount of England. After a series of remarkable adventures he awakes during a seance and realises that the entire experience has been merely a vivid dream. *Parham*.

PARLOAD [R. A. Gregory]. Clerk to a solicitor in Overcastle and a close friend of William Leadford. He was 'a tall, flaxen haired, gawky youth, with a disproportionate development of neck and wrist, and capable of vast enthusiasm . . . physiography was his favourite subject'. He infects Leadford with his enthusiasm for socialist and rationalist ideas; Leadford gives an amusing and detailed description of Parload's living room. *Comet*.

PARSONS. An apprentice at the Port Burdock Drapery Bazaar and a close friend of Mr. Polly. He introduces Polly to the delights of literature, and the two enthuse over Rabelais and Boccaccio. Eventually Parsons is dismissed for assaulting his employer during an argument and Mr. Polly, to his great regret, loses track of him. *Polly*.

PENGE. Richard Remington, the narrator of *Machiavelli*, lived at Penge during his schooldays. 'After my father's death a large and very animated and solidly built uncle in tweeds from Staffordshire . . . got us into a small villa at Penge within sight of that immense façade of glass and iron, the Crystal Palace.' *Machiavelli*, Book 1, 3.

PENTSTEMON, UNCLE. An aged relative of Mr. Polly. 'There was something potent about this old man. . . . He seemed a fragment from the ruder agricultural past of our race, like a lump of soil among things of paper.' He is a vocal presence at both the funeral of Polly's father and Polly's wedding, and gives the latter the benefit of his advice on matrimony. *Polly*.

PLUMP WOMAN. The licensee of the Potwell Inn. 'Many people

would have called her a fat woman, but Mr. Polly's innate sense of epithet told him from the outset that plump was the word.' A kind-hearted and trustful woman, she employs Mr. Polly as a general handyman at the Inn but is terrified that he will be scared away by the villainous Uncle Jim. After Uncle Jim has been routed she and Polly settle down to a life of happy companionship. *Polly*.

POLLY, ALFRED. Romantic by nature and convinced that 'somewhere—magically inaccessible perhaps, but still somewhere—were pure and easy and joyous states of body and mind', Mr. Polly goes through life a misfit. After six years as an apprentice in a drapery emporium at Port Burdock [Southsea], he establishes his own haberdashery shop at Fishbourne, where he is unhappily married to his cousin Miriam Larkins. Unable to endure his life any longer, he abandons his wife and shop and eventually finds happiness as general factotum at a country inn. *Polly*.

PONDEREVO, EDWARD. Uncle of George Ponderevo and inventor of Tono-Bungay. He had 'a young fattish face behind gilt glasses, wiry hair that stuck up and forward over the forehead, an irregular nose that had its aquiline moments . . . the body betrayed an equatorial laxity, an incipient "bow window" as the image goes'. He progresses from a young, inpecunious chemist at Wimblehurst [Midhurst] to a wealthy financier with a country estate and numerous interlocking business interests. Eventually he is made bankrupt by the collapse of his financial empire and he dies at Luzon Gare in the Pyrenees. *Tono-Bungay*.

PONDEREVO, GEORGE. Nephew of Edward Ponderevo and the narrator of *Tono-Bungay*. After being apprenticed at his uncle's chemist's shop George is offered a leading role in the Tono-Bungay enterprise and is active for some years in its promotion. Later he withdraws from a too-demanding involvement in order to conduct experiments in aeronautics. He is unhappily married to Marion Ramboat. In his scepticism and general attitude to life George is a faithful reflection of Wells himself. *Tono-Bungay*.

PONDEREVO, MRS. [Sarah Wells]. Mother of George Ponderevo and housekeeper at Bladesover House. She is a devoted, religious woman who knows 'with inflexible decision her place and the place of everyone in the world'. She dies soon after George is apprenticed to his uncle Edward; George, realising for the first time the intensity of her love for him, is grieved by her death. *Tono-Bungay*.

PONDEREVO, SUSAN. Wife of Edward Ponderevo. A delightful and pretty woman, she has a 'disposition to connubial badinage, to a sort of gentle skylarking'; she has a lively sense of humour and takes a keen interest in her husband's ideas and ventures. She is genuinely fond of her nephew George and concerned for his happiness. *Tono-Bungay.*

POPE, MARJORIE. Wife of Richard Trafford and the second of the Pope children. She is extremely attractive, with 'an abundance of copper-red hair, which flowed back very prettily from her broad, low forehead and over her delicate ears, and she had that warm-tinted clear skin that goes so well with reddish hair'. She accepts Will Magnet's offer of marriage but breaks this off in favour of Trafford. When Trafford becomes disillusioned with conventional society she agrees to travel to Labrador with him in order to think out life afresh. *Marriage.*

PORNICK, ANN. Wife of Arthur Kipps and daughter of a New Romney haberdasher. She is Kipps's childhood sweetheart; as a girl she gives him half a sixpence as a token of her undying affection. When they meet again in later life he breaks off his engagement to Helen Walshingham in order to marry her. *Kipps.*

PORNICK, SIDNEY. Brother of Ann and a close boyhood friend of Kipps. As children he and Kipps are inseparable companions. Later Sid Pornick becomes a bicycle repairer and opens a shop in Hammersmith. *Kipps.*

PORT BURDOCK [Southsea]. Mr. Polly was apprenticed 'in one of those large, rather low-class establishments which sell everything from pianos and furniture to books and millinery, a department store, in fact, the Port Burdock Drapery Bazaar at Port Burdock, one of the three townships that are grouped round the Port Burdock naval dockyards'. Chapter 1 of *Polly* contains numerous references to the town and to its surrounding countryside. (Wells was apprenticed at a drapery emporium at Southsea for two years, 1881–1883.) The town also figures briefly in *Visit* and *Invisible. Polly*, 1; *Visit*, 2; *Invisible*, 17, 26–7.

PORT STOWE [Portsmouth]. The home of Griffin's friend Doctor Kemp, with whom the Invisible Man seeks refuge. Port Stowe is the scene of the hunting and death of Griffin, and nearby is the inn of which Thomas Marvel becomes the landlord. *Invisible*, 14–18, 24–28.

POTWELL INN, THE [Beetle and Wedge Inn, Moulsford]. After various adventures as a tramp Mr. Polly settles down at the Potwell Inn as a ferryman and general 'odd man about the place'. He defeats Uncle Jim in a series of battles and ultimately finds his haven at the Inn. 'All the Potwell Inn betrayed his influence now, for here, indeed, he had found his place in the world.' *Polly*, 9, 10.

PREEMBY, ALBERT EDWARD. Husband of Chrissie Hossett and nominally the father of Christina Alberta. He becomes convinced that he is a reincarnation of Sargon, King of Sumeria, sent back to earth to reunify the world. He dies after realising that this is a delusion, and that 'the real thing was to be just a kingly person and work with all the other kingly persons in the world'. *Christina.*

PREEMBY, CHRISTINA ALBERTA. Daughter of Christina Hossett and Wilfred Devizes, brought up as the daughter of Albert Edward Preemby. 'She had little or no tact, and there was always something remote and detached, something of the fairy changeling about her. Even her personal appearance was tactless. . . . As she grew up the magic forces of adolescence assembled her features into a handsome effect, but she was never really pretty.' It is not until she is a grown woman that she discovers her true parentage. *Christina.*

PRENDICK, EDWARD. A gentleman of independent means who sojourns for a period on the island of Doctor Moreau. Formerly a student of biology under Huxley, he is an unwilling prisoner on the island and is both fascinated and repelled by Moreau's experiments. After Moreau's death he succeeds in returning to civilisation and writes an account of his experiences which is subsequently published by Charles Edward Prendick, his nephew and heir. *Moreau.*

R.A.C. The dedicatee of *Conversations.* Apparently a misprint for 'R.A.G. ' (R. A. Gregory) a close friend of Wells's from student days onwards.

RAMAGE. A stockbroker and neighbour of the Stanleys at Morningside Park. He was a 'square-faced man of nearly fifty, with iron-grey hair, a mobile, clean-shaven mouth and rather protuberant black eyes'. Ann Veronica seeks his advice after her flight to London: he lends her money and attempts to seduce her. *Veronica.*

RAMBOAT, MARION [Isabel Mary Wells]. Wife of George Ponderevo. A 'very gracefully moving figure of a girl', she first meets Ponderevo when he is a science student in London. He finds her irresistibly attractive but recognises that there are profound temperamental differences between them. Their married life is one of increasing difficulty and frustration; finally he is unfaithful to her and they are divorced. She finds happiness in managing a farm, and later a robes shop. (Cf. *Experiment,* 421–34). *Tono-Bungay.*

RATZEL. Leader of one of the rival factions in a civil war, and opponent of Bolaris. When Ratzel is taken prisoner he and

Bolaris realise that they have far more in common than either had appreciated and that, in fact, they are brothers. *Brothers*.

REDWOOD [Nyewood]. After his fight with Archie Garvell, George Ponderevo 'went into exile in the dog-cart to Redwood station, with Jukes the coachman, coldly silent, driving me, and all my personal belongings in a small American-cloth portmanteau behind'. *Tono-Bungay*, Book 1, 1.

REDWOOD, PROFESSOR. One of the discoverers of Herakleophorbia, the Food of the Gods, and father of the first of the Giant Children. He was 'entirely ordinary in his appearance' and until he and Bensington discovered the Food both had led lives of 'eminent and studious obscurity'. *Food*.

REMINGTON, ARTHUR [Joseph Wells]. Father of Richard Remington, a science teacher at the Bromstead Institute, 'a lank-limbed man in easy shabby tweed clothes and with his hands in his trouser pockets'. He 'carried a natural imcompetence in practical affairs to an exceptionally high level'. He shares many of his son's interests and encourages him in his reading; Mrs. Remington, on the other hand, is intolerant of her husband's scepticism and untidiness. He falls to his death while pruning a grape-vine when Richard is thirteen years of age. (Cf. *Experiment*, 52–62, 108, 192–8.) *Machiavelli*.

REMINGTON, MRS. [Sarah Wells]. Mother of Richard Remington. She is devoted to her son but intensely religious and conventional in her outlook. She is unable to tolerate her husband's scepticism and constitutional waywardness. 'My mother had been trained in a hard and narrow system that made evil out of many things not in the least evil, and inculcated neither kindliness nor charity.' She dies of appendicitis some years after her husband's death. (Cf. *Experiment*, 43–76, 175–6.) *Machiavelli*.

REMINGTON, RICHARD. The only son of a Bromstead [Bromley] science teacher, he wins a scholarship to the City Merchants School and then becomes a student at Cambridge. He marries Margaret Seddon and becomes M.P. for the Kinghampstead division. Throughout his life he is torn between intellectual and emotional predilections, between a passion for constructive statesmanship on the one hand and the desires of his heart on the other. Ultimately the two prove to be incompatible; his elopement with Isabel Rivers leads to the destruction of his political career. *Machiavelli*.

RIVERS, ISABEL [Amber Reeves]. A close admirer of Richard Remington and ultimately his mistress. When he first meets her she is 'a rather ugly and ungainly, extraordinarily interesting school-girl with a beautiful quick flush under her warm brown skin, who said and did amusing and surprising things'. She assists Remington with his constituency work and with the editing of his journal, the 'Blue Weekly'. Their friendship develops into a love affair and finally the two run away together to Italy, thus ending Remington's political career. *Machiavelli*.

ROPEDEAN [South Harting]. One of the dependent villages of Bladesover (*q.v.*) The rector of Ropedean was 'vindictively economical because of some shrinkage of his tithes'. *Tono-Bungay*, Book 1, 1.

RUMBOLD. A china-dealer at Fishbourne and neighbour of Mr. Polly. During the fire on the High Street Polly rescues Rumbold's deaf mother-in-law. As a result of this act of heroism Rumbold renews his friendship, which had for many years been estranged as a result of a disagreement. *Polly*.

RUSPER. An ironmonger at Fishbourne and neighbour of Mr. Polly. He has an egg-shaped head and a defect of the palate which caused 'a peculiar clinking sound, as though he had something between a giggle and a gas meter at work in his neck'. His friendship with Mr. Polly ceases after Polly accidentally knocks over the pails outside his shop. *Polly*.

RYLANDS, CYNTHIA. Wife of Philip Rylands, a sensitive, thoughtful woman, she is acutely conscious of her need for intellectual and emotional fulfilment. While staying at her Italian villa she invites a number of guests who assist her in her quest for a purpose in life. The character of Cynthia Rylands is based in part on that of Wells's wife Jane (Amy Catherine Robbins). *Meanwhile*.

SANDGATE. *See* FOLKESTONE.

SARNAC, *See* SMITH, HARRY MORTIMER

SCROPE, EDWARD (Bishop of Princhester). Brought up in a conventional religious environment, he spends some years as curate, vicar, and then as bishop. He begins to have profound doubts of the relevance of the church's teachings and has a series of visions, culminating in his secession from the Church of England. *Bishop*.

SEDDON, MARGARET (Wife of Richard Remington). A quiet, studious, graceful woman, she first meets Remington when she is twenty. Five years later they meet again at the Bailey's house and shortly after this are married. Their marriage becomes estranged, first by the change in his political views and, more seriously, by his infidelity with Isabel Rivers. *Machiavelli*.

SELENITES. Insect-like inhabitants of the moon. Living in vast underground caverns, their complex and highly specialised civilisation is a parody of features of English society in 1900 which

Wells found distasteful. The ruler of the Selenites is the Grand Lunar. *First Men.*

SHALFORD, EDWIN. Proprietor of the Folkestone Drapery Bazaar, 'an irascible, energetic little man with hairy hands, for the most part under his coat tails, a long, shiny bald head, a pointed aquiline nose a little askew, and a neatly trimmed beard'. He is obsessed with the need for system and efficiency. (Cf. *Experiment*, 152–9). *Kipps.*

SHERE. Stephen Stratton and Rachel More were married in Shere parish church on 8 November 1906. William Benham spent the night at a 'friendly little inn' at Shere whilst on a walking tour of Sussex and Surrey. *Friends*, 9; *Research*, 2.

SIDDERMORTON [South Harting]. In describing Siddermorton and its neighbouring villages Sidderton and Sidderford, Wells is apparently referring to South Harting and its close neighbours East Harting and Nyewood. Siddermorton House [Up Park], the home of Lady Hammergallow, 'is a mile and a half out of Siddermorton'. *Visit, passim.*

SKINNER, MR. AND MRS. ALFRED. The 'extremely dirty' couple engaged by Mr. Bensington to manage the Experimental Farm at Hickleybrow. Mr. Skinner was 'a large-faced man, with a lisp and a squint that made him look over the top of your head, slashed slippers that appealed to Mr. Bensington's sympathies, and a manifest shortness of buttons'. Mrs. Skinner was ' a very little old woman, capless, with dirty white hair drawn back very very tightly from a face that had begun by being chiefly, and was now, through the loss of teeth and chin, and the wrinkling up of everything else, ending up by being almost exclusively—nose'. Eventually she leaves the farm and goes to live with her daughter, Mrs. Caddles, taking with her a supply of Herakleophorbia. *Food.*

SLAUGHTER, OLIVE. Daughter of an Oxford tobacconist and close friend of Arnold Blettsworthy. She and Blettsworthy have an idyllic courtship, but separate when he discovers her with his friend Lyulph Graves. Shortly after she marries a pork butcher and has several children by him. *Blettsworthy.*

SMALLWAYS, ALBERT PETER. Son of a Bun Hill [Bromley] greengrocer, 'a vulgar little creature, the sort of pert, limited soul that the old civilisation of the early twentieth century produced by the million in every country of the world'. He is accidentally carried to Germany in a balloon, where he is mistaken for Butteridge, a famous inventor. He lives to see the world devastated by warfare and pestilence. *Air.*

SMITH, FANNY. Elder daughter of Martha and Mortimer Smith of

Cherry Gardens. A voracious reader, she encourages her brother Harry in his literary ambitions. Her mother disowns her when she runs away from home to live with Richard Newberry. *Dream*.

SMITH, HARRY MORTIMER. Youngest son of Martha and Mortimer Smith of Cherry Gardens, and brother of Fanny. Rebelling against the conventional and narrowly religious atmosphere of his home, he obtains an editorial post in the huge publishing enterprise at Thunderstone House, where he achieves rapid promotion. After serving in the First World War he is shot dead by Sumner, the lover of his first wife. Two thousand years later Sarnac has a dream in which he experiences Smith's life and death. *Dream*.

SOUTH HARTING. One of the dependent villages of Up Park (*q.v.*) Wells's mother worshipped regularly at South Harting church during the years when she served as housekeeper at Up Park. The village figures in *Visit* as 'Siddermorton'. William Benham in *Research* spends a walking holiday in the area and encounters Amanda Morris near Harting. *Research*, 2; *Visit, passim. See also* UP PARK *and* ROPEDEAN.

SOUTHSEA. *See* PORT BURDOCK

SPADE HOUSE. Wells's house at Sandgate near Folkestone, from 1900 to 1909. The house was designed by the distinguished architect C. F. A. Voysey, and its planning and construction mark the inception of Wells's intense interest in architectural matters (cf. for example *Anticipations*, Chapters 3 and 4, and *Kipps*, Book 3, 1). The menage at Spade House is described in detail in Meyer, M. M., *H. G. Wells and his Family*, and the house itself appears in *Christina* as 'Udimore'.

STANLEY, ANN VERONICA [Amber Reeves]. Youngest child of Peter Stanley, she is an attractive girl of twenty-one with 'black hair, fine eyebrows, and a clear complexion; and the forces that had modelled her features had loved and lingered at their work and made them subtle and fine'. Eager for life and experience, she leaves home in order to study biology in London. There she falls in love with her tutor, Capes, and agrees to live with him though aware he is already married. *Veronica*.

STRATTON, STEPHEN. The only son of the rector of Burnmore, he spends much of his childhood at Burnmore Park (Up Park) where he meets and falls in love with Lady Mary Christian. Stratton serves in South Africa throughout the Boer War, and on his return becomes Mary's lover, though she is married to a wealthy financier, Justin. When the affair is discovered by Justin, Stratton is banished from England for three years. Eventually he marries Rachel More, a young woman who has loved him for some time, and, reflecting on his past life, decides to write his autobiography. *Friends.*

STOKE ON TRENT. Wells stayed in the Potteries for three months in the spring of 1888 (at 18 Victoria Street, Basford) whilst convalescing after an illness. The district made a deep impression upon him, and is featured in a number of his novels and stories. See especially the short story 'The Cone' (set in Etruria), the 'Margaret in Staffordshire' chapter of *Machiavelli*, and *Comet*. (Cf. also *Arnold Bennett and H. G. Wells*, pp. 33–35; and *Experiment*, pp. 306–10.) *Machiavelli*, Book 2, 1; *Comet, passim.*

The identification of the place names in *Comet* and *Machiavelli* is as follows:

Bantock Burden Pit	Deep Pit, Hanley
Bladden's Ironworks	Shelton Iron & Steel Co., Hanley
Clayton	Burslem, but located as Basford
Clayton Crest	Basford Bank
Four Towns	Potteries—Arnold Bennett's 'Five Towns': Tunstall, Burslem, Hanley, Stoke-upon-Trent, Longton.
Glanville Blast Furnaces	Earl Granville's Furnaces, Etruria
Leet	Leek
Overcastle	Newcastle-under-Lyme
Swathinglea	Hanley

Wells uses actual names in *Machiavelli*: Burslem, Five Towns, Hanley, Longton, Newcastle-under-Lyme, Potteries and Staffordshire. The only slightly disguised names are 'Bursley Wakes'—Bursley is a Bennett name for Burslem, contrived from Burslem and Hanley. (Burslem Wakes, equivalent of Nottingham Goose Fair, is held at the end of June, and Wells would know of it (and mentions it in the penultimate paragraph of 'Triumphs of a Taxidermist')—and 'Lord Pandram's Works'; this is Earl Granville's Steelworks; the fictitious name is abbreviated from 'Panjandrum', which Earl Granville was known as in this area.

STUART, NETTIE. Daughter of Mrs. Verrall's head gardener and childhood friend of William Leadford, to whom she is related. She is extremely attractive, with 'a sort of gravity in her eyes' and a 'grave, sweet smile'. Leadford is deeply infatuated with her, and when she runs away with her lover, Edward Verral, he follows her to Shaphambury. *Comet.*

STUBLAND, PETER. The only child of Arthur and Dolly Stubland. A sensitive, thoughtful boy, he is brought up under the care of his guardian, Oswald Sydenham, following the death of his parents by drowning. After being educated at Caxton [Oundle] and Cambridge he marries Joan Debenham, a beautiful girl with whom he had been brought up. *Joan.*

SUNDERING ON SEA [Leigh on Sea]. Job Huss spends a vacation at Sea View, Sundering on Sea, prior to his operation for suspected cancer. From the house can be heard 'the dull thudding of the gun practice at Shorehamstow [Shoeburyness]'. *Undying Fire*, passim.

SWATHINGLEA. *See* CLAYTON.

SYDENHAM, LADY CHARLOTTE. Aunt of Oswald Sydenham, 'one of those large, ignorant, ruthless, low-church, wealthy and well-born ladies who did so much to make England what it was in the days before the Great War'. She has Joan and Peter secretly christened but lives in fear of Oswald, their guardian, whose ideas on the education of his wards are totally different from hers. *Joan.*

SYDENHAM, OSWALD. Cousin of Dolly Stubland (née Sydenham) and guardian of Joan Debenham and Peter Stubland. On his return from Africa he supervises the education and upbringing of Joan and Peter; the children call him 'Nobby' because of his resemblance to Peter's doll. *Joan.*

TEWLER, EDWARD ALBERT. Only son of Mr. and Mrs. Richard Tewler. A selfish, unimaginative child, he is brought up in complete sexual ignorance until he becomes emotionally involved with Evangeline Birkenhead. After his divorce from Evangeline he marries his house-keeper Mrs. Butter, and lives in suburban respectability at Morningside Prospect. (Wells asserts that *Homo sapiens* exists as yet 'only in the dreamlands of aspiration', and that mankind is in reality *Homo Tewler.*) *Careful.*

TRAFFORD, RICHARD ANDREW GODWIN. Husband of Marjorie Pope. An ambitious young professor of physics, he is consumed with a passion for scientific research. Dissatisfied with the emptiness and conventionality of life in Edwardian London, he persuades Marjorie to travel to Labrador with him in order to think out afresh their fundamental attitudes. *Marriage.*

TRUMBER. Lecturer in English literature at Clayfoot College, Camford. 'He was the quintessence of the intellectually genteel, though that word would have crucified him.' While lecturing one day he is interrupted by an unseen voice, demanding to know 'What is this literature you are talking about?' The experience unsettles him, but with the passage of time he convinces himself that it was merely a vivid dream. *Camford*.

TWAIN, GEMINI. Husband of Stella Kentlake. An Oxford graduate, he writes criticism for a weekly paper. He was 'something of a pug about the face, with disarming brown eyes, a lot of forehead and a resolute mouth'. After witnessing war atrocities in Poland and Finland he has a breakdown in health, and emerges profoundly disillusioned with human life. His wife Stella wins him back to health and confidence. *Babes*.

UP PARK. (West Sussex, near Petersfield). It is one of the most famous and beautiful English country houses built in the late seventeenth century, and a symbol *par excellence* of the squirearchy of the Age of Reason. Wells stayed at Up Park frequently whilst his mother was housekeeper there, and the house played a very important part in stimulating his youthful imagination.

Up Park figures as 'Bladesover' in *Tono-Bungay*, 'Checkshill' in *Comet*, 'Siddermorton House' in *Visit*, 'Burnmore Park' in *Friends* and 'Mowbray' in *Clissold*. (Cf. *Experiment*, pp. 135–8). *Tono-Bungay*, Book 1, 1; *Comet*, 1, 2; *Visit*, 28; *Friends*, 2; *Clissold*, Book 2, 1.

VILLA JASMIN. The Provencal home of William Clissold, described in detail in Book One, 15, of *Clissold*, 'View from a Window in Provence'. It is at this villa, 'a small farmer's house set upon a hillside among olive terraces not far from Grasse', that Clissold writes his autobiography. The description of the house and its surrounding scenery corresponds with Lou Bastidon, Wells's winter home during the years 1923–6. (Cf. *Experiment*, 739–41.) *Clissold*.

WADDY, MR. Arthur Kipps's paternal grandfather. He leaves Kipps a fortune, as a result of which Kipps is enabled to leave the drapery emporium to which he was apprenticed and become a member of society. Also the central character in *Waddy*. *Kipps*.

WALSINGHAM, HELEN. The beautiful daughter of a Folkestone solicitor; she is a member of a county family and 'related to the Earl of Beaupres'. Kipps first meets her at a woodcarving class and, after being attracted to her for a considerable time, becomes engaged to her after inheriting his fortune. At last he realises the incongruity of his attempts to become a member of polite society and breaks off his engagement to marry his childhood friend Ann Pornick. *Kipps*.

WATERS, DORIS THALASSIA. A mermaid, 'born ages and ages ago in some dreadful miraculous way in some terrible place near Cyprus'. She comes ashore at Sandgate to acquire a soul, or so she claims, but in reality to meet Harry Chatteris. Chatteris falls in love with her and breaks his engagement to Adeline Glendower for her sake. *Sea Lady*.

WATSON, H. B. MARRIOTT. The dedicatee of *The Stolen Bacillus and other Incidents*. Watson was literary editor of the *Pall Mall Gazette* in the 1890s and gave Wells much encouragement as a short story writer in his early years.

WEENA. A fragile member of the Eloi whom the Time Traveller rescues from drowning. She is childlike and affectionate, following him persistently on his journeys. She is killed during a fight with the Morlocks, but before her death presents the Time Traveller with a bunch of flowers which he takes back with him to his own time. The narrator of the story reflects that the flowers 'witness that even when mind and strength had gone, gratitude and a mutual tenderness still lived on in the heart of man'. *Time Machine*.

WETMORE. *See* WINDSOR.

WEYBRIDGE. Weybridge and Shepperton were destroyed by the Martians in *Worlds*. The narrator gives a detailed eyewitness account of the Martian attack and his subsequent escape. *Worlds*, 12.

WHITLOW, RUDOLF. Brother of Samuel and Alfred Whitlow, he is educated at Camford University and becomes extremely interested in politics. A splenetic, ambitious young man, he eventually achieves the leadership of a world movement of open conspirators pledged to unify the earth. *Holy Terror*.

WHORTLEY, *See* MIDHURST.

WILBECK, DOLORES [Odette Keun]. Wife of Stephen Wilbeck. A shrewish, argumentative woman, alternately endearing and exasperating, she involves her husband in a series of increasingly embarrassing incidents. She is acutely jealous of Lettice, his daughter by his first marriage, and suspects him of being unfaithful to her. After her death he has inscribed on her gravestone the words: 'Dolores, Pax.' *Dolores*.

WILBECK, STEPHEN. A successful publisher, husband of Dolores Wilbeck. He first meets Dolores while staying at a Riviera hotel, and subsequently tells the story of their tempestuous marriage and travels in the form of an intimate journal. Exasperated by the increasingly illogical and shrewish behaviour of Dolores, he administers to her a fatal overdose of drugs. He speculates that mankind is divided into two distinct species, *Homo Doloresiform*, 'emphatic, impulsive and implacable', and *Homo Wilbeckius*, 'observant, inhibited and disingenuous'. *Dolores*.

WILKINS, EDGAR. Novelist and Fabian. He is 'a man of a peculiar mental constitution; he alternates between a brooding sentimental egotism and a brutal realism, and he is as weak and false in the former mood as he is uncompromising in the latter'. The character is apparently a facetious representation of Wells himself. (Also mentioned in *Veronica, Machiavelli, Harman* and *Britling.*) *Boon.*

WIMBLEHURST. *See* MIDHURST.

WINDSOR. Wells was apprenticed for a brief period (July 1880) to Messrs. Rodgers and Denyer, drapers, of 25 High Street, Windsor, and knew the surrounding district well. His 'uncle' Thomas Pennicott kept a riverside inn, Surly Hall, near Clewer. 'And yet that nocturnal tramp along the Maidenhead Road, which I took whenever I could, is real and living to me still. I could draw a map of the whole way down the hill and through Clewer. I could show you where the road was wider and where it narrowed down.' (*Experiment*, 124.)

Windsor is sketched in *Friends* as 'Wetmore', and Eton as 'Harbury'.

Peter Stubland in *Joan* attends the High Cross Preparatory School near Windsor. *Joan*, 8; *Friends*, 2.

WOLDINGSTANTON [Oundle]. The public school of which Job Huss is the Headmaster and to which he dedicates his life. (Cf. Wells, *The Story of a Great Schoolmaster.*) *Undying Fire, passim.*

WOODCOCK, SIR BUSSY [Max Beaverbrook]. A business tycoon, 'one of those crude plutocrats with whom men of commanding intelligence, if they have the slightest ambition to be more than lookers-on at the spectacle of life, are obliged to associate nowadays'. He is a close friend of Mr. Parham and together they embark on a study of psychic research, culminating in Parham's dream during a seance. *Parham.*

ZELINKA, PRINCE MICHAEL. Leader of patriotic Clavery. He attempts to involve Paul Zelinka in his military campaigns but is killed by Paul, who is intent on avoiding war. *King.*

ZELINKA, PAUL. King of Clavery and rival of his brother, Prince Michael. He takes the initiative in imposing a world control of calcomite, and establishes peace between the warring kingdoms of Clavery, Saevia and Agravia. He marries his cousin, Princess Helen. *King.*

Appendix: Film Versions

The following is a list of the principal film versions of Wells's novels and stories.

1909 *The Invisible Thief* (silent) (based upon *The Invisible Man*). Pathé, France.
1919 *The First Men in the Moon* (silent). Gaumont. Directed by J. L. V. Leigh, with Hector Abbas, Heather Thatcher and L. d'Aragon.
1921 *The Wheels of Chance* (silent). Stoll. Directed by Harold Shaw, with George K. Arthur and Olwen Roose.
1922 *The Passionate Friends* (silent). Stoll. Directed by Maurice Elvey, with Milton Rosmer and Madge Stewart.
1922 *Kipps* (silent). Directed by Harold Shaw, with George K. Arthur and Edna Flugrath.
1927 *Marriage* (silent) (also entitled *The Wedding Ring*). Fox. Directed by R. William Neill, with Virginia Valli, Allan Durant and Edward Davis.
1928 *Bluebottles, The Tonic* and *Daydreams* (silent). Anglo. Directed by Ivor Montague, with Elsa Lanchester, Charles Laughton and Harold Warrender.
1932 *Island of Lost Souls* (based upon *The Island of Doctor Moreau*). Paramount. Starring Charles Laughton and Bela Lugosi.
1933 *The Invisible Man*. United Artists. Directed by James Whale, with Claude Rains.
1935 *Man Who Could Work Miracles*. London Films. Directed by Lothar Mendes, with Roland Young, Ralph Richardson and Joan Gardner.
1936 *Things to Come*. London Films. Directed by William Cameron Menzies, with Raymond Massey, Ann Todd and Ralph Richardson.

1941   *Kipps.* Twentieth Century Fox. Directed by Carol Reed, with Michael Redgrave, Phyllis Calvert and Diana Wynyard.

1948   *The Passionate Friends.* Rank. Directed by David Lean, with Ann Todd, Claude Rains and Trevor Howard.

1949   *The History of Mr Polly.* Two Cities. Directed by Anthony Pelissier, with John Mills and Finlay Currie.

1953   *The War of the Worlds.* Paramount. Directed by Byron Haskin, with Gene Barry.

1953   *The Door in the Wall.* Experimental film by Associated British and Pathé, and the British Film Institute.

1960   *The Time Machine.* Metro Goldwyn Mayer. Directed by George Pal, with Rod Taylor, Alan Young and Yvette Mimieux.

1964   *The First Men in The Moon.* Columbia. Directed by Nathan Judd, with Lionel Jeffries, Martha Heyer and Edward Judd.

1967   *Half a Sixpence* (musical based upon *Kipps*). Paramount. Directed by George Sidney, with Tommy Steele.

1977   *Empire of the Ants.* American International. Directed by Bert I. Gordon, with Joan Collins.

1977   *The Island of Doctor Moreau.* American International. Directed by Don Taylor, with Burt Lancaster, Michael York, Nigel Davenport, Barbara Carrera and Richard Basehart.

For a detailed discussion of the film versions of Wells's novels the reader is referred to *The Films of H. G. Wells* by Alan Wykes (Jupiter Books, London, 1977).

References

BACKGROUND

1. Wagar, *H. G. Wells and the World State*, (Yale University Press, 1961) 269.
2. *Experiment in Autobiography*, 64.
3. Ibid., 65.
4. Introduction to *World Natural History*, by E. G. Boulenger (Batsford, 1937).
5. *Experiment in Autobiography*, 193.
6. Ibid., 136.
7. Ibid., 137.
8. *Tono-Bungay*, 118.
9. Ibid., 17–18.
10. *Experiment in Autobiography*, 136.
11. Introduction to *Shop Slavery and Emancipation*, by William Paine (King and Son, 1912).
12. *Experiment in Autobiography*, 181.
13. Ibid., 186.
14. Ibid., 201.
15. 'Scepticism of the Instrument', printed as an appendix to *A Modern Utopia*, 376.
16. *Experiment in Autobiography*, 240.
17. Ibid., 303.
18. Ibid., 306.
19. Letter to Elizabeth Healey, March 1888.
20. *A Modern Utopia*, 378.
21. *Textbook of Biology*, 131–2.
22. *Experiment in Autobiography*, 376.
23. Introduction to *The Book of Catherine Wells*, 1928.
24. *Certain Personal Matters*, 179.
25. *The War of the Worlds*, 22.
26. Ibid., 57.
27. *The First Men in the Moon*, 65.
28. Bergonzi, *The Early H. G. Wells* (Manchester University Press, 1961),

165–74; Bloom, *Anatomies of Egotism: A Reading of the Last Novels of H. G. Wells* (University of Nebraska Press, 1977).
29. *Cornhill Magazine*, London, July 1945.

WELLS'S LITERARY REPUTATION

1. Introduction to *H. G. Wells: A Sketch for a Portrait* by Geoffrey West (Howe, 1930).
2. *Tono-Bungay*, 6, 8.
3. *The Book of Catherine Wells*, 25.
4. *Experiment in Autobiography*, 737–41.
5. *The New Machiavelli*, 157.
6. *Marriage*, 191.
7. *Experiment in Autobiography*, 627.
8. *An Englishman Looks at the World*, Chapter 9.
9. This is not meant to imply that Wells's later works are lacking in literary merit. Indeed, many of the later novels—as will be demonstrated—possess considerable literary and imaginative power. Cf. Robert Bloom, op. cit.
10. *Henry James and H. G. Wells*, Hart-Davis, 1958.
11. *Experiment in Autobiography*, 493.
12. *The World of William Clissold*, 84.
13. *Tono-Bungay*, 250.
14. Preface, *The Sleeper Awakes* (1910 edition). Cf. *Experiment in Autobiography*, 499.
15. *You Can't Be Too Careful*, 113–14.
16. Amber Pember Reeves and Odette Keun respectively.
17. *The New Machiavelli*, 335.
18. 'The Betterave Papers', *Cornhill Magazine*, July 1945.
19. Margaret Cole, *Growing Up Into Revolution*, 147 (Longmans, Green, 1949).

THE SHORT STORIES

1. Introduction, *The Country of the Blind and Other Stories*.
2. Ibid.
3. *Experiment in Autobiography*, 645.
4. Bates, H. E., *The Modern Short Story: A Critical Survey* (The Writer Inc., 1950).
5. Introduction, *The Country of the Blind and Other Stories*.

THE ROMANCES

1. *The Review of English Studies*, New Series, vol. XI. no. 41, February 1960: 'The Publication of *The Time Machine* 1894–5'.

2. *Experiment in Autobiography*, 515–19; Geoffrey West, *H. G. Wells*, 289–94.
3. *The Puritan* (1899), 219.
4. *The Island of Doctor Moreau*, 61.
5. Ibid., 123.
6. Ibid., 216–17.
7. Ibid., Chapter 9. Cf. *Experiment in Autobiography*, 295; *Tono-Bungay*, 50–1; *The Dream*, 40–50.
8. *The Island of Doctor Moreau*, 154.
9. *Arnold Bennett and H. G. Wells* (Hart-Davis, 1960), 258–9; *George Gissing and H. G. Wells* (Hart-Davis, 1961), 64.
10. *Experiment in Autobiography*, 100–2; 693.
11. Ibid., 582.
12. Preface, 1910 edition.
13. Preface, 1921 edition.
14. Wells to Gissing, 22 January 1898. Wells to Bennett, 9 September 1902.
15. *Experiment in Autobiography*, 473.
16. Ibid., 738–40.
17. Ibid., 468.
18. Reprinted as an appendix to *Mankind in the Making*.
19. *The Food of the Gods*, Book 2, Chapter 1.
20. See Norman and Jeanne Mackenzie, *The Time Traveller* (Weidenfeld and Nicolson, 1973), Chapters 14–16.
21. Preface to 1921 edition.
22. *Experiment in Autobiography*, 138.
23. *A Year of Prophesying*, 271.
24. 'H. G. Wells' (1957). Reprinted in *Principles and Persuasions* (1958), and in *H. G. Wells: A Collection of Critical Essays* (ed. B. Bergonzi), (Prentice Hall, 1976).
25. *Joan and Peter*, 342; *The World of William Clissold*, 92, 699–700; *Star Begotten*, 50–1; *Brynhild*, 79; *The Bulpington of Blup*, 315.
26. *The War of the Worlds*, 46.
27. *The King who was a King*, 10.
28. *Things to Come*, 1935; *Man Who Could Work Miracles*, 1936.
29. 'The Probable Future of Mankind': reprinted as Chapter One of *The Salvaging of Civilisation*, 'The Way to World Peace', (Ernest Benn, 1930).
30. *Experiment in Autobiography*, 643.
31. *The Book of Catherine Wells*, 27.
32. *Anticipations*, 69.
33. *The Croquet Player*, 29, 47.
34. Ibid., 53.
35. Ibid., 73. Cf. *Joan and Peter*, 501–3.
36. *The Island of Doctor Moreau*, 216–19; *The Croquet Player*, 73, 79; *Mr. Blettsworthy on Rampole Island*, 269, 272.
37. *Star Begotten*, 171.
38. Introduction to 1914 edition, *Anticipations*.

39. *The Happy Turning*, 6.
40. Ibid., 6. The 'long series of drawings and writings' would presumably include the short stories 'A Vision of Judgement', 'The Story of the Last Trump' and 'Answer to Prayer'.
41. For many years Wells had been interested in his own dreams. Cf. *The Way the World is Going*, Chapter XIX, 'New Light on Mental Life'.
42. *The World of William Clissold*, 840. Cf. ibid., 27–8.
43. *The Way the World is Going*, 49–50.

THE NOVELS

1. *Experiment in Autobiography*, 543.
2. Ibid., 171–2.
3. *Love and Mr. Lewisham*, 23.
4. *Experiment in Autobiography*, 468.
5. Letter to his agent, J. B. Pinker, October 1898.
6. Atlantic Edition, vol. 8, Preface.
7. *Experiment in Autobiography*, 499–500.
8. Ibid., 639.
9. *Daily Telegraph*, 10 February 1909.
10. *Tono-Bungay*, 25.
11. 'Draft for an Obituary', *Coronet*, January 1937.
12. *Tono-Bungay*, 249–50.
13. Ibid., 77.
14. Ibid., 491–2.
15. Ibid., 482–3.
16. Ibid., 276.
17. Lovat Dickson, *H. G. Wells: His Turbulent Life and Times* (Macmillan, 1969), Chapters 11 and 12; Norman and Jeanne Mackenzie, *The Time Traveller*, Chapter 16.
18. Later re-titled 'The Contemporary Novel' and included in *An Englishman Looks at the World*.
19. Geoffrey West, *H. G. Wells*, 181.
20. *A Modern Utopia*, 47.
21. *H. G. Wells*, 271.
22. Letter to Frederick Macmillan.
23. Cf. *The War of the Worlds*, Book One, Chapter 11. 'It was the strangest spectacle, that black expanse set with fire. It reminded me, more than anything else, of the Potteries seen at night.'
24. *Experiment in Autobiography*, 736, 739.
25. *Tono-Bungay*, Book Three, Chapter 4, §2.
26. Geoffrey West, *H. G. Wells*, 142.
27. Leon Edel and Gordon N. Ray (ed.), *Henry James and H. G. Wells* (Hart-Davis, 1958), 172–7; Harris Wilson (ed.), *Arnold Bennett and H. G. Wells*, 185–6.
28. *Tono-Bungay*, 4–5; *Experiment in Autobiography*, 611; M. M. Meyer,

H. G. Wells and his Family (International Publishing Co., 1956), 35, 85.

29. Gordon N. Ray, *H. G. Wells and Rebecca West* (Macmillan, 1974), *passim*; Norman and Jeanne Mackenzie, *The Time Traveller*, Chapters 18–19; Lovat Dickson, *H. G. Wells*, Chapter 13.
30. *Experiment in Autobiography*, 498.
31. Leon Edel and Gordon N. Ray (ed.), *Henry James and H. G. Wells*, 157–64.
32. A French translator, unfamiliar with the subtleties of the English language, rendered the title as *Mr. Britling Sees Through It*.
33. In retrospect we can now see that its much-publicised religious element (Mr. Britling's 'discovery' of God towards the conclusion) is of far less significance. For a fuller discussion of this aspect of Wells's thought see the chapter on *The Soul of a Bishop*.
34. *The World of William Clissold*, 92; *Experiment in Autobiography*, 671–7.
35. *Experiment in Autobiography*, 677.
36. Ibid., 500.
37. Preface to Atlantic Edition, vol. 23.
38. *Babes in the Darkling Wood*, Introduction: 'The Novel of Ideas'.
39. Atlantic Edition, vol. 25, Preface.
40. Gordon N. Ray, *H. G. Wells and Rebecca West*, 100–3.
41. *The Dream*, 137.
42. *Experiment in Autobiography*, 739.
43. *Arnold Bennett and H. G. Wells*, 232.
44. 'The Betterave Papers', *Cornhill Magazine*, July 1945.
45. See Wagar, W. Warren, *H. G. Wells and the World State*, for a fuller discussion of Wells's theory of world revolution.
46. *Experiment in Autobiography*, 501.
47. *Mr. Blettsworthy on Rampole Island*, 222, 247.
48. *Experiment in Autobiography*, 501.
49. Robert Bloom, *Anatomies of Egotism*, 83.
50. *Experiment in Autobiography*, 624.
51. Reprinted in *An Englishman Looks at the World*, 1914, and also in Leon Edel and Gordon N. Ray, *Henry James and H. G. Wells*.
52. For a discussion in depth of the Jamesian elements in *Brynhild* see Bloom, Robert: *Anatomies of Egotism*.
53. For an interesting fictional account of the affair, written by the son of Wells and Rebecca West, see Anthony West, *Heritage* (Random House, 1955) in which Wells appears as 'Max Town' and Odette as 'Lolotte'.
54. *Apropos of Dolores*, 49, 347.
55. *The Holy Terror*, 23. Cf. *Experiment in Autobiography*, 100–7, 693; *Tono-Bungay*, 31–2; *The New Machiavelli*, 83–4.
56. *The Holy Terror*, 442.
57. Introduction, *Babes in the Darkling Wood*.
58. *Experiment in Autobiography*, 487–504.

59. Anthony West, *Principles and Persuasions* (London, 1958).
60. See Bergonzi, *The Early H. G. Wells*, 172, and Bloom, *Anatomies of Egotism*, 162.
61. Anthony West, 'H. G. Wells', *Principles and Persuasions* (Eyre and Spottiswoode, 1958). Reprinted in Bergonzi (ed.): *H. G. Wells: A Collection of Critical Essays*.

Select Bibliography

THE WORKS OF H. G. WELLS

There is no uniform edition of Wells's works. The following editions are recommended:

The History of Mr. Polly, edited with an introduction by Gordon N. Ray (Houghton Mifflin Company, U.S.A. 1960).
Kipps, with an introduction and notes by A. C. Ward (Longmans Heritage of Literature series 1960).
Tono-Bungay, with an introduction and notes by A. C. Ward (Longmans Heritage of Literature series 1961).
The Invisible Man, with an introduction by Frank Wells (Collins Classics, 1954).
The First Men in the Moon, with an introduction by Frank Wells (Collins Classics, 1954).
Selected Writings of H. G. Wells, with a preface by Wells and an introduction by George Sampson (Heinemann/Octopus, 1977). This volume contains *The Time Machine, The Island of Doctor Moreau, The Invisible Man, The First Men in the Moon, The Food of the Gods, In the Days of the Comet, The War of the Worlds*.
The Complete Short Stories of H. G. Wells (Ernest Benn, 1927).
The Last Books of H. G. Wells, edited with an introduction and an appendix by G. P. Wells (H. G. Wells Society, London, 1968). This volume contains *The Happy Turning* and *Mind at the End of its Tether*.
H. G. Wells: Early Writings in Science and Science Fiction, edited by Robert Philmus and David Y. Hughes (University of California Press, 1975).

THE LETTERS

Henry James and H. G. Wells: a record of their friendship, their debate on the art of fiction, and their quarrel. Edited with an introduction by Leon Edel and Gordon N. Ray (London, Hart-Davis, 1958). This volume contains the correspondence between Wells and James, 1898–1915.

Arnold Bennett and H. G. Wells: a record of a personal and a literary friendship. Edited with an introduction by Harris Wilson (London, Hart-Davis, 1960). This volume contains the correspondence between Wells and Bennett, 1897–1931.

George Gissing and H. G. Wells: their friendship and correspondence. Edited with an introduction by Royal A. Gettmann (London, Hart-Davis, 1961). This volume contains the correspondence between Wells and Gissing, 1896–1903.

BIBLIOGRAPHY

Herbert George Wells: An Annotated Bibliography of His Works, by J. R. Hammond (Garland, New York 1977).

The Works of H. G. Wells 1887–1925: A Bibliography, Dictionary and Subject-Index, by Geoffrey H. Wells (London, Routledge, 1926).

Catalogue of the H. G. Wells Collection in the Bromley Public Libraries, Edited by A. H. Watkins (London, Bromley Public Library, 1974).

BIOGRAPHY

Norman and Jeanne Mackenzie, *The Time Traveller: The Life of H. G. Wells* (Weidenfeld and Nicolson, London 1973). This is now accepted as the standard life of Wells, and was the first to make extensive use of his unpublished private papers. It does not claim to be a *critical* biography: there is little attempt to discuss Wells's contribution to English literature or to assess his achievement as a thinker and polemicist. It is a straightforward account of his life and times, illuminated throughout by penetrating insight and lively scholarship.

The Mackenzies are particularly skilful in tracing the

sociological background to the various phases in Wells's career: his birthplace at Bromley; his student days at the Normal School of Science; his encounter with the Fabian Society; his role in the First World War; and so on. At each stage in his life he is placed in the context of his times against the backcloth of his contemporaries in the world of literature and ideas. The biography is well researched, and is also notable for its frankness in describing Wells's complicated emotional life.

Lovat Dickson, *H. G. Wells: His Turbulent Life and Times* (Macmillan, London, 1969). This is a well-written and highly readable account, particularly valuable for the chapters on *Ann Veronica* and *The New Machiavelli*, and for its insight into the relationship between Wells and Macmillan. The account of the last twenty years of Wells's life is rather inadequate, otherwise this biography is difficult to fault.

Geoffrey West, *H. G. Wells: A Sketch for a Portrait* (London, Howe, 1930). The biography by Geoffrey West has the inestimable advantage that it was written with the full co-operation of Wells himself, who contributed a preface. The account of Wells's early life—his struggles to earn a living, and his succession of illnesses—is particularly well done. West also includes numerous quotations from Wells's correspondence, much of it unavailable elsewhere. The book has the great merit that Wells the man seems to come to life again in its pages and animate each episode, in a way which is not so true of the Mackenzies' biography, excellent though it is. There is a useful appendix on student writings and on the early versions of *The Time Machine*.

CRITICISM

Bernard Bergonzi, *The Early H. G. Wells* (Manchester University Press, 1961). A perceptive and useful study of the scientific romances and short stories. Bergonzi is particularly skilful in tracing the genesis of *The Time Machine* and in discussing the allegorical and thematic elements in the early romances. Included as appendices are the texts of 'The Chronic Argonauts' and 'A Tale of the Twentieth Century'.

Bernard Bergonzi (ed). *H. G. Wells: A Collection of Critical Essays*

(Prentice Hall, 1976). This is a most important collection of critical studies, and a valuable contribution to Wells scholarship. Included are Anthony West's seminal essay on Wells's fundamental pessimism, and '*Tono-Bungay* and the Condition of England', by David Lodge, a wholly excellent piece of literary analysis. Bergonzi contributes an interesting introduction which provides an overview of Wells's life and work.

Robert Bloom, *Anatomies of Egotism: A Reading of the Last Novels of H. G. Wells* (University of Nebraska Press, 1977). This is a scholarly study of the later novels: *The Bulpington of Blup, Brynhild, Apropos of Dolores,* and *Babes in the Darkling Wood.* By deliberately concentrating on the later work the author does much to balance the emphasis on the early romances which is so prevalent in current literary criticism. Bloom's approach is to assume that the reader has little or no knowledge of the novels in question and to simulate the experience of reading them—commenting and reflecting on them as they unfold. The result is a most thorough and competent study.

  In addition to the chapters on the individual novels the author contributes a lengthy and fascinating examination of Wells's approach to the novel. The handling of the Wells–James debate is particularly accomplished and reveals a shrewd grasp of the literary and intellectual issues involved. Throughout the book the intention is to demonstrate the literary and imaginative qualities of the later novels—an aim in which the author admirably succeeds. Not all readers will agree with Bloom's dismissal of *You Can't Be Too Careful* as 'by all odds the weakest of the whole group', but *Anatomies of Egotism* remains a penetrating and strikingly original critique which is unlikely to be superseded.

Patrick Parrinder, *H. G. Wells* (Oliver and Boyd, 1970). This is a concise introduction to the novels and scientific romances, concentrating in particular on *Love and Mr. Lewisham, Kipps, The History of Mr. Polly* and *Tono-Bungay.* The author's approach is thorough and scholarly, and the book contains an excellent bibliography of writings by and about Wells.

Patrick Parrinder (ed.), *H. G. Wells: The Critical Heritage* (Routledge and Kegan Paul, 1972). This is a collection of contemporary criticism of Wells's fiction, ranging from *The Time Machine* (1895) to the *Complete Short Stories* (1927). The volume also includes a number of important retrospective articles published after his death.

The articles and reviews possess considerable intrinsic interest: it is fascinating, for example, to read Arnold Bennett's opinion of *Tono-Bungay* and T. E. Lawrence's appraisal of the short stories.

Ingvald Raknem, *H. G. Wells and his Critics* (Allen & Unwin, 1964). This is a comprehensive re-appraisal of Wells's fiction seen in the light of the literary criticism of his age. It includes six main sections: 'Towards Public Recognition', 'Wells in his Novels', 'Social Problems, Science, and Character-Creation', 'Wells and the Spirit of the Age', 'Wells and the Art of Character-Creation', and 'Originality or Plagiarism'. This comprehensive and well-documented study examines critically the suggestion that the characters in Wells's novels are Wellsian self-projections, and analyses the impact modern thought had on Wells's mind. It includes particularly useful and original material on the autobiographical elements in *Tono-Bungay*, *The New Machiavelli*, and *Mr. Britling Sees It Through*, asserting that these are the only Wells novels which can be accurately described as autobiographical. The book continues with some illuminating character studies of Wells's heroes and heroines, and a perceptive chapter on Wells as the recorder and interpreter of his age. These are the most valuable sections of the book.

It would be fair to say that the book is marred by serious defects. It has no index—surely indispensable in a scholarly work of this nature. The author seems unaware of any book about Wells published since 1954. Moreover, he rarely refers to first editions, being content to use later editions of Wells's works: this is an important point, for *First and Last Things* (for example) went through THREE different editions, with some important textual alterations in the process. Dr. Raknem's discussion of Wells's ideas seems rather superficial, and contains little or no acknowledgement of the complexity of his thought.

Perhaps the most permanently valuable part of the work is the splendid bibliography of books and articles about Wells which forms one of the appendices to the book. Much of this material will be indispensable to future students of Wells's writings.

W. Warren Wagar, *H. G. Wells and the World State* (Yale University Press, 1961). This is a comprehensive survey of Wells as a prophet of world order. The study ranges over the whole field of Wells's thought on sociology, education and world revolution, culminating in a balanced and penetrating assessment of his achievement as a social prophet. As an introduction to, and critique of, the sociological writings *H. G. Wells and the World State* is indispensable. There is a useful bibliography of primary and secondary sources of information.

Jack Williamson, *H. G. Wells: Critic of Progress* (Mirage Press, Baltimore, 1973). This is a scholarly study of the scientific romances from the point of view of Wells as a utopist and social critic. In spite of its brevity the intellectual range of the work is remarkably comprehensive, and reveals a thorough understanding of the subject. The author rightly emphasises the profound pessimism of the early romances and asserts that Wells's fiction is far more complex and imaginatively coherent than is usually acknowledged.

CRITICAL ARTICLES

Odette Keun, 'H. G. Wells—The Player', *Time and Tide*, 15 (1934), pp. 1249–51, 1307–9, 1346–8.

Christopher Caudwell, 'H. G. Wells: A Study in Utopianism', *Studies in a Dying Culture* (London, 1938), pp. 73–95.

George Orwell, 'Wells, Hitler and the World State', *Critical Essays* (London, 1946), pp. 83–8.

Sir Arthur Salter, 'H. G. Wells, Apostle of a World Society', *Personality in Politics* (London, 1947), pp. 120–37.

Edward Mead Earle, 'H. G. Wells, British Patriot in Search of a World State', *Nationalism and Internationalism* (New York, 1950), pp. 79–121.

Anthony West, 'H. G. Wells', *Encounter*, 8 (1957), pp. 52–9.

J. B. Coates, 'H. G. Wells', *Ten Modern Prophets* (London, 1944), pp. 167–83.

David Lodge, '*Tono-Bungay* and the Condition of England', *Language of Fiction* (London, 1966), pp. 214–42.

Frank Swinnerton, 'Herbert George Wells', *The Georgian Literary Scene 1910–1935* (London, 1969), pp. 49–67.

H. G. Wells, 'The Betterave Papers', *The Cornhill Magazine*, 965 (July 1945), pp. 349–63.

Gordon N. Ray, 'H. G. Wells Tries to be a Novelist', *English Institute Essays*, 1959.

ADDITIONAL RECOMMENDATIONS

F. H. Doughty, *H. G. Wells: Educationist* (London, 1926).

Vincent Brome, *Six Studies in Quarrelling* (London, 1958).

M. M. Meyer, *H. G. Wells and His Family* (Edinburgh, 1956).

Kenneth B. Newell, *Structure in Four Novels by H. G. Wells* (The Hague and Paris, 1968).

Mark R. Hillegas, *The Future as Nightmare: H. G. Wells and the Anti-Utopians* (New York, 1967).

J. P. Vernier, *H. G. Wells Et Son Temps* (Rouen, 1971).

Index